Praise for *The Wildflower Meadow Book* ...

"... this new (American Horticultural) Society-endorsed book is a must for any individual interested in wildflowers or meadow gardening." — *American Horticulture*

"In this fascinating new book Laura Martin shows how to capture the natural beauty of grasslands or alpine meadows in your own backyard." — *The Garden Book Club*

"Very few questions are left unanswered. This book is thoroughly researched, well-documented and truly inspirational." — *The Garden Club of America*

"This well-written volume fills a need in horticultural literature by providing practical guidelines for developing a wildflower meadow. It is obvious that the author has hands-on experience and has made an effort to learn about the state-of-knowledge on the subject. She is an expert on plant material applications around the country."
— *Audubon Naturalist News*

"... her enthusiasm is catching. Any green thumber looking through the book will be anxious to have a try at meadow gardening." — *Library Journal*

"With its detailed descriptions and instructions, this title will easily become the wildflower gardener's 'bible.' " — *The Midwest Book Review*

"... should be in the library of every serious plant enthusiast." — *Naturalist Review*

"With the growing interest in wildflowers and ecological preservation, (this book) is a timely resource that will educate both beginning and experienced gardeners."
— *MS Outdoors*

"Laura Martin has skillfully managed to take the mysticism out of wildflower gardening in a clear and straightforward way." — *Springfield (VA) Journal*

"... an excellent presentation for anyone interested in native or wildflowers or in lawn substitutes." — *Atlanta Journal & Constitution*

"... for the gardening enthusiast who wants to convert a few hundred feet — or even a few acres — into a wildflower meadow." — *San Francisco Examiner & Chronicle*

To David

Everyone
who is seriously involved
in the pursuit of science
becomes convinced that a spirit
is manifest in the laws of the universe—
A spirit vastly superior
to that of man, and one
in the face of which
we with our modest powers
must feel humble.

Albert Einstein

T·H·E
Wildflower
MEADOW
B·O·O·K

A
Gardener's
GUIDE

Laura C. Martin

EAST WOODS PRESS

Library of Congress Cataloging-in-Publication Data

Martin, Laura C.
　　The wildflower meadow book.

　　Includes index.
　　1. Wild flower gardening　2. Meadow gardening
I. Title.
SB439.M365　1986　　　635-9'676　　　85-45699
ISBN 0-88742-073-7
ISBN 0-88742-065-6 (pbk.)

Design by Anna E. Birkner
Line drawings by Mauro Magellan
Cover photographs by David Martin
Copyedited by Linda Benefield

Typeset by RJ Publishing Co.
Printed in the United States of America

East Woods Press Books
Fast & McMillan Publishers, Inc.
429 East Boulevard
Charlotte, NC 28203

Acknowledgments

The sharing of knowledge is a wonderful thing, and I am thankful to the people all across the country who were so generous in sharing their wisdom with me. From the country's finest universities to the isolated fields and grasslands of rural America, you responded to my plea for information with an enthusiasm that was both astounding and touching. I salute you and the work that you are doing so well.

There are some individuals whose support and contributions deserve extra recognition. Special thanks goes to: Stephen Davis with the American Horticultural Society for his initial inspiration for this project, and to Barbara Ellis with the American Horticultural Society for her help with the pronunciation guide; Ray Nelson of McLaughlin Seed Company for sharing his extensive knowledge of the Western wildflower species; Dr. David K. Northington, director of the National Wildflower Research Center for sharing his knowledge of both botany and horticulture, and serving as a technical consultant, and answering a multitude of questions; Dr. Joseph L. Collins of the Tennessee Valley Authority for his support and encouragement and for his recommendations for the Southeastern regional section; Harry R. Phillips of the North Carolina Botanical Garden for being a much-needed sounding board and for his suggestions for the Southeastern regional section; Laura Quatrochi of Environmental Seed Producers for sharing her comprehensive knowledge of wildflower seed production; Barbara Emerson of Union Carbide Agricultural Products Company for her sensitive insight into meadow gardening and her recommendations for the Northeastern regional section; Dr. Arthur R. Kruckeberg of the University of Washington for his ideas and suggestions for growing native plants in the Pacific Northwest; Lisa Johnston of the Plant Materials Center, Los Lunas, New Mexico, and Judith Phillips of Bernardo Beach Native Plant Farm for their enthusiasm, for information about growing wildflowers, and for their recommendations for the Southwestern regional section; Gene and Dee Milstein of Applewood Seed Company for sharing their expertise on growing wildflowers from seed; Kathryn Kennedy for her contributions and recommendations for the Texas regional section; Lauri Lindquist of Fernwood Nature Center for her suggestions for the Midwest regional section.

A different kind of thanks but certainly one just as important, goes to my publisher, Sally McMillan, for her support and friendship and especially to my husband, David, and my children, David, Jr. and Cameron, for their patient understanding and love.

Contents

Foreword

Looking out my window at the American Horticultural Society's six-acre meadow garden here at River Farm makes me wish that this book had been available several years ago. Our meadow, which reaches almost to the shores of the Potomac River, represents several seasons of learning about meadow gardens and the plants that inhabit them — learning that had to be accomplished largely by trial and error.

In November, 1983, Laura Martin came to the American Horticultural Society's 39th Annual Meeting in San Antonio, Texas, with many questions about meadows and meadow gardening. After talking to Society Grounds Director Steve Davis about his own experiences with the meadow at River Farm, she decided to take his advice and read all that she could about meadow gardening when she returned home. This she did; it took all of twenty minutes. After recovering from her amazement at how little information there was available on the subject, she set about to rectify this deficiency in our horticultural literature. This comprehensive and authoritative book is the result of her endeavor. It not only represents countless hours of research, but it also incorporates the experiences and wisdom of many individuals across the country who have experimented with meadow gardening. American gardens will be more diverse and interesting in the future because of her contribution.

Some months ago, Laura came to visit River Farm to talk to members of the Society's staff about her book, and to find out more about our meadow and what we had learned from it. It is exciting to know that our experiences here in northern Virginia, by virtue of their being included in *The Wildflower Meadow Book,* will help other gardeners.

The Society was especially pleased to become involved in Laura Martin's project, because *The Wildflower Meadow Book* helps mark an important turning point in American horticulture. Americans have only recently begun to appreciate the beauty of this country's wildflowers, and native plants are being used in American gardens at unprecedented levels today. The fact that we no longer need to go abroad to appreciate the most promising cultivars of our asters and goldenrods in garden settings is just one indication. Yes, the tide is finally turning, and this book will further convince Americans that some of their greatest gardening resources lie in or near their own meadows.

The revelation that native plants enhance the distinctiveness of our nation's various geographic regions is all the more important, coming as it does in an age of otherwise increasing conformity and standardization of our public landscapes. Native plants and plantings offer an important alternative to plants and landscape styles often thrust upon us from afar and, together with the continued use of exotic plants and plantings, will make our gardening world more interesting and enjoyable.

Landscaping with native plants is a manifestation of our common sense as well as our aesthetic sense. Year in and year out, native plants are more suited to the climate, soils, and other growing conditions of the region in which they evolved naturally. For this reason, they require less care, generally, than introduced exotic plants, and are a good choice for low-maintenance landscapes.

Although meadow gardening is an outgrowth of prairie restoration work that has been going on in the midwestern United States for some time, it is a very recent phenomenon on a home landscape scale. In addition to an increased appreciation for the beauty and finiteness of native plants and natural landscapes, the development of meadow gardening is due in large part to an increasing interest in low-maintenance gardening with less dependence on environmentally sensitive methods of garden management. For example, one of the reasons for developing the wildflower meadow here at River Farm was the vast amount of labor and material we would save each season in terms of mowing, spraying, and other care that a well-manicured lawn requires.

There will be those who belittle the concept of meadow gardening as just another passing fad, but it is an important manifestation of man's continuing need to maintain intimate contact with nature. It is also indicative of our increasing realization that we must be more mindful of long-term natural cycles if we are to have any positive affect on the conservation of the earth's natural resources. The burgeoning interest in native plants in this country is an indication of a newly found maturity in our outlook about the natural world and its importance in our everyday lives. This bodes well for the future of wildflower meadows and promises a prominent place for them in American gardening.

Meadow gardening is destined to become increasingly appreciated by those seeking to create seemingly effortless, uncontrived gardens. Only the most dedicated and patient wildflower enthusiasts will probably ever succeed in this delusion, however, given the need to accept nature as the more influential yet less predictable partner in meadow gardening. Regardless of one's degree of success in feigning

I do not think that the measure of a civilization is how tall its buildings of concrete are, but rather how well its people have learned to relate to their environment and fellow man. — Sun Bear of the Chippewa Tribe

14

naturalness, meadow gardening will provide all who attempt it with a worthwhile challenge to influence nature responsibly on a small scale and an opportunity to understand firsthand the complexity and omnipotence of natural forces.

While *The Wildflower Meadow Book* is intended for the average gardener who is interested in using native plants in the home landscape, particularly in planting a meadow, it does more than serve as a ''how-to'' reference to meadow gardening. Historical perspective and current concepts in American horticulture blend to create a wholistic view of meadow gardening and its far-reaching benefits to the American scene and beyond. Laura Martin explains in a delightful, refreshing, and easily understandable manner everything an avid gardener will want or need to know to establish and enjoy a meadow garden, including the many and varied uses of meadows — as a source of cut flowers, a haven for birds and butterflies and other forms of wildlife, and an outdoor classroom for firsthand study of natural history.

This book comes at an important time. Today gardeners are faced with a plethora of tempting wildflower mixes and a dearth of information about how to grow them successfully. Laura Martin has skillfully managed to take the mysticism out of wildflower gardening. In a clear and straightforward way, she has explained many of the technical terms gardeners must understand if they are going to have a successful and satisfying experience with meadow gardening. *The Wildflower Meadow Book* includes a comprehensive body of taxonomic and geographic information that has considerable practical value to wildflower enthusiasts throughout the nation. Nearly half the book is devoted to a thorough treatment of individual taxa that might be suitable for growing in meadowlike environments. This section includes valuable information on the cultural requirements, methods of propagation, and growth characteristics of each species. The seven chapters devoted to growing wildflowers in the different regions of the country give this book a special strength rarely found in gardening books of this nature. Laura Martin is to be admired further for taking a stand on the suitability of plants for meadow projects in different geographical regions and cultural situations. While not everyone will always agree with her, all should applaud her for providing us with an important baseline for improving and refining future wildflower recommendations. However, it would be a great mistake for readers to focus only on the chapter that pertains to their region in addition to the introductory chapters. Many interesting ideas and inspirations are threaded throughout the book. Read all its chapters, and enjoy.

Just as experienced gourmets go beyond cookbooks which concentrate on formula recipes for success in the kitchen, so will serious gardeners appreciate Laura Martin's emphasis on understanding the factors and variables of wildflower gardening rather than adhering to simplistic formulas for achieving success in the meadow. The principles and basic ingredients alike for success in meadow gardening have been admirably presented in this treatise; it is up to each of us as gardeners to come up with our own recipe for successfully creating and managing our own meadow. Bon appetit!

CHARLES A. HUCKINS

River Farm, Mount Vernon, Virginia
November, 1985

Part One

Introduction

A meadow has been called nature's most abundant and expansive garden. If it is true, as Emerson suggested, that the earth laughs in flowers, then a meadow is the earth laughing right out loud. To capture nature at one of her most glorious stages is the idea behind the popular concept of meadow gardening.

To create a meadow garden is to create a bit of wilderness in your own backyard. How often have you driven across the countryside, seen a bright patch of wildflowers and wished that you could take it home with you? If you have a meadow garden you can do this, if not literally, then at least in theory. While it may not be possible to actually dig up a particular plant for ethical or legal reasons, it is possible to find out what that plant is and find the seeds to plant in your own meadow.

A meadow could serve as a remembrance of things past, a nostalgia center, and it should be filled with the flowers that you have a fondness for. A field of black-eyed Susans might remind you of summers at your grandmother's farm; a patch of goldenrod might make you think of trips back to college in the fall. You might remember plucking daisy petals off to see if he or she really does love you, or you might recall picking a fistful of wild poppies to give your mother on Mother's Day. Our native wildflowers are special to people for different reasons, but they have won an affectionate place in nearly everyone's heart.

In addition to creating an air of nostalgia for us, the wildflowers in our meadow gardens remind us of our historical roots. Wildflowers are an important part of our national heritage, for many of our native plants played a crucial role in the everyday lives of the pioneers and settlers of this country. Because they were often far from the "civilized" world, these pioneers frequently needed to rely on the plants that grew close by for food and medicine. By borrowing from the skills of the Indians, by piecing together bits of information remembered from the old country, and by a great deal of trial and error, the early settlers found plants to satisfy their needs. Seeds from the sunflower were used for food and for cooking. The young shoots of fireweed were eaten in early spring and considered quite a delicacy. Tea was made from the leaves of goldenrod and bee balm. Joe-pye weed was used to treat typhoid fever, improve the appetite, soothe nerves, and clear the complexion. Through the force of their needs and the strength of their own ingenuity, the settlers were able to use the wild plants to satisfy many of their day-to-day needs, from magic to medicine.

However, it was the beauty of the American wildflowers, rather than their medicinal or culinary value, that meant most to those early Americans. From the woods of New England to the seemingly endless stretch of the prairies, flowers were abundant everywhere, inviting the settler, by their beatuy, to make a home there. That same beauty can grace your already "civilized" backyard, in a meadow garden.

Planting your own meadow garden also makes good common sense. Although non-native species certainly will always have their place, it is advantageous for many reasons to use the native plants as the backbone of your landscape plan. Plants native to your own region will be ideally suited to the climate and weather conditions in your area. If you mimic the natural habitat closely and provide growing conditions suitable for each kind of plant, your garden will have little need for extra watering, fertilizer, or intensive maintenance.

Natural landscaping has been called a compromise between the chaos of the wilderness and the rigid structure of a formal garden. One of the most exciting kinds of natural landscapes that can be easily and successfully put in by an individual is a wildflower meadow. Borrowing from the beauty of the garden and the freedom of the wilderness, meadows are a good choice of landscape design for many people. A meadow garden does not require a huge area of land. An existing lawn or perhaps only a corner of a lawn can be transformed from the monoculture of grass to the exciting diversity and beauty of a meadow. A meadow garden is merely a sunny area planted with wildflowers and grasses, and this area can be as large as several acres or as small as a few hundred square feet. While a meadow garden requires less maintenance than many other forms of landscaping, it is not a magical "no-work" deal; it is important to choose an area small enough for you to work with and control easily.

Writers and philosophers throughout the ages have discussed the benefits of staying close to nature, and even modern writers have spoken of the necessity of wildness. As populations increase and urban areas sprawl, acres of green are quickly changing to acres of blacktop and it is often difficult to get a taste of nature. The quiet of a garden provides a therapeutic touch — a haven for the harried. Although any garden will provide this to some extent, a patch of freely flowing wildflowers that departs from the strict geometry of evenly spaced rows or neatly bordered beds of flowers might make the mysteries of nature a little more tangible. A British gardener said of meadows that they " ... allow the enclosed mind, no less than the feet, freedom and movement."

A meadow garden provides a window on nature. It invites you to become an intimate part of the change in the seasons, the fluctuations of the weather, and the migration of birds and butterflies that visit your area. More than any other kind of gardening, meadows need a wholistic approach — and in return they will teach you the true meaning of ecology. Carol Smyser in her book *Nature's Design* says that meadows "react to seasons and climate with a unity that is at once random and uniform." It will add to your knowledge as a gardener and to the stability and beauty of your meadow if you can learn to treat the whole rather than the parts, for there will be many variables within even the smallest meadows. No matter how or what you plant in your area, you will have a combination of wildflowers and grasses unlike any other. Rather than a row of marigolds and a row of zinnias that could be found anywhere in the nation, you will have a gentle sea of wildflowers and grasses, unique to your own geographical region, that flow with and into one another.

Planning and planting a meadow garden involve time and effort. There are no magical formulas to make wildflowers grow quickly and produce a profusion of blossoms; you must work at it. The most important factor in establishing a meadow is choosing wildflowers and native grasses that will be compatible with one another and will thrive in the particular environmental conditions that make up your site. This book is designed to help you master this trick and allow you to have a little piece of wilderness right outside your door. There are no strict rules about what can and cannot be put into a meadow. As long as you choose plants with a sensitivity toward conservation and ecology, you can make it what you like. The meadow is your canvas and you are the artist. The plants, with their wonderful diversity of color and texture, are your paints. With careful planning, a little well-placed common labor, and a big dose of patience, your wildflower meadow can look like the magic shown on the cover of the seed catalogs. And finally, when with calloused hands and bent back you are standing admiring the breathtaking beauty of your meadow in full bloom, someone will walk by and say "Isn't it amazing that all these wildflowers just popped up here this summer!" Take it as a compliment. After all, in planting a meadow we are trying to mimic nature, and the highest praise for a mimic is to be taken for the real thing.

Happy meadowing!

CHAPTER ONE

What Is
A
Meadow?

Just what is a meadow garden? Picture, if you will, stepping outside your door on a morning in early June. Full of exciting colors and textures, your meadow is dominated by the white of the daisies but is also enriched with generous sprinklings of blue from the bachelor's buttons and yellow from the black-eyed Susans. The maroon buds of calliopsis blossoms contrast nicely with the other colors and are a hint of good things yet to come. As you move closer and walk along the path through the meadow, you look down and discover a myriad of plants which had been obscured by their taller neighbors. Red from the annual phlox peeks out from the base of the taller plants, and the little toadflax blossoms look like jewels sprinkled throughout the area.

This mental image is one that can easily become a reality. A meadow could just as well be called a wildflower planting or a field of wildflowers, a naturalized lawn or even, depending on your point of view, a bunch of pretty weeds! The word meadow conjures up such lovely images, however, that it has become the favorite term for describing any naturalized planting of wildflowers and grasses in a sunny, open area. This area is usually planted in such a way as to mimic naturally occurring grasslands or alpine meadows.

The Audubon Society book *Grasslands* defines a meadow as a grassland that is cut periodically for hay and describes a pasture as a grassland or field that is continuously grazed. Webster adds another definition to these: "a low, level grassland near a stream or lake." The word *meadow* comes from the words "to mow" and has the same origin as the word "mouth," for the first meadows and pastures were mowed by the mouths of grazing animals. Meadows occur naturally in many parts of the world — wherever the climate can support a combination of grasses and wildflowers, yet some limiting factor prevents the area from turning into a woodland. The best-known naturally occurring meadows are alpine

There are some who can live without wild things and some who cannot. — Aldo Leopold

23

meadows, where the altitude and temperature extremes keep the area open, and wildflowers are profuse during the short growing season. It is this type of meadow that we try to imitate in our home landscapes.

A LITTLE HISTORY

The idea of meadow gardening probably grew out of the enthusiasm shown for restoring prairie areas in the Midwest. The word *prairie* is from the French word for meadow; the American prairies were named when the early pioneers saw this beautiful, extensive grassland. Many different types of prairies are found in this country, mainly in the central sections, and each has its unique flora. Variations in vegetation are due primarily to the amount of available moisture. Although at one time prairies covered millions of acres, the number of existing original prairie communities is depressingly low. Concerned about the disappearance of the prairies and determined to do something about it, several universities and botanical gardens in the Midwest began the study of prairie restoration. Foremost among these were the University of Wisconsin; the University of Iowa; the Morton Arboretum in Lisle, Illinois; and the Boerner Botanical Garden in Hales Corners, Wisconsin. This study not only resulted in many successful restoration projects but also created a very popular landscape design adaptable to the home garden. Although it takes a great deal of space to do a proper prairie restoration, it was found that smaller areas could mimic the effect of a prairie and the results were not only beautiful, but also economically attractive. The *Prairie Propagation Handbook,* published by Wehr Nature Center in Wisconsin, lists some benefits of prairie restoration:

"(1) Preserving the native vegetation
(2) Providing an aesthetically pleasing plant community with rich textures, colors, and plant forms
(3) Providing for easy maintenance"

These benefits, combined with the energy crunch of the seventies, made homeowners begin to pay attention to the idea of turning their yards into naturalized prairie areas. Gardeners all over the country began to look toward the Midwest with envy. What could be better than ''rich textures, colors and plant forms'' with easy maintenance? Although in the United States prairies occur only in certain areas, people began to realize that the same concepts could be applied to their own landscapes and that naturalized plantings could work in other areas.

The major difference between a prairie and a meadow is that a prairie is a naturally occurring balanced plant community — a climax community. There are different types of prairies but in each, the climax state is a combination of grasses and forbs, or wildflowers. In areas other than the prairie states, a grassland is merely one stage in the process called natural succession. In most parts of the country, if you leave a grassland or a meadow untended for many years, it will go through various stages of

There wouldn't be such a thing as counterfeit gold if there were no real gold somewhere. — Old Sufi proverb

The old prairie lived by the diversity of its plants and animals, all of which were useful because the sum total of their co-operations and competitions achieved continuity. — Aldo Leopold

succession. Woody species will invade, and the area will soon look very different from the original meadow. Successful meadow projects are planted and must be maintained either mechanically or chemically to prevent succession and for this reason could be more accurately called meadow gardens rather than meadows.

There is quite a difference in restoring a prairie and planting a meadow garden. To properly restore a prairie you must be quite knowledgeable about the plants that are native to your area and use only those species. You must establish a delicate balance between the native grasses and forbs, and you must plant a great diversity of species in order to fill different niches within the prairie. In creating a meadow garden we are trying to put Mother Nature on hold at one of her most beautiful stages. But usually we try to improve on Mother Nature at this stage, so we change the concentration of grasses and wildflowers. Instead of a field of grass sprinkled here and there with wildflowers, we try for a field of wildflowers with occasional clumps of grass.

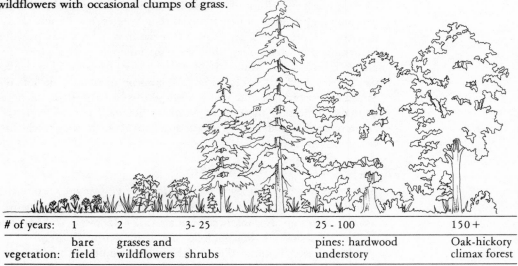

# of years:	1	2	3- 25		25 - 100	150 +
vegetation:	bare field	grasses and wildflowers	shrubs		pines: hardwood understory	Oak-hickory climax forest

Because we cannot hope to establish a climax community, we are not bound by as many rules in planting a meadow garden as we are in restoring a prairie. As long as we are cautious about the number and amounts of non-native species that we use and are aware of their potential to become pests, we can plant the species we like the best. And what glorious fun it is! Plant annual phlox for a bed of red, black-eyed Susans for a splash of yellow, and asters for a streak of purple. If you are out of town every summer, plant for a glorious spring show. If you entertain a lot in the autumn, plant for color in the fall. I happen to be an impatient gardener and can't wait to see the first spot of color in the spring, so I have planted a profusion of early bloomers in my meadow. Make your meadow your own personal project and treat yourself to the colors, textures, and seasonal bloom that will give you the greatest pleasure.

STAGES OF NATURAL SUCCESSION

This chart shows ''old field'' succession as it would occur in the southeastern United States. The type of vegetation and the rate of succession vary from one part of the country to another. Each new type of vegetation creates the proper environmental conditions (shade and soil type) for the next stage of succession.

Perhaps my lawn in itself is more interesting than lawns in general. The soil is sandy with a very little peat, and the fine grasses and little flowers that grow in it are the grasses and flowers of the wild heath-land that I have always loved. — Gertrude Jekyll

Using native plants for home landscaping has become increasingly popular. The native plants are beautiful and varied, and you can find plants to fit your every need. Using plants native to your region will help preserve the integrity of the local vegetation. But to use them, you must first learn what plants are native to your region. Show a little regional pride when you plant your meadow. If you live in the Southeast, then grow a Southern meadow, using Southern plants. Let's keep the wonderful diversity of flora that is unique to each section of the country.

You might want to find out what your state wildflower is and make sure you include that in your meadow. If your garden club or botanical society is named for a wildflower, plant this in your meadow. This can work in reverse as well. If you club plants a meadow and has an extraordinary show from some particular wildflower, you might want to rename your club to commemorate your success. You might also try your hand at growing wildflower species that are threatened or endangered in your area — particularly if your meadow already has the environmental conditions necessary for succesful growth of any of these species. Just be very careful that you acquire your seeds or plants in the most ethical way possible. Remember that we are trying to increase the numbers of these plants. Do not do anything that would in any way decrease the population. Unless you are involved in an organized plant rescue operation, **do not dig** threatened or endangered plants from the wild. The department of natural resources in most states or many botanical gardens will have botanists on their staff to help answer questions about growing threatened wildflower species.

HELPFUL DEFINITIONS

As soon as you begin to learn about native plants, you will encounter a variety of terms that can be somewhat confusing. Is a plant native? naturalized? escaped? introduced? Is it a weed? wildflower? There are few cut-and-dried answers, but the following definitions might help.

Wildflower: Traditionally the definition of wildflower has been that it is any flowering plant that grows without intentional cultivation by man. With the increased popularity of wildflower gardening, this definition has become somewhat outdated. Perhaps a more modern definition is that a wildflower is a flowering plant that can grow without the aid of man. According to this definition, species native to or naturalized within an area are considered wildflowers. Any species that cannot survive without cultivation should not be considered a wildflower within that region.

Native: A native plant is generally thought to be one that evolved in a particular area without having been moved by man. Some experts say that it is a plant that grew in an area of North America before the arrival of the white man. Basic to this definition is the realization that with the arrival of Europeans the landscape began to change drastically and the habitat for many species was destroyed. As the habitats changed, plants that the settlers brought with them took root, and it soon became difficult to tell what was native and what had been introduced, particularly among the grassland and meadow species. Woodland wildflowers seem to be more exacting about their environmental conditions and are thus unable to grow in as many different locales as their less particular, sun-loving cousins. In addition, the grassland wildflowers seem to reseed more readily and grow more quickly, making it easier to establish themselves in a new area. For these reasons, when you walk into an open, grassy area you will probably see a great many more aggressive non-native species there than you would in a woodland area within the same vicinity. This is a point which needs to be considered when planning our meadows, for although there are an abundance of roadside and grassland species that will grow in our meadows, often these are non-native species that can easily outgrow their welcome and are thus not as horticulturally desirable as many of our true natives.

There is some question as to when a plant stops being considered a native plant and is considered a cultivated flower. After all, if we continue to cultivate wildflowers, then what makes them wild? The dividing line seems to come at selective breeding. If we begin to breed for certain characteristics such as height or flower size, then the plants become different genetically from the original strain. If nature does this selective breeding, then it is still considered a wild strain.

Naturalized: A species that is not native to an area but can grow there without the aid of cultivation is considered naturalized. These plants can exist in ecological balance, which means the plant finds a niche within the ecosystem and competes well with, but does not crowd out, the native vegetation. On the other hand, naturalized species can become invasive, outcompeting the native vegetation for available space and nutrients, filling habitats normally filled by native plants. Sometimes the same species can be in ecological balance in some areas and be an invasive problem in others, depending on environmental conditions and the existing vegetation. An example is the common ox-eye daisy. This plant was brought from England and was cherished by the early settlers, for it reminded them of the fields they had left behind. Adapting easily to growing conditions in the New World, the ox-eye daisy eventually found its way all across the continent. In some areas of this country it found conditions so attractive that it has become something of a pest and has become so aggressive that it is not considered to be in balance with the existing native vegetation. In other areas the daisy seems to fit in well within its environmental niche and is a welcomed part of the landscape.

Introduced: An introduced plant is one that was not native to a region but was brought in either intentionally or by mistake. Sometimes species that were brought in intentionally turned out to be a mistake. For example, kudzu was intentionally introduced to the United States from

Japan and was featured at the 1876 Philadelphia exposition. It was planted in the southeastern United States and was thought to be the answer to erosion problems there. Now kudzu is a severe pest, for it overpowers the native vegetation and spreads at an alarming rate.

Escape: A plant that was brought into an area for cultivation but was able to grow and reproduce in the wild without the aid of man is known as an escape plant. Some escape plants are found within close range of cultivated areas; others have been able to spread great distances because of their adaptability. An example of this is Japanese honeysuckle, which was once cultivated for its lovely gold and white blossoms. Finding growing conditions here good, it escaped from cultivation and is now a fast-growing pest, able to grow up to 30 feet in a single growing season. Do not be tempted by its pretty, sweet-smelling blossoms, for once established, it is extremely difficult to eradicate.

Exotic: An exotic is a plant growing in areas other than its natural geographic range. This term usually refers to an ornamental or cultivated garden plant. Cosmos is a good example of an exotic plant that is often included in wildflower seed mixtures. Although it can withstand environmental conditions suited to other meadow plants, it is not native to this country nor is it naturalized here — yet. Perhaps in years to come, cosmos will naturalize in balance with our native vegetation and become a welcomed spot of beauty along our roadsides. However, its great adaptability and its ability to reseed readily, might someday make it a pest and a serious threat to naturally balanced plant communities. The problem is that we just do not know what will happen. But until we do know, we would be well advised not to inadvertently spread across the countryside large amounts of seeds from exotic species.

A weed ... 'a plant whose virtues have not yet been discovered.' — Emerson

Weed: A weed is a plant growing where you do not want it to grow. The word *weed* usually connotes a plant that grows in profusion, is a fast colonizer, and is found in a disturbed area.

Most of these terms are relative. A flower can be a weed in some areas and a prized cultivated specimen in another. A good example is the common sunflower *(Helianthus annuus)*. The sunflower is sometimes grown in agricultural regions for its seed, and in gardens for its flower, thus making it a cultivated plant. In many parts of North America, it grows profusely and spreads rapidly into areas where it is not wanted, thus making it a weed. In parts of its natural geographic range where it is not considered a pest, it is a native wildflower. In European gardens where they pamper and care for it, it is an introduced or exotic species. If it found growing conditions suitable in the countryside outside of European gardens and spread there, then it would be an escape. If it were able to spread and grow in many different locations throughout the countryside, then it would be naturalized. None of these terms is absolute; geography, environmental conditions, existing vegetation, and the extent of man's intervention are all factors that influence the definitions of these terms.

CHAPTER TWO

Planning
Your
Meadow

CHOOSING A SITE

Of the many factors you must consider when planning a meadow, two of the most important are how you are going to use it and where you are going to put it. These two decisions depend one on another: if you plan to use your meadow often for observation or for cutting flowers, then you will want to choose a site that is close by and easily accessible.

Although the word *meadow* connotes large, open spaces, you can have a meadow in a very small area. Just consider it a condensed landscape. Instead of having a big field sprinkled here and there with wildflowers, you can have a very small "field" overflowing with wildflowers. It is actually easier to plant and control a small naturalized area than it is to maintain a large expanse of land, and control is a very important part of planning a meadow. When you let an area revert back to nature you lose control. When you let it return to nature and maintain control, the result can be a breathtakingly beautiful naturalized planting.

Control, of course, is a relative term. Even though I feel that I keep my meadow area under good control, it might look like utter chaos to someone else. The key point to the control issue is being able to prevent one or two aggressive species from taking over the entire meadow and to prevent the invasion of woody species which could transform your meadow into brambles in a very short time. The size meadow you are able to control will depend on the resources available to you and the amount of time you want to spend on it. My meadow covers approximately 2,000 square feet and is a comfortable size for me to take care of by myself. By spending roughly one-half hour per week weeding during the active growing season, and mowing once at the end of the season, I can keep grasses and aggressive weeds in check. As the meadow matures and becomes more established, necessary weeding time should become

If you have built castles in the air, your work need not be lost; that is where they should be. Now put the foundations under them. — Henry David Thoreau

Things tasted better in small houses. — Queen Victoria

less and less. For extensive roadside plantings or large meadow projects hand weeding is, of course, not possible. Control over these plantings is still important, however. If aggressive weeds become a problem, selective spraying or mowing might be necessary. Don't be tempted to plant huge expanses of land unless you have the resources to do it properly. Choose a site that is only as large as you are willing to work with and retain control of.

A meadow can serve a variety of purposes in the landscape. It can take the place of an existing lawn, particularly one that is seldom used or that is at the side or back of the house. It can provide open spaces to attract birds and small wildlife and to view and study during all parts of the year. Pocket meadows can provide islands of color and interesting texture to contrast with existing lawns or formal garden beds.

The meadow should look, ideally, as if it had occurred naturally. Any open sunny space can be converted into a meadow, but some adapt more gracefully than others. I chose to put my meadow into a side yard where we had planted several small dwarf apple trees. The remainder of the area was covered with a mixture of lawn grasses and weeds. It was the beauty of the clumps of weeds that first got me thinking about converting the area into a meadow. Because it was already supporting many of the plants I desired, it converted quite easily and gracefully. As the trees grow and produce more shade, I will introduce more shade-loving species.

Choose a site that will blend in well with both architectural structures and with the existing landscape plan. Take advantage of features of the landscape that are already there. Fences make good boundary lines and add to the country look that the meadow will create. Fences are particularly useful as dividing lines between formal and naturalized plantings. Although small rocks might be a nuisance, large boulders or groups of rocks can be used to advantage. Plant low-growing, rock garden plants among the boulders. Many species thrive in a situation of full sun and well-drained rocky soils.

Paths are important even in a small meadow. They beckon people into the area and invite them to enjoy the colors and scents of the wildflowers. You can make a simple path by merely mowing a track through the flowers and grass, or a more elaborate path with gravel or stepping stones.

Paths and architectural structures are particularly useful if lawn laws are a problem in your community. As you plan your meadow, remember that not everyone likes wildflower plantings. Laws in many cities and towns limit the height of grassy areas. These laws were designed to protect property values at a time when tall grass indicated neglected and abandoned houses and buildings. As philosophies in horticultural design change, it will be necessary to educate lawmakers as well as complaining neighbors and to prove that naturalized plantings indicate concern for conservation rather than neglect. There are ways to prevent trouble and keep the complaints to a minimum; foremost among these is to be educated yourself and know what the laws are in your community before you put in a meadow. Talk to your neighbors, let them know what you are doing, and encourage them to enjoy your meadow. One neighbor asked me to include one of her favorite wildflowers that she remembered from her childhood home. Treat your meadow as a treasured part of your landscape plan and not as a neglected child. Using paths and walkways and including fences and benches within the meadow area will not only enhance the beauty of the site, but will also convince your neighbors that you worked and planned and hoped for these wildflowers to bloom — and that you did not simply forget to cut the grass.

Noxious weed laws are another potential problem. Nearly every state has weed laws listing plant species that are potential pests and problems in that particular state. It is easy to get a plant included on one of these lists, and several species are listed that should not be. However, to be on the safe side, get a copy of the noxious weed list in your state and abide by its restrictions. There are many beautiful native plants that can be used for every type of growing condition without using species found on these lists. Noxious weed lists can be obtained from each state's Department of Agriculture, from the United States Department of Agriculture, or from county extension agencies.

Meadows can be planted anywhere from the inner city to the wilderness. A meadow in the city is a glorious thing. It presents such a strong contrast to the surrounding concrete and tall buildings that it can be a real oasis of beauty and color. Small meadow gardens within a formal home landscape can provide wonderful spots of interest with the added advantage of being small enough to maintain so that they can be attractive during all seasons of the year. If treated as gardens, they can provide a taste of wilderness but can be weeded and pampered so that they do not detract from more formal areas of the landscape.

When we see land as a community to which we belong, we may begin to use it with love and respect. There is no other way for land to survive the impact of mechanized man, nor for us to reap from it the esthetic harvest it is capable, under science, of contributing to culture.
— Aldo Leopold

If you live in a rural area and are lucky enough to have grand vistas beyond your home, a meadow provides a wonderful transition from inside the house through the home landscape to the natural areas beyond. A meadow in front of a mountain house will not only make the mountains seem closer and more approachable, but will also seem to make the house reach out and be a part of the landscape.

CREATING PLANT COMMUNITIES

Within nature a transition zone between two different environments provides the greatest diversity of plants and animals because the organisms can take advantage of the best of both worlds. Areas between woods and an open field can support species that need full sun as well as those that need shade. Areas between field and water can support species that need dry conditions as well as those that need a great deal of moisture. For this reason, plant your meadow in a transition zone if possible.

A meadow garden between a well-kept lawn and a wooded area provides a buffer between a formal area and a natural one. Many of the meadow plants can take full sun or partial shade and are well suited to growing between the woods and the open meadow. Many home landscapes have more shade than sun. A border of shade-tolerant meadow plants can provide a little color and a great deal of beauty to the woodland edge. You might also want to plant a series of native shrubs at the edge of the wooded area to help sustain the idea of a natural transition and to help keep seedlings from the wooded area from taking root in the meadow. Lists of shade-tolerant species suitable for each region are given in Part Two.

Meadows also work well at the edge of the water, whether it is a pond or stream or lake. Many meadow species naturally occur in this environment where they get plenty of sun and abundant moisture. Not only will it be easy to grow many of these plants, but they will also look very much at home. Lists of moisture-loving plants are given in Part Two.

... every plant must bear its part, and they must fall into their places like the notes in music. — John Evelyn

Wherever you put your meadow, pay attention to the types of plants that you are putting in, and if at all possible, plant species together that occur together naturally, thus planting communities rather than individual specimens. Get to know your meadow and learn about the different ecosystems that can exist within even a small area. Plant species that will thrive in the type of soil, the amount of moisture, and the temperature ranges that exist in your area. Don't try to plant wildflowers or grasses that are not suited to your region or to your particular conditions. Trying to grow plants where they cannot survive is a frustrating experience. Save your time and money for those species that will be able to repay you by growing well. The meadow plants, on the whole, are quite adaptable. You should be able to find many, many species that will adapt to your conditions no matter where you live.

DETERMINING GROWING CONDITIONS

One of the real advantages to planting a meadow area is that many of the meadow and roadside plants can grow under truly adverse conditions; they actually thrive in dry, poor soils and can withstand drought conditions. However, you need to know what the growing conditions in your meadow are to be able to determine which plants to put where. Species that will grow in very poor soils with little moisture might languish in rich, moist soils, growing tall, spindly stems, or they might grow lush foliage with few blossoms. When using any native plant, the rule of thumb is to put it in growing conditions that resemble as closely as possible those of its natural habitat. Rather than trying to change the conditions that you have, it is a lot easier and makes more sense to choose plants that will grow in your situation. The variety and adaptability of the meadow plants make it possible to find lovely flowers that will grow in many different kinds of environments.

The four environmental factors that are most important to know about your area are: soil type and pH, the amount of sunshine, the amount of moisture available, and temperature ranges.

MOISTURE AND TEMPERATURE

If you have done any gardening at all in your area then you will be somewhat aware of general climatic conditions in your region. If you know the temperature ranges within your area, you can tell not only what to plant but when to plant it. Available moisture will vary from one locale to another, sometimes even within a small area — it depends on terrain. The amount of available moisture will also depend on your own resources: can you give your meadow extra water when needed? Although many plants are drought tolerant, remember that all plants need water to get established, whether you sow seeds or transplant seedlings. Unless you want to take your chances with Mother Nature, you'll need a water supply when you first establish the meadow.

Praised be my Lord for our sister water, who is very serviceable unto us, and humble, and precious and clean. — Saint Francis of Assisi, Hymn to Creation

THE SPRING MEADOW

Many of the plants blooming during the spring are woodland plants that are delicate and lightly colored. This would be a good season to spotlight a woodland border at the edge of your meadow. Leave the wide open spaces for the bolder and hardier summer blooming plants that need full, intense sunlight.

spring beauty .... 4-6 inches	*blue eyed grass* .. 6-10 inches
Johnny jump up .. 5-8 inches	*larkspur* .... 36 inches
baby blue eyes .... 10 inches	*columbine* ..... 12-24 inches
dwarf crested iris . 4-10 inches	*beard tongue* ..... 48 inches
wild geranium .. 12-24 inches	

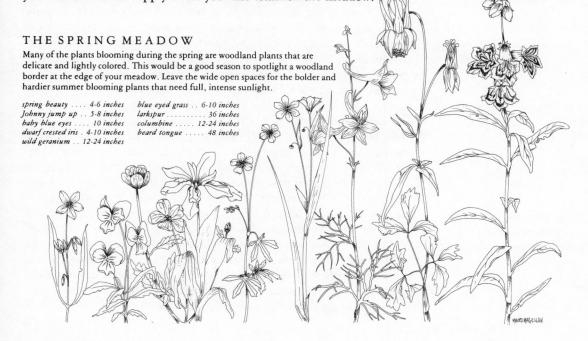

SUNSHINE

Most meadow plants need a lot of sun. When growing conditions specify full sun, that means *full* sun. With insufficient light, plant growth will be sparse and flowering will be disappointing, particularly during the first few years when the greatest show will be from the sun-loving annuals. Many species can tolerate light or partial shade, but this means that they still need several hours of sunlight each day. Many of the shade tolerant plants require abundant moisture. Numerous species, however, seem to be unaffected by the amount of light and moisture they receive and will thrive in sun or shade, moist or dry conditions. Look at your meadow area before you plant and determine how many hours of sunlight it gets every day (remember to check during the summer when the leaves are out and think about the winter months when the midday sun is lower and may be blocked by nearby trees, etc.).

SOIL

While many plants can tolerate very poor and infertile soil, good drainage seems to be an essential growth requirement for most meadow wildflowers. Drainage is directly dependent on the makeup of the soil. To determine which kind of soil you have, dig up a shovel of soil from your meadow site. If the soil feels gritty and does not hold together when moist, you have sandy soil. This type of soil drains very quickly, often leaching out important nutrients. Sandy soils are easy to work with, will dry out quickly after a rain, and will heat up quickly in the spring. If your soil feels greasy when wet and forms hard, rocklike clods, you probably have soil with a high clay content. Clay soils drain very poorly, retaining much more moisture than sandy soils, and are difficult to work with. The ideal growing medium is loamy soil, which is a combination of sand and clay and high proportion of organic matter. If your soil breaks apart well but can hold its shape, you probably have loamy soil. This type of soil does not drain so quickly as to leach out necessary nutrients nor does it become hard and compacted as does poorly draining clay soil. Although it is rarely necessary to improve the fertility of the soil to have a wildflower meadow, it might be advantageous to add organic matter to extremely heavy, clay soils to allow them to drain better. Choosing the correct plants for your meadow will be easier if you know the pH (the amount of acidity or alkalinity) of your soil. There are native plants that will grow in alkaline soils and others that grow in acidic soils, but you need to know which type of soil you have so you will know which plants to use. Easy-to-use pH indicator sets designed for the home gardener are available at local gardening centers, and many county extension agencies offer a soil analysis service.

CHOOSING PLANTS

The most important thing to remember as you plan your meadow is to be sure to choose the types of plants that you can easily control. Part of the problem with controlling an area is the aggressive behavior of some of the non-native species that have naturalized across our country. Although many of these species are included within wildflower seed mixtures, you should take care that they do not become a threat to the balance of the meadow or to an existing plant community. Some wildflowers, particularly those that have been introduced from other countries, spread with alarming speed. If you plant an abundance of these wildflowers, they are going to spread from your meadow to neighboring areas and, in some instances, may become a real pest. Aggressive species can be held in check to some extent by giving them plenty of competition from other plants. In parts of the country where prairies are found, the spread of non-native plants poses a particular threat, for they can quickly destroy the balance of the prairie plant community. For these reasons, each of us has a responsibility to plant wisely and to use non-native species cautiously. Learn what plants are native to your region and make these the backbone of your meadow, using the non-native plants for accent and special effects only. (See Part Two for lists of species that are native to each region.)

THE SUMMER MEADOW

Summer meadow flowers are characterized by their bright, bold colors and their love of sunshine.

ox-eye daisy	*24 inches*	*lupine*	*12-26 inches*
annual phlox	*20 inches*	*bachelor buttons*	*24-36 inches*
forget me not	*6-15 inches*	*milkweed*	*24-60 inches*
black-eyed Susan	*12-36 inches*	*Queen Anne's lace*	*12-48 inches*

You will have a more natural-looking area if you choose plants that fit the scale of your meadow garden. If you have a small, confined meadow you certainly will not want to plant large, overpowering species. Small meadows look best planted with flowers that are small, do not spread too rapidly, and are low growing. Conversely, if you

The garden should fit its master or his tastes, just as his clothes do; it should be neither too large nor too small, but just comfortable. — Gertrude Jekyll

have a very large, wide-open space to fill, choose plants that are large and showy and will make a big splash of color. If you want to include some low-growing plants within a large area, plant them toward the front so that they will not be overshadowed by taller species. Even if you use a packaged mixture of seeds, you might want to obtain extra seeds or plants of a size that best suits your meadow.

In addition to size, you should pay careful attention to when the different species bloom, so you can get a longer blooming season. Ideally you should have some plants that bloom during each part of the growing season, beginning in early spring and lasting until fall. How long you will actually have color depends on where you live, of course, for the growing season will be limited by temperature changes and the amount of available moisture. If you live in a very dry area you can extend the period of bloom of many species by giving them extra water. To have the best display of color and to keep the meadow looking as neat as possible, group plants according to when they bloom and mow different sections as they set seed. You might concentrate spring-blooming plants in one section, summer flowers in another, and fall-blooming species in another. When you place these sections remember that spring flowers are generally much shorter than summer- or fall-blooming species and should be placed toward the front of the meadow.

MIXTURES VERSUS INDIVIDUAL SPECIES

There are advantages to using a premixed wildflower blend as well as to choosing individual species to plant. By choosing individual plants to put in, you can retain better control over the flowers that you have planted. You can group them to have a better show of color. It is easier to recognize groupings of the same kind of plants as they germinate and begin to grow, and this makes it easier to distinguish them from the weeds. You can choose individual plants that are best suited to your meadow's particular environmental needs, and you can mow sections of the meadow planted with the same flowers as they set seed, eliminating the seed heads if you find them unattractive.

On the other hand, a seed mixture designed for your particular region is an easy and fun method of establishing a naturalized area. The more specific a mixture is, the better results you will have. For example, a mixture composed of native wildflowers that grow in acidic soils in Georgia will produce more abundant and healthier plants there than a general mixture designed for the Southeast, and it will certainly give better results than a broad mixture of seeds designed for the entire country. You can generally get a greater variety of plants by using a mixture, and you will probably discover new species that you had not thought of including. A mixture of evenly distributed seeds will produce the most natural-looking meadow, for you will get a random distribution of species. Using a mixture is also a great way to find out which plants grow best in which parts of the meadow and will show you where to reseed if you want more of the same species. One problem with using a mixture is that some very desirable species are not included in premixed blends because their seeds are difficult to collect, because they are quite expensive, or because they are unavailable commercially. Foremost among these are the seeds of asters and goldenrods. Both these plants are wonderful for fall color, and there are species of both flowers that are suited to each region of the country. Don't leave these plants out of your meadow because they don't happen to be in your mix: either buy the seeds separately, collect seeds from the wild, or buy plants from a local source and put them in yourself.

THE AUTUMN MEADOW

   Although the meadow in Autumn is usually dominated by asters and goldenrods with careful planning, a variety of plants will bloom during the fall months.

grey goldenrod	*24 inches*
yarrow	*12-36 inches*
purple coneflower	*24-36 inches*
tickseed sunflower	*12-60 inches*
blackberry lily	*18-48 inches*
evening primrose	*24-60 inches*
New England aster	*36-72 inches*
Joe-Pye weed	*24-72 inches*

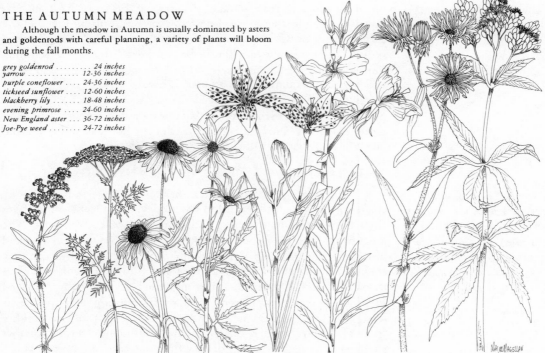

Be wary of the amount of grass seed and the amounts of potentially invasive species included in the mix. Although it is important to have grasses within the meadow, only certain kinds should be used so they won't overpower the wildflowers. Lawn grass seed is inexpensive and is sometimes used as a filler so that the consumer gets a bigger package. Avoid seed mixtures that include grasses such as tall fescue, annual rye, orchard grass, Timothy grass, and bluegrass. However, there are some non-spreading grasses that are often included within mixtures, and moderate amounts of these grasses are acceptable. Both Chewing's fescue and blue fescue are acceptable, as well as many kinds of native grasses such as big bluestem, blue grama, side oats grama, buffalo grass, and Indian ricegrass. Before you start to curse the seed companies for including grass seed that has taken over your meadow, identify the problem grass to make sure that it was one included in your mixture. If not, complain to Mother Nature but not to your seed company. The seeds of many non-native plants are also inexpensive because they are so abundant and are sometimes used in quantity. Ask for a list of species and relative amounts before you buy a mixture.

The wildflower seed industry is relatively new, and better and more varied mixtures will come on the market as the industry grows. You can help by letting the seed companies know what you want and what grows best in your area. Many seed companies will mix a custom blend for you if you ask, so take advantage of this service. Although it is easy to put together a list of desirable species, putting together the correct blend of wildflowers in the correct proportions is an acquired skill. There are many variables to be considered, including germination rate, time of bloom, necessary pretreatment of seeds, and when and where the mixture will be used. Share your knowledge of what works in your area with the seed companies and your local native plants societies, garden clubs, or botanical garden. Landscaping with native plants is a new and exciting part of the horticultural world and our best information will come from you, the gardener.

THE MEADOW IS ALWAYS CHANGING

It is fortunate, perhaps, that no matter how intently one studies the hundred little dramas of the woods and meadows, one can never learn all of the salient facts about any one of them. — Aldo Leopold, A Sand County Almanac

It is difficult to get bored with a meadow because it is constantly changing. It looks different from day to day, and it certainly changes from one season to the next and from one year to another. The amount of change in your meadow will greatly depend on you and how you manage it. If you don't manage it at all it will certainly change, for you will have a great many weeds that will soon choke out the wildflowers. During the growing season of a properly managed meadow, a few species seem to dominate during each particular season. Ideally these dominant species should begin to fade as other species begin to bloom so that you have continuous color. Remember that if you have a spectacular display from one type of flower all at the same time, these flowers are all going to go to seed at the same time, and for every blossom that you have now, you will have a brown seed head later on. It is very difficult to have a meadow that looks spectacular during the entire growing season, but by creating a balance of wildflowers and grasses you can have a meadow that looks good all the time.

A balanced meadow should include both perennial, biennial, and annual wildflowers and grasses. Perennial wildflowers, those that live and flower for more than two years, usually spend the first one or two years developing a root system before they are able to bloom. If you plant perennial seeds, don't expect to see flowers until at least the second growing season. Some perennials take even longer before they are able to bloom; others are able to produce limited bloom by the end of their first season. Annuals complete their life cycle within one growing season, so you will get color the first year from the seeds of these species. Biennial plants take two years to complete their cycle, developing a root system the first year and then producing blooms the second year. When planning your meadow, remember that during the first year you will have color only from the annual plants, but by the second or third year you should have flowers from the biennials and perennials as well. The annuals should reseed themselves from one year to the next. Whether they actually do or not depends on growing conditions in your meadow and when you cut your area. If you wait until all the flowers have set seed before you cut, your chances of the annuals' reseeding will be much greater. However, to guarantee continuous color and diversity year after year, you should reseed some annuals yearly and reseed perennials every three to four years.

In a Nutshell

(1) Choose a site small enough for you to plant and control easily.

(2) If possible, put your meadow in a transition zone, for example an area between woods or water and a more formal landscape.

(3) Plant species together that occur together naturally in the wild.

(4) Pay attention to the time of bloom and the size that different plants will attain, and group them accordingly.

(5) Learn the soil type, amount of sunshine and moisture, and temperature ranges of your meadow. Use only those plants that will grow under these conditions.

(6) Be responsible: plant wisely and use non-native species cautiously.

(7) Carefully weigh the benefits of using a premixed blend of wildflower seeds or choosing individual species to plant, and determine the method that best fits your needs.

(8) Realize that the meadow is in a constant state of change due to seasonal variations and the natural influx of new plants from seeds that blow in.

(9) Remember that it takes time to establish a meadow. Annuals will give good color the first year, but most biennial and perennial plants take at least two years before they will bloom.

The Meadow in the first three years

First year

Second year

Third year

The meadow during the first year will be characterized by color from the annual wildflowers. During the second year the biennials and many perennials will begin to bloom, adding to the diversity of the meadow. The third year should present even greater diversity and good color and texture from a variety of perennials and from annuals that have reseeded.

CHAPTER THREE

Obtaining Seeds
And
Plants

CHOOSING A NURSERY OR SEED COMPANY

One of the best parts of establishing a meadow is choosing the plants that you want in it. It is also one of the most crucial parts. It is frustrating to spend time and money on something that does not work. The best assurance for success is to choose your plants wisely. Not only is it important to choose plants that are well suited to your own particular environment, but it is also important to choose your source for these seeds and plants with care. Although the wildflower seed industry is relatively new, there are many excellent sources for quality seeds and plants in all parts of the country. There are also many seed companies that "jumped on the bandwagon" as wildflower gardening became popular and are not as reputable as they should be. As with anything else, you get what you pay for. Wildflowers seeds are not cheap, but if you invest your time and effort into preparing a site for a meadow garden, don't throw it all away by buying poor-quality seeds or plants. Whether you establish your area by sowing a seed mixture or the seeds of individual species or by plugging in plants is your personal preference, but the basis of all methods should be quality merchandise.

When choosing a seed company one criterion is the amount of information that the company is willing and able to give you about its product. You should be able to get a germination rate for each variety of seed. If you purchase a mixture, the company should supply you with a list of the species included and a percentage by weight of grasses and wildflowers.

Although pretty pictures are fun to look at, don't choose a company based on how slick its product looks. Many small companies do not have the time, money, or inclination to produce fancy catalogs, but this does not mean that their products are inferior.

The Greeks, and Milton, alike speak of violets as growing in meadows or dales. But the Greeks did so because they could not fancy any delight except in meadows; and Milton, because he wanted a rhyme to nightingale — and was, after all, London bred. But Viola's beloved knew where violets grew in Illyria — and grow everywhere else also, when they can — on a bank, facing south . . . — John Ruskin Prosperina

Although wildflower seed mixtures are quite popular, a good mixture cannot be put together by just anyone. A good, working mixture is both an art and a science. The art is including species that work together aesthetically and will produce the best show for the longest amount of time. The science of putting a mixture together is much more difficult and requires a great deal more knowledge. Factors that must be considered include competition among the plants themselves, germination rates, growing conditions for the region where it will be used, when to plant to break dormancy of the greatest number of seeds, the soil conditions of the proposed site, and the aggressive behavior of many species. Read about the mixture you are buying and ask questions. Be a knowledgeable consumer.

Will locally produced seed be better suited to a particular region than seed from plants grown across the country? For plants with a wide natural range and great adaptability, the origin of the seed seems to make little difference. For those species that have a small geographical range or that are very exacting in their environmental conditions, buying seeds from a non-local source might result in a reduction of cold hardiness, heat and drought tolerance, and general adaptability. Most wildflowers included within a meadow mixture are characterized by their adaptability, and a local seed source is not a necessity. In general the quality of the seed is more important than the source.

A seed company cannot guarantee a beautiful flower from every seed (just as a company that sells photographic film cannot guarantee a beautiful picture). There are too many variables involved, many depending on the consumer, others depending on nature. There are certain things that a seed company can guarantee, however: purity of the seed and germination rate. The consumer should expect a reasonable degree of purity — there should be no mold or insects, and no substantial amount of dust, chaff, or dirt.

Optimal conditions for germination will vary greatly from one species to another. Many seeds have a dormancy period which can be broken only by high or low temperatures. Some need alternating high and low temperatures, some need constant light, some need absolute darkness to germinate. Each species has a specific germination rate which should be listed on the label of your seed package. This rate is based on the number of seeds that germinate within a laboratory under optimal conditions. Usually an acceptable germination rate is seventy-five percent or higher, but some species have a lower acceptable rate. Seeds of species with low germination rates must be planted in greater quantities to produce the same number of plants as species with high germination rates. Use the sowing rate suggested by the seed company.

HOW TO HANDLE THE SEEDS

The time needed for germination for many species may be decreased by

If an Arctic summer is exceptionally cold, some "snow-bed" plants may not emerge at all from underneath deep drifts. But they survive, biding their time for another, more favourable year . . Buried in permafrost, they can survive millennia. A lemming's cache of Arctic lupine seeds, hidden deep in the frozen ground more than ten thousand years ago, was recently discovered by botanists. Given earth and light and water, these seeds, asleep for one hundred centuries, awoke to life; they germinated, grew roots and flowers and new seeds. These delicate, lovely plants were older than mankind's recorded history.
— Fred Bruemmer, Seasons of the Eskimo

breaking the dormancy period of the seeds. Seed dormancy is a natural condition that is beneficial to the plants, for in nature seeds drop as they mature. If they were not dormant, many of these seeds would germinate during a season when there were severe temperatures or insufficient moisture, and the seedlings would not survive. Seed dormancy is nature's way of guaranteeing that the seeds germinate at the correct time. If seeds are collected or purchased in the fall but you don't want to sow them until spring, they should be stored in the refrigerator to help break dormancy and reduce the chance of early germination.

Seeds that are produced dry on the plant should be thoroughly air dried for a few days after collection to make sure that no moisture is present in the seeds before they are stored. Moisture can cause mold to grow or seeds to germinate while in storage. Seeds stored dry can be placed in freezer containers or clean, dry jars and kept in the refrigerator until you are ready to plant them in the spring. Some seeds need to be stratified, or placed between layers of a moist substance. An efficient way to do this is to pack the seeds in layers of damp sphagnum moss and keep them in the refrigerator until spring.

Seeds with a very thick, hard seed coat can be scarified, or broken, to allow the seed to absorb water. This can be done by scratching the surface of the seed coat with a file, by softening the seeds in hot or boiling water, or by treating the seeds with acid. For example, the germination rate of most lupines will be greatly increased by soaking the seeds in hot water for several hours.

Many members of the legume family (such as clovers and lupines) have certain types of bacterium on their roots that make the conversion of atmospheric nitrogen into a usable form possible. This process, called nitrogen fixation, is necessary for the growth of these plants. To insure that the proper bacteria are present, the seeds of these plants should be inoculated with the correct bacterial mixture. Many regulations exist concerning the chemical treatment of seeds, so seedsmen generally will not treat seeds that are sold outside their state. For this reason, seeds bought out of state will rarely be treated chemically.

Not all seeds will need to be stratified, scarified, or inoculated. Check individual requirements for different species in Part III of this book. To store a mixture of seeds, keep them dry in the refrigerator until planting time. Remember, however, that quick germination is not always what you want. For example, the National Wildflower Research Center recommends not scarifying lupine seeds, for by doing so you are destroying the seed's protective coat. Once this seed coat is broken, if the seed does not germinate soon, it will not be able to survive climatic conditions to be able to germinate another year. Be patient. Mother Nature knows what she is doing.

June 5, 1852: The Lupine is now in its glory. It is the more important because it occurs in such extensive patches, even an acre or more together . . . It paints a whole hillside with its blue, making such a field (if not a meadow) as Proserpine might have wandered in . . . Such a profusion of the heavenly, Elysian Fields. That is the value of the Lupine. The earth is blued with them . . . You may have passed along here perchance, a fortnight ago and the hillside was comparatively barren. But now you come, and these glorious redeemers appear to have flashed out here all at once. Who planted the seeds of Lupines in the barren soil? Who watereth the Lupines in the field?
— *Henry David Thoreau, Journals*

COLLECTING SEEDS FROM THE WILD

An inexpensive and informative way to decide what you want in your meadow is to collect seeds from the wild. By choosing plants that you see growing in the wild, you will know how they look and what their natural habitat is. Theoretically, collecting seeds from wild plants will neither harm the parent plant nor decrease the plant population in any way. However, as with any activity involving the native plants, a cautionary note must be added. First, be sure to get the property owner's written permission to collect from his land. Collect only from plants that are common and locally abundant and be sure to gather only a few seeds from each of many plants. Take care not to harm any other part of the plant, and disturb the surrounding vegetation as little as possible. Start looking for desirable species in the spring and keep looking throughout the growing season. Inconspicuously mark plants that you want to collect seed from. A tag of colored yarn or flagging tape tied near the base of the plant will not get blown away or broken off. Tagging at the base of the plant allows you to know where to look but does not advertise your plant for poachers. It is also helpful to tag a fence post or other landmark and make notes about where your tagged plants are. Come back often to check on their progress, for some species hold their seeds for a very long time and other types of seeds seem to be green one day and are mature and gone by the next. Dry seeds are usually mature when the seeds or seed pods are dark and brittle and when the seeds and surrounding tissue are dry, and moist seeds are ripe when the berries or fruit are most brightly colored. Depending on local weather conditions, seeds from summer-blooming species can usually be collected in August or September. Keep notes on where and when you collect seeds from different species, and you can save a great deal of time and effort in subsequent years.

After collection, the seeds should be air dried for a few days in a draft-free, dry spot. Don't put the seeds in the hot sun where temperatures would get to 100 degrees or more, and do not leave them outdoors all night. During this time, check carefully for insects among the seeds. When they are thoroughly dry, the seeds should be cleaned. Seeds formed in capsules or pods can be separated by placing the split capsule in a paper bag and shaking vigorously. Adding a bit of pea gravel to this bag will help loosen the seeds. Some seed capsules are so hard that they must be crushed with a rolling pin. A series of wire screens in varying sizes from 1/32 inch to 1/2 inch is useful in separating the seeds from surrounding tissue and chaff. Although the seeds should be as clean as possible, a small amount of litter will not effect the viability of the seeds.

BUYING NATIVE PLANTS

Many of our native plants, and particularly woodland species, are being collected from the wild at a frightening rate. Do not dig plants from the woods to use in a wildflower garden. Many of the woodland species are

To you the earth yields her fruit, and you shall not want if you but know how to fill your hands. It is in exchanging the gifts of the earth that you shall find abundance and be satisfied. — Kahlil Gibran, The Prophet

By plucking her petals, you do not gather the beauty of the flower. — Rabindranath Tagore

difficult to propagate and may take years to grow from a seed to a blooming plant. Purchase these plants only from wildflower nurseries that have a policy of not digging from the wild. If you don't know where they get their plants, ask them. If they don't give you a direct answer, don't give them your business.

The science of propagating native plants is advancing, and one of the great pioneer institutions in this science is the North Carolina Botanical Garden at Chapel Hill, North Carolina. Alarmed at the rate that the wildflowers and native plants were being removed from their area, this botanical garden began actively working to practice and promote alternative approaches of plant rescue and plant propagation. Their aim is to make propagated plants and seeds of the native species so widely available that collection from the wild will no longer be profitable.

Luckily roadside and common meadow wildflowers are generally easy to grow from seed and to propagate by other methods. They are less expensive to buy than most woodland species and are readily available from a great number of native plant nurseries. Any plants that you want to establish quickly can be bought from a reputable nursery and plugged into the meadow garden.

PROPAGATING METHODS

TRANSPLANTING SEEDLINGS

And what is it to work with love? ... It is to sow seeds with tenderness and reap the harvest with joy ... — Kahlil Gibran, The Prophet

Although most meadow plants can be easily grown from seed, some of them need a bit of extra care and should not be directly sown into the meadow plot. Sowing individual species indoors or in outdoor seed beds and allowing them to become established before planting in the meadow will give the most reliable results from seeds. The plants that have very slow-growing seedlings will need the extra pampering of being sown indoors and protected until they have established a root system. To avoid damage to the soft, newly formed tissue, do not transplant seedlings until they have grown at least two pairs of leaves.

DIVISION

A very easy way to get new plants is to divide an established one. For best results, spring-blooming plants should be divided in the fall and fall-blooming plants should be divided in late fall or early winter while they are dormant. The entire clump should be dug and, depending on the species, either separated gently by hand or cut apart with a knife or spade. Cut off part of the top growth to minimize water loss. The divisions should be replanted immediately and watered thoroughly.

ROOT AND STEM CUTTINGS

Though it's a little more complicated than dividing plants, root or stem cuttings are another means of propagating plants. To determine which species are most easily propagated by cuttings, check Part III. One advantage of both plant division and root and stem cuttings is that these are a sexual means of propagation, so the new stock will be genetically identical to the parent plant. Often plants grown from seeds show quite a variation in appearance from the parent plant. There are several good resource books available that will explain in depth the procedures necessary for taking successful root and stem cuttings. One of the best in reference to the wildflowers is Harry Phillip's *Growing and Propagating Wildflowers*, published by the University of North Carolina Press.

In a Nutshell

(1) Choose a seed company or nursery carefully, making sure that they are knowledgeable about their product.
(2) Read the label on your seed package, and make sure you are getting what you asked for. Examine the seeds to see that they are clean and free of bugs.
(3) Store your seeds correctly. If you have purchased a mixture, store it dry in the refrigerator until you are ready to use it. If you have bought individual species, store each according to its own requirements.
(4) Collect seeds yourself from the wild to become familiar with the appearance and habitats of different species. Allow them to dry thoroughly and then clean carefully and store properly.
(5) DO NOT BUY from nurseries that dig their plants from the wild.
(6) Try planting techniques other than direct seeding. Transplanting seedlings started indoors, division of established plants, and root and stem cuttings are all good methods of propagation.

CHAPTER FOUR

Planting The Meadow

God grant me patience ... but I want it now!

— Anonymous

Growing wildflowers is a lesson in patience. Although many of our native plants are hardy, this does not mean that they are indestructible. They need good soil-to-seed contact and plenty of moisture to germinate, and they need relief from overcrowding by weeds, just as any other plant would. Wildflowers are beautiful and exciting and wonderful, but they are not magic. You cannot sit in the rocking chair on your back porch, throw wildflower seeds into the yard and expect a meadow to appear the next day. It takes work to establish and maintain a meadow garden year after year, just as it does for every other type of garden.

The late Carroll Abbott, noted wildflower enthusiast and founder of Green Horizons Nursery in Texas warned his customers that "Raising wildflowers is like rearing children: time and love are the key factors. Time is essential because it allows for unhurried and sturdy growth; love is necessary because it breeds patience and salves the passing pains of inescapable heartbreak. Instant success is rarely — if ever — possible with wildflower plantings." There are guidelines that one can follow, however, that will create better conditions for success.

A sower went out to sow. And as he sowed, some seeds fell along the path, and the birds came and devoured them. Other seeds fell on rocky ground, where they had not much soil, and immediately they sprang up, since they had no depth of soil, but when the sun rose they were scorched; and since they had no root they withered away. Other seeds fell upon thorns, and the thorns grew up and choked them. Other seeds fell on good soil and brought forth grain some a hundredfold, some sixty, some thirty. — Matthew 13:3

PREPARING THE SOIL

It is never too early to begin preparing the area for a meadow garden. The biggest problem that confronts meadow gardeners is competition from weeds. Much of this problem can be eliminated by preparing the site correctly to begin with. There are several methods of soil preparation, but the goal of each method is to get as many seedlings or plants established in the area with the invasion of the fewest number of weeds. Plowing deeply will result in better growing conditions for the wildflowers but will produce equally good growing conditions for the weeds with the added disadvantage of digging up weed seeds that have lain dormant in the soil for many, many years. Sowing directly, without any surface preparation, will not produce additional weeds, but conditions for the germination of the seeds will be poor. Just as every cook has a favorite recipe, so does every meadow gardener seem to have a favorite way of establishing a meadow. The following methods are some that are used most often. Choose the one that best suits your conditions and resources.

(1) Shallow or surface tilling of the soil allows for good seed-to-soil contact but pulls up relatively few weed seeds. It is a bit more difficult for the seedlings to become established because only the first inch or two of earth is tilled.

The plough is one of the most ancient and most valuable of man's inventions; but long before he existed the land was in fact regularly ploughed, and still continues to be ploughed by earthworms. — Charles Darwin

(2) Rototilling (plowing, or somehow breaking up the soil to a depth of 6 to 8 inches) and then killing off weeds before planting the seeds is the method most often recommended. The idea is to create as clean a seed bed as possible. For the best results from this method, you should do it during the active growing season. After tilling, allow the area to remain fallow for at least three weeks and let the weed seeds germinate. You might even want to water the area during this time because you want as many as possible of the weed seeds to germinate. After three to four weeks have passed, the entire area should be sprayed with a general herbicide. Ideally you should wait another three weeks and spray again to rid the area of any additional weeds that have come up. Depending on the type of herbicide used and the climate of the region, you usually need to let the area sit after the last spraying for at least two more weeks. Check with a local gardening center to determine the recommended length of time to wait after spraying before planting in your area. The disadvantages to tilling or plowing any area are that you will lose any wildflower plants that might occur in the site naturally, and you will pull up weed seeds that have lain dormant but are now exposed to light and air and will begin to germinate.

(3) A similar method rototills or plows the area, and instead of spraying, the entire site is covered with black plastic during the summer months to smother the weeds. The disadvantage to this, of course, is having black plastic as a part of your landscape for two months.

(4) If you object to black plastic, an alternative method is to rototill or plow the area early in the spring and plant a cover crop of buckwheat. Plant it heavily enough so that the leaves touch and effectively shade out any grasses and weeds that come up. You must till this crop under before it sets seed and plant another crop immediately. Once you have tilled the second crop under, during the fall, you will be able to immediately plant the meadow seeds. The advantages of buckwheat over black plastic are many. First of all, it is much more attractive. Second, the tilled buckwheat adds organic matter to the soil. The disadvantage is that you

have to begin to prepare the area one year ahead of time. Be sure that you do not allow the buckwheat to go to seed; if it does you will always have volunteer buckwheat plants.

(5) A single deep tilling (6 to 8 inches) followed by successive shallow tillings will succeed in breaking up the soil quite well, but it may bring up a new crop of weed seeds every time you till. For the shallow tillings, make sure you go only deep enough to turn under the existing plants.

(6) If resources are available, you can plug in established plants throughout the meadow area. This eliminates the need to disturb large sections of soil and cuts down considerably on the weed problem.

(7) One other possibility is to do soil preparation and no planting, stop mowing and merely maintain an area that is at a grassland stage. This has been found to be effective for very large tracts of land, particularly in the Northeast. The area is mowed annually to keep it at a grassland stage. Naturally this type of area will not have the concentration of wildflowers that planted areas have, but it does have the advantage of low maintenance.

> For larger areas of an acre or more: Do not plow. If you are direct seeding, scarify or surface till the area only. Get the greatest seed-to-soil contact possible but disturb the soil as little as you can.

It would indeed be worthwhile to leave many parts of the grass unmown for the sake of growing many beautiful plants ... We want shaven carpets of grass here and there, but what a nuisance it is to shave it as often as foolish men shave their faces! ... Who would not rather see the waving grass with countless flowers than a close surface without a blossom.
W. Robinson, The Wild Garden

Recommendations

The best method of preparing the soil for the home gardener with a relatively small area seems to be tilling deep and killing the weeds with a general herbicide spray. Till and spray on the following schedule:
 (1) Rototill or plow to a depth of 6 to 8 inches.
 (2) Wait three weeks and spray with a safe, general herbicide.
 (3) Wait approximately two weeks and plant the seeds.
The longer you wait and work with the weeds, the fewer weeds you will have to contend with. Two sprayings are better than one. Three will rid the area of even more weeds.

AMENDING THE SOIL

Under most circumstances, meadow flowers will perform better if you do not amend the soil in any way. There are, or course, exceptions to this. If your soil is completely infertile, adding small amounts of fertilizer might

Ten Steps
to a
Successful Meadow

1. **PLOW** (till, harrow, scarify) or somehow break up the surface of the soil to get good seed-to-soil contact.

2. **SPRAY** an herbicide on any weeds that appear on the site. Wait at least three weeks after you till the soil to get rid of as many weeds as possible.

3. **RAKE** the area to smooth the seed bed and eliminate more weeds and roots.

4. **SCATTER SEEDS** evenly throughout the meadow site. Use the recommended seeding rate for the particular seeds or mixture you have chosen. Use species of wildflowers that are native or naturalized in your area. For even distribution, mix the seeds with damp sand or sawdust.

5. **TAMP** down the seeds by gently walking over the seeded area.

6. **MULCH** lightly with weed-free straw, pine-straw, or sawdust. Do not mulch too heavily; this hampers penetration of the seedlings.

7. **WATER** the area regularly until the seedlings are established. Even wildflowers that are drought resistant need water to get established.

8. **WEED** out the undesirable grasses and plants that will appear in your meadow. A little weeding early in the growing season will make a big difference later on.

9. **ENJOY** your wildflowers! You worked for them; you deserve them.

10. **CUT** the meadow at the end of the summer or in later winter. This prevents many weed problems, opens up the area to more light and air, and sets the scene for another year of meadow gardening.

be beneficial. However, you can choose wildflowers that will grow quite well in poor soil, and fertilizing usually results in bigger foliage but fewer flowers and better growing conditions for the weeds. There are certain species of wildflowers that prefer more fertile conditions. If you want to grow these species, amend the soil only where these particular plants will grow.

Although most species suitable for a meadow environment can thrive in relatively infertile soils, most require well-drained soils, and it might be necessary to amend the soil to meet this requirement. Poor drainage is most often caused by heavy soils with a high clay content. Adding organic matter is a much more efficient way of helping the situation than adding sand.

If the soils in your area are extremely acidic, adding lime to the soil will help this condition. Many species of wildflowers, however, seem to be unaffected by the acidity of the soil.

PLANTING SEEDS AND PLANTS

Choose your seeds and plants carefully and make sure you have healthy materials to plant. You will have greater success if you use species native to your area or those that are naturalized in balance. See Part Two to find lists of plants suitable to your region and to your conditions.

Many people have found that the most effective way to establish a naturalized area is to "plug" in plants without tilling the soil. The advantages of this method are many. You know exactly what plants you are putting in, and you can better match their cultural requirements to specific areas in the meadow with the correct conditions. By not disturbing the soil, you are working with "known enemies"; the chance of a surprise crop of weeds is greatly reduced. The disadvantages are obvious — it takes a great deal of time and money to grow plants from seed or purchase plants from a nursery and then plug them into the area. However, if you have the resources, this is the method that will give you the best and quickest results. Remember to purchase your plants from a reputable source that propagates rather than digs from the wild.

You can also do a combination of plugging in established plants and direct seeding. This method is particularly good if you are using a pre-mixed blend of wildflowers; desirable species that are not included in the mixture can be plugged in separately. By plugging in perennial plants, you can have color from these species the first year, whereas from seeds perennials usually take at least two years to bloom. Even if you are plugging in plants for all the wildflowers, you may still want to seed native grasses or a cover crop to help hold the soil until the plants become established.

The least expensive way to establish a meadow is to use all seeds. Choose whatever seeds you prefer. The only guidelines that should be followed are:

(1) Use as many species native or naturalized in your region as possible.

(2) When you buy a premixed blend of seeds, choose one that is as specific for your circumstances as possible.

(3) Do not plant large amounts of species that are potentially invasive, and do not plant any species listed on your local noxious weed list.

(4) Use seeds bought from a reputable source.

Once the soil is prepared, rake it thoroughly to get a very even seed bed. When you are ready to plant, examine your seeds and make sure that they are clean and free of insects. For better distribution, mix the seeds with clean, dry sand or sawdust. This not only makes them easier to sow but also allows the seeds of varying sizes and weights to be evenly mixed and distributed. You can either broadcast by hand or with a mechanical sower or spreader. If you are establishing large areas, a seed drill or rangeland drill may be helpful. Be sure to broadcast seeds on a windless day.

Hydroseeding and hydromulching are methods of seeding that apply a slurry of seed and water or seed, water, and wood fiber to the soil. Where available, this is an excellent means of broadcasting the seed, but be careful not to use too much fiber in the initial broadcast, for the seeds have a tendency to become hung up in the fiber. Recommendations are to use 10 percent of the fiber in the initial planting and then apply the remainder in a separate procedure. Check with local landscaping companies for information on hydroseeding.

After the seeds have been sown, rake the area lightly to assure good soil-to-seed contact. Then firm and tamp the area. There are various ways to do this, depending on the size of area you are working with. A hand-pushed, water-filled sod roller works quite well.

The amount of seeds that you will use depends entirely on the types of seeds that you are sowing. Suggested planting rates will vary depending on many different factors, including the germination rate, how easily the species compete with other plants, and how quickly they are able to spread. If you have bought your seeds from a reputable source, follow their planting suggestions. Do not make the mistake of seeding too sparsely. If there are not wildflower or native grass seeds available to fill the niches, Mother Nature is going to fill them with weeds. On the other extreme, if you are using a mixture, there is a danger of overseeding and having the annual species crowd out the small perennial seedlings during the first year of growth before the perennials have a chance to become established. However, if you must err on one side or the other, over seed rather than seed sparsely.

Too much of a good thing is wonderful. — Mae West

RESEEDING

Although most studies have shown that plant diversity in the meadow stays high year after year, some studies have shown that after a few years, one or two flowering species begin to dominate and diversity is greatly reduced. In these circumstances, reseeding of desired species is recommended. A general recommendation is to use a wildflower seed mixture the first year and find out what wildflowers you like and which ones will do well in your meadow. Remember that the first year will give you color from the annuals only. Two or even three years will be necessary to obtain color from the biennials and perennials. Once you have determined which species are best suited to your own individual tastes and to the conditions present in your meadow, purchase or gather seeds of these species to reseed as needed and wanted. It is not necessary to have twenty different species blooming all at once; five to six different species blooming during each season will give you great interest and diversity.

Just as when you planted originally, it is important to get good seed-to-soil contact, but when you reseed you want to disturb as few of the existing plants as possible. The most efficient way of doing this is to choose various spots within the meadow to seed again, rake the soil, and broadcast the seeds. In other areas, you can use a dethatching rake to break up the soil but avoid hitting the perennial plants. Spot hydroseeding is also a viable means of reseeding.

USING MULCH

Although a mulch is not a necessity, a very light covering of mulch is useful to keep the seeds from blowing away, to retain better moisture, and to cover the seeds and protect them from birds as well as adverse weather conditions. Do not mulch heavily, for many seeds need light to germinate, and the mulch should not hamper penetration of the seedlings. Various materials can be used for mulch, but all should be weed free. Both bagged compost and peat moss make excellent mulches. Straw, when you can get it free of weed seeds, also is useful. Wood chips or wood bark can be used, but they often deplete nitrogen from the soil as they decay, so take this into consideration and amend the soil if you use these products. Wood products generally work better in warm, humid areas where plants grow more quickly.

On steep slopes, coarse gravel can be used as a mulch. It should be put in place first, and then the area can be seeded and soaked thoroughly. Seedlings come up through crevices in the rocks. Be sure to plant only those species that will thrive in this type of environment.

Where a full mulch is not necessary or desired, twiggy branches placed over the planting will discourage birds from getting the seeds.

Sweet April showers — doo spring
Maie flowers. — Tusser

MAINTAINING THE MEADOW

After seeding or planting, the area must be kept moist at least until the seedlings or plants have become established. Although many of the native plants are considered drought tolerant, they still need moisture to germinate and become established. If you are planting an area too large to water effectively or too far from a water source to get moisture to it, plant during the season of the year that receives the most rainfall — and be prepared for disappointing results if nature chooses not to cooperate. Once the plants are growing well, watering will be necessary only when the plants show stress. If you live in a very dry area, choose plants that are native to your area and are adapted to dry conditions. Do not overwater, for this will tend to produce more leaves than flowers.

Particularly during the first few years, you must control the weeds that will invade your meadow garden. The number and type of weeds coming in will depend on how you did your initial soil preparation. One of the biggest weed problems is usually caused by perennial grasses. These are difficult to get rid of because they occur in such large numbers. Each part of the country seems to have a set of particularly noxious weeds from kudzu in the Southeast to thistles in the Northeast to blackberries in the Pacific Northwest. Keep a diligent watch for any noxious weeds, and to not let them get a foothold in your meadow. Prevention is the best maintenance. It is often difficult to tell the wildflowers from unwanted weeds in the seedling stage. No doubt you will pamper and weed around a special plant only to find out that it is a despised and dreaded plant in your area. I've done it many times. When you do weed, weed from the base of the plant. If you start grabbing at leaves, you will probably end up with a handful of something that you did not mean to pull up.

Many of the perennial plants will need to be divided periodically (usually every three to four years) to retain their vigor. By dividing the clumps you will increase the number of plants in the meadow as well as continue to have healthy, freely blooming wildflowers.

Choose your plants carefully before you plant them. If you are un-sure about using any species (particularly ones that spread rapidly) use them in moderation. It is much easier to add a variety of plants in later years than to pull up flowers you realized you don't want. Usually when you decide you don't want a particular species in your area, you will find it in every nook and cranny of your meadow.

At least once each year you must mow or burn the meadow. This clearing serves many purposes. In parts of the country where the invasion of woody species is a problem, an annual mowing keeps them in check. Mowing also opens up the area and allows sufficient sunshine to penetrate to the low-growing plants. If it's done at the correct time of year, mowing will help to disperse seeds set by the plants during the growing season. Depending on where you live, mowing should be done sometime be-tween the end of August and late winter. A fall mowing will make the area look neater, but leaving the seed heads until late winter will create winter color and interest and will provide food for the birds.

By the time March comes you should look out for weeds. Of course you must learn to know your weeds, just as you must learn to know your flowers, and you must know them, too, in quite a young state. — Gertrude Jekyll, Children and Gardens

An initial mowing should be relatively high: 6 to 8 inches or higher. You can do a second mowing at a lower level to thoroughly break up the resulting litter. Do not cut too low (below about 3 to 4 inches) or you might damage the perennial plants. Traditional home lawn mowers are not the best tools for the initial mowing. A lawn mower simply can not handle the amount of vegetative materials in a meadow at the end of the growing season. For small areas, either a hand scythe or swingblade or a saw blade on a weed eater are very effective and work surprisingly quickly to cut the meadow. If a great deal of vegetative material has been produced during the growing season, it's a good idea to rake at least part of this off the meadow area after mowing.

Within the prairie states, the most effective tool to clear the meadow or prairie is fire. Fires have been an important part of the growth cycle of a prairie area for centuries, and prairie plants are well suited to the conditions produced by a fire. They actually seem to benefit from a burning every two to three years. The best time to burn prairie areas is late March to early April. Not enough research has been done at this time to determine whether or not fire is a beneficial tool for clearing meadow areas in other parts of the country. Although some species of plants used in meadow gardens also grow in the prairies, most of the plants are quite different, with different growth habits and root systems. At this point, it seems best to mow areas outside of the prairie states rather than to burn to maintain a meadow garden.

In summary, there is no single best way to establish a meadow garden. The use of native plants within the home landscape and the establishment of meadow gardens in particular is a relatively new chapter in the book of American horticulture. This is a big country full of hundreds of different kinds of growing conditions and characterized by a wonderful diversity of native flora. Each of you will want something different from your meadow garden, and each of you will have different resources available to you. The information in this chapter is a compilation of methods most often used by experts in different regions. It is my sincere hope that research and the resulting knowledge on using native plants will greatly increase within a very short time. It seems a shame that we know more about growing exotic species than we do about growing the plants native to our own country. Because native plant landscaping is a new concept, it is important that we all share our knowledge about what grows best in our own areas. As more research is done and more knowledge shared, clear-cut guidelines will emerge for different regions as to what plants grow best in the area and the most effective ways of preparing the soil, planting seeds, and maintaining the area. You can take part in this research by sharing your knowledge and experiences with the experts.

Few if any of our native plants add more to the beauty of the midsummer landscape than . . . the gorgeous butterfly-weed, whose vivid flowers flame from dry sandy meadows with such luxuriance of growth as to seem almost tropical. Even in the tropics one hardly sees anything more brilliant than the great masses of color along some of our New England railways in July . . The Indians used it as food and prepared a crude sugar from the flowers; the young seed-pods they boiled and ate with buffalo-meat . . . Oddly enough, at the Centennial Exhibition Philadelphia, 1876 much attention was attracted by a bed of these beautiful plants which were brought from Holland. Truly, flowers, like prophets, are not without honor save in their own country. — Mrs. William Starr Dana, How to Know the Wild Flowers.

In a Nutshell

(1) Be patient when planting a wildflower meadow. Realize that it will take a few years for the perennials to bloom and for you to have a really good display.

(2) Prepare the soil correctly initially to get a headstart on the weed problem. If you till, start preparing the soil at least six weeks before you plan to plant.

(3) Choose your plants or seed varieties carefully so that they meet your site's individual conditions. The majority of the plants you choose should be native or naturalized to your region.

(4) Plant the amount of seeds recommended by your (reputable) suppliers.

(5) Pamper your seedlings and new plants until they become established.

(6) Watch out for noxious weeds that will invade the meadow garden. Prevention is the best maintenance.

(7) Mow (or burn) your meadow area annually to retard the growth of weeds, to open up the area to allow more sunshine in, and to scatter seeds.

(8) Reseed as often as necessary to guarantee good color and diversity every year.

(9) Share your knowledge and experience with the experts.

Timetable for establishing a meadow area:

(1) If you are in a hurry . . . (minimum of six weeks).
   A. Rototill or plow your area.
   B. Wait three weeks for weeds to come up. Water if necessary — you want weeds up at this point.
   C. Use a general herbicide to kill all the weeds that have appeared. (Repeating the plow/spray routine will eliminate more weeds.)
   D. Wait two weeks, then rake lightly, sow seeds, and rake again. Tamp soil.
   E. Water until seedlings are established.

(2) If you are in a hurry and have sufficient funds and manpower . . .
   A. Purchase enough plants from a reputable dealer to give your meadow good cover.

B. Plug plants into existing vegetation, disturbing the soil as little as possible.

C. Seed native grasses or some sort of cover crop to help hold the soil until the plants are established.

D. Water until plants are established.

(3) If you are patient . . . (and patience does pay off).

A. In early spring plow or rototill to a depth of 6 to 8 inches.

B. Immediately sow large amounts of buckwheat (or other cover crop).

C. Plow under before buckwheat goes to seed (mid-summer).

D. Immediately sow another heavy crop of buckwheat.

E. Plow under before it goes to seed (mid-fall).

F. Rake smooth and immediately sow wildflower and native grass seed into a virtually weed-free seed bed.

Dealing
With
Uninvited Guests

No matter how carefully we plan and design our meadows, they are never going to be exactly what we had in mind because Mother Nature steps in whether we invite her or not. It is difficult to fill every niche in the meadow with seeds or plants. Seeds germinate at different times and at different rates, and plants will grow at different rates. The local weather and our own inputs of watering and weeding will create different growing conditions for the various plants, beneficial to some and detrimental to others. This variation in growth will result in bare or weak spots in the meadow which nature will be delighted to fill with a weed. The goal in establishing a meadow garden is to create as balanced a plant community as possible. Part of this balance is achieved by making sure that weeds don't crowd out the desirable plants. Of course, there can be some question as to which are the weeds and which are the wildflowers! In meadow gardening, especially, beauty is in the eye of the beholder. When I told my father that I had been weeding my meadow, he harrumphed and mumbled that they all looked like weeds to him. A traditional gardener might consider my field of wildflowers all weeds, but the definition of a weed is a plant growing where you don't want it to grow. I wanted those plants in my meadow, so they are wildflowers to me and not weeds. I do have weeds in my meadow, however, for there are many plants there that I definitely do not want. Most of these I want to get rid of because they pose a threat to the balance of the plant community. Unless a plant is particularly ugly, or out of proportion to the rest of the plants, or holds the potential to crowd out more desirable plants for space and nutrients, it's best to just let it stay. It will do no harm, and you will have plenty to do controlling other plants that will take over if you let them. The trick, of course, is knowing which ones will become invasive and which ones are no problem. Since growing conditions will be different in every meadow, what might be a real pest in one area would be no problem at all in another. Some weeds might actually turn out to be so attractive that you

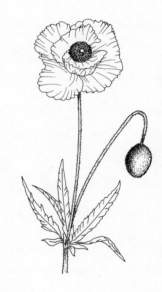

Spring comes and the grass grows by itself. — Tao Te Ching

want to encourage their presence. I look forward to the bright yellow heads of dandelions that appear in my meadow in the spring. I certainly would not have thought of planting them there, but they add color at a time that is not particularly showy, they do not grow or spread prolifically, and I am always glad to see them.

Because the invasion of weeds is such a problem to meadow gardeners in every part of the country, it is important to rid the area of as many weeds as possible before you plant and then to keep them in check during the growing season. It will be difficult to spray herbicide on the weeds after the meadow has been planted for by doing so you are sure to lose some wildflowers as well as the weeds. At the end of the growing season, if you have spaces in the meadow that appear to be all weeds and grasses, spot spray these and replant.

Prevention is the best maintenance. If you prepare your soil correctly, keep the weeds in check during the growing season, and reseed or replant areas of the meadow every three or four years to keep the number and diversity of wildflowers high, you should have a lovely meadow. If things should get out of hand and you have a year when the weeds win, you might consider starting over and replanting entirely. If you decide to do this, salvage what you can by digging up perennial species to replant after you plow.

If for some reason you decide that a meadow is not for you, it is relatively easy to convert your meadow back into a lawn. Sow grass seed heavily, fertilize and mow regularly, and the grasses will soon crowd out the wildflowers.

The following is a list of uninvited guests that most often appear in meadows throughout the country. Though some of them might turn out to be welcome, keep a sharp lookout for these plants and keep them in check. In addition to these plants, each region seems to have its own particular troublesome weeds. Talk to gardeners within your area to find out what these are and watch out for them. Meadows are too beautiful and too much fun to let them go to the weeds.

PLANTS WITH GRASSLIKE LEAVES

Yellow foxtail *(Setaria glauca):* Annual that spreads by seeds.

Bermuda grass *(Cynondon dactylon):* Perennial that spreads by seeds and creeping rootstock.

Annual bluegrass *(Poa annua):* Annual that spreads by seeds.

Large crabgrass *(Digitaria sanguinalis)* and smooth crabgrass *(Digitaria ischaemum):* Annuals that spread by seed.

Goose grass *(Eleusine indica):* Annual that spreads by seeds.

Quack grass *(Agropyron repens):* A perennial that has become a real pest in some parts of the country. It spreads rapidly by underground stems that grow great distances just beneath the surface and root at every node.

Johnson grass *(Sorghum halepense):* This can be a more serious pest than any of the other perennial grasses. It has roots that go very deep and spread quite rapidly.

All of the grasses can be controlled with applications of a general herbicide. Spraying can be done most effectively in the spring. Other means of getting rid of these pests include smothering with a mulch and spading under.

VINES AND SHRUBS

Poison ivy *(Rhus radicans):* An unfortunate but good example of a native plant that has gotten out of control. Its growth is rampant in some areas, and it can smother out shrubs and small trees as well as wildflowers and ferns. This is one pest that you should not allow a foothold in your meadow. Attack it with a vengeance and stay on top of the situation. Hand weed (with gloves) small areas. If you have a large stand of the pest, spray with an appropriate herbicide, but remember that the leaves can remain poisonous to the touch for a year. The seeds are commonly eaten by birds and dropped throughout the countryside. Do not burn areas containing poison ivy or poison sumac, for inhaling the fumes can cause serious problems.

Kudzu *(Pueraria lobata):* The curse of the Southeast! Kudzu can spread very quickly (up to 60 to 80 feet in a single growing season). Although this introduction from Japan is a real problem if unchecked, small areas are relatively easy to eradicate by persistent spraying with a general herbicide and pulling up the roots. Do not allow this to get into your meadow.

Japanese honeysuckle *(Lonicera japonica):* Introduced from Japan in the early 1900s as an ornamental vine, honeysuckle soon proved to be quite a pest. It spreads rapidly, particularly in sunny, open areas, so watch out for it in your meadow and don't allow it to take root. The yellow and white blossoms are pretty and some people still plant it, unaware of its ability to strangle and smother anything in its path. Do not be tempted. It could overtake a meadow or field in very short order. Eradication of the plant in large areas involves repeated sprayings of an herbicide such as 2,4-D. The plants should be sprayed while in active growth during the summer months.

Blackberry *(Rubus species):* Easily spread by bird droppings, blackberry bushes usually appear during the second or third summer in both managed and unmanaged open areas.

Note: 2,4-D is nontoxic to people and animals, is noninflammable, and has little effect on the soil, but do not plant seeds immediately after spraying with this chemical.

PERENNIALS

Yellow wood sorrel *(Oxalis stricta):* This plant spreads by seeds but has fragile stems and roots and is eaily pulled up. It is very low growing, only three to six inches high. The small bright yellow flowers are fully opened at midday but close up during cloudy weather and in the evening.

Broad-leaved plantain *(Plantago major):* This plant spreads by seeds and can be controlled with 2,4-D.

Mouse-eared chickweed *(Cerastium vulgatum):* Though some of its larger cousins (such as *Cerastium bierbersteinii* or *Cerastium tomentosum)* are actually included within some wildflower seed mixtures, the mouse-eared chickweed spreads too easily by seed and has too insignificant a flower to make it attractive.

White clover *(Trifolium repens):* This plant spreads both by seeds and creeping stems. There are several types of clovers, some of which (such as crimson clover, *Trifolium incarnatum)* are considered desirable meadow flowers and good soil stabilizers. Other clovers, such as low hop and white clovers, can become persistent pests.

Ground ivy *(Glechoma hederacea):* The wrinkled, kidney-shaped leaves of this plant should be well known, for they are very often found in lawns. This plant prefers moist, rich soil and should not be a problem in the more arid areas of the country. It spreads by seeds and creeping stems.

Dandelions *(Taraxacum officinale):* One of the reasons dandelions are so successful is that they have a very deep taproot, making them impervious to drought, grazing animals and weeders. Other reasons for their success include the fact that the seeds are easily dispersed and that they take only three days to germinate. Dandelions rarely become a serious problem in the wildflower meadow.

Canadian thistle *(Cirsium arvense):* The Canadian thistle has become such a problem in some areas that there are legal controls to halt its spread. The thistle does not seem to know there's a law against its growth, however, and it can spread from a single plant to a large patch within a single growing season. It can become a very serious pest, and you should try to keep it out of the meadow. Once the plant is in the bud or blooming stage, it is difficult to eradicate. It can be effectively sprayed with an herbicide early in the spring when the plants are between 6 and 15 inches tall.

ANNUALS

The most important control of annuals is to prevent their going to seed.

Lady's thumb *(Polygonum persicaria):* When the plant is not growing so prolifically that it outgrows its welcome, the small red or pink flowering heads of lady's thumb can be quite attractive. These plants, with basal reddish leaves, are quite easy to pull up by hand.

Shepherd's purse *(Capsella bursa-pastoris):* The triangularly shaped seed pods of this annual give it its common name. There is a basal rosette of leaves that looks somewhat like that of dandelion. It spreads easily and quickly by seeds.

Common groundsel *(Senecio vulgaris):* The leaves of the groundsel look very much like those of dandelion or chicory. There are numerous small, yellow, dandelion-like flowers, and the seed head looks like that of the dandelion, also. Be sure to pull this up before it goes to seed for the seeds are easily dispersed.

Calliopsis, Indian blanket, and lupines create a wonderful show of color on the banks of this lake in Texas.

Dennis Fagan, Wildseed

This and the following photographs show a variety of possible settings for planting a meadow.

Applewood Seed Company   Wildflowers can be used in small areas as well as large ones. This small grouping of wildflowers dominated by Indian blanket gives a touch of the wild to a more formal landscape.

Indian paintbrush and bluebonnets create a spectacular entrance for this home in central Texas.

Dennis Fagan, Wildseed

Texas State Department of Highway and Public Transportation

Springtime in Texas is made glorious when the bluebonnets begin to bloom along the roadsides and in home meadows such as this one.

Poppies and bachelor's buttons naturalize easily and create quite a display of color in this sideyard meadow in Colorado.

Applewood Seed Company

David S. Martin The author and her daughter enjoy a profusion of calliopsis in their
Georgia meadow.

The meadow in front of the house at River Farms — the national headquarters for the American Horticultural Society in Mount Vernon, Virginia — is proof that low-maintenance gardening and beauty go hand in hand.

Barbara Ellis, American Horticultural Society

Meadows need not be confined to rural areas. These wildflowers in the Bronx bring a little wilderness to the center of New York City.

Applewood Seed Company

CHAPTER SIX

Using
The
Meadow

Nearly everyone plants a meadow garden primarily for its beauty, but other attributes of the meadow should not be overlooked. In addition to providing a spot of peaceful beauty, meadows will also create a boundless supply of cut flowers and ingredients for many kinds of nature crafts. Meadows create habitats for birds and butterflies, and by planting particular species, it is possible to attract certain kinds of wildlife. Perhaps the best use for a meadow, however, is for the study of the wondrous intricacies of nature. A meadow is an unparalleled outdoor classroom, allowing for hands-on experience and the field study of many different disciplines. So enjoy your meadow for its beauty, but take advantage of other bounties that your meadow offers, too.

God gave all men earth to love but since our hearts are small, ordained for each one spot should prove beloved over all. — Rudyard Kipling

CUT FLOWERS

Most of the meadow plants are quite showy and have stout stems, so they serve well as cut flowers. Most members of the Compositae Family, commonly found in meadows (daisies, sunflowers, asters), retain their color and form for several days and are excellent flowers to bring indoors.

Following some general guidelines might help your cut flowers last longer. Cut plants with soft stems with a sharp knife at an angle. Strip off the excess leaves and place the flowers in cool water for several hours before using. For plants with milky sap, strip off the excess leaves and sear the bottom of each stem quickly with a match or candle, or place the ends of the stems in boiling water for ten to twenty seconds. For plants that are excessively juicy, dip the stems in salt water after cutting. For woody stems, crush or split the bottom of them stem one inch from the base with a sharp knife.

Aster: Cut when about half the flower buds are opened. Strip off the excess leaves, and split the stem 1 inch from the bottom with a knife.

To see a world in a grain of sand And heaven in a wild flower Hold infinity in the palm of your hand And eternity in an hour. — William Blake

65

Pressed wildflowers can be used in bookmarks, notecards, or in miniature frames. Violets, clovers, Queen Anne's lace, and annual phlox are especially good for pressing.

Bellflower: Burn the ends of the stems by placing them in 1 inch of boiling water for twenty seconds. Then put them in a container full of cool water and allow them to drink for several hours.

Columbine: Pick after the first blossoms are open and immediately dip the stems into salt water and then into warm water to the base of the flowers.

Delphinium: Be sure to pick before all the flower buds are open. The upper buds will not open, but the lower ones seem to last much longer. Delphiniums can also be dried by hanging them upside down in a dry place.

Sweet William: This requires no special treatment but should never be allowed to dry out.

Foxglove: Pick the flowers when the first blooms open. Place the ends of the stems in warm water for several hours.

Grasses: Perennial grasses make unusual and very lovely additions to wildflower arrangements. Plunge them into cool water immediately after picking.

Sunflower: Pick sunflowers when the blossoms open, strip off the excess foliage, and split the stems. Place them in warm water for twenty-four to forty-eight hours.

Lupine: Stand the stems in weak starch solution so that they will not lose petals. This solution can be added to the water that holds the arrangement.

Forget me not: Cut when the flowers first open, and plunge the stems into cool water.

Poppy: Cut when in tight bud. The stems should be burned either with a match or by placing the stems in 1 inch of boiling water. Then place the stems in cool water for many hours. The seed heads dry nicely and should be allowed to dry on the stem, but you must protect them from hungry birds.

Beard tongue: Conditioning for this plant is very important. Cut when the flowers are in full bloom, place the stems in 1 inch of boiling water, and then place them in cool water for many hours — at least overnight.

Phlox: No special conditioning is necessary for phlox, but they should be placed in warm water for several hours before they are arranged. They should not be allowed to wilt, for they will never recover.

Black-eyed Susan: Bruise the ends of the stems and then place them in cool water for several hours.

Flowering sage: The stems should be placed in 1 inch of boiling water for twenty seconds and then placed in cool water.

NATURE CRAFTS

A meadow is a special blessing to scout leaders, naturalists, parents, or teachers who want to do nature crafts with children, for it will provide easy access to an abundant supply of materials for several kinds of crafts. If you use plants and wildflowers that are not in your meadow, make sure of their identity and do not use species that are threatened, endangered, or poisonous. The following crafts give quick results and are suitable for a variety of age groups.

PRESSED FLOWER CRAFTS

Many of the meadow flowers press very well and can be used in a variety of crafts. There are some species, however, that will not press well, so avoid these. For instance, flowers that have large, firm flower heads (such as black-eyed Susans or sunflowers) will not press flat, so they are unsuited for use in this craft. Generally, smaller flowers will do better. Annual phlox, spurred snapdragon, evening primrose, violets, clovers, and Queen Anne's lace are some wildflowers that press very well. For best results, the flowers should be pressed as flat as possible. Flowers can be pressed in phone directories or other heavy books, but they often lose their color quickly this way. A better method is to place them between corrugated paper or blotting paper in a plant press. This can be purchased through many different catalogs or from gift shops at nature museums or other shops specializing in nature or flower paraphernalia. A plant press can also be made by using two pieces of wood and several sheets of blotting paper joined together with twine, string, or wire.

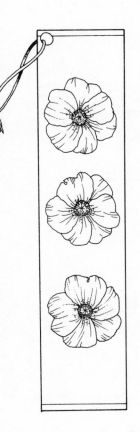

Depending on the variety of plant used and the moisture conditions when it was picked, the flowers should be ready to use in one to three weeks. The thicker the plant, the longer you will need to press it. Don't overlook the wonderful forms and textures of the grasses. They will lend an air of grace to your pressed flower creations.

Once the flowers are pressed, they can be used for a variety of crafts. They can be artfully arranged in pictures or made into bookmarks or notecards or can be used in miniature frames for kitchen magnets. The easiest way to attach the pressed flowers is to arrange them on a board or card and then cover with clear adhesive shelf paper, which is found in hardware or craft stores. Once the board is covered, trim the edges of the paper even with the edges of the card or board.

Pressed Queen Anne's lace can be used to make lovely Christmas tree ornaments. Spray the pressed flower with spray adhesive (available at art supply or hardware stores) and then sprinkle with glitter. Tie satin ribbons on the stems and hang them on the Christmas tree for a delicate and unusual ornament.

DYEING CLOTH AND YARN

There are many good books about using natural materials to dye cloth and yarn. The shades and hues of colors obtained from these materials cannot be duplicated by synthetic dyes. For a quick craft and a good lesson about the "olden days", you can collect seeds and flowers, extract their pigment, and use this solution to color fabric or wool without going through elaborate methods. However, unless you use mordants to set the pigments and follow rather precise procedures, it will be a temporary dye that cannot be washed. It gets the idea across, though, and is a great learning experience. The basic procedure is to pick plant materials (brightly colored blossoms and colorful fleshy fruits do best). Work with one type of plant at a time. Place the blossoms or seeds in a pot and just barely cover them with water. Boil them for ten to fifteen minutes. Strain the plant material off and discard it. Replace the resulting colored water in the pot and add clean, pure wool or cotton cloth or yarn. Bring the water back to a boil, and boil until desired color intensity is reached (usually about ten to fifteen minutes). The amount of color you get in your fabric will depend on the type of plants used, the length of time you leave it in the colored solution, and the capability of your fabric to absorb the pigment. Experiment with different blossoms and fruits to find the ones you like the best.

NATURAL "CRAYONS"

This is the best nature craft I know of for preschoolers. Pick brightly colored petals and let them rub them across a piece of white paper. Pigments from the petals will come off on the paper. They love it, and it is a fail-proof, quick craft for little fingers.

NATURE STUDY

When you create a small piece of wilderness in your back yard, you can closely study nature from your kitchen window. Not only will the flowers and grasses present you with an ever-changing landscape, but visiting wildlife will add interest and a chance to study nature as a system rather than one piece at a time.

The most desirable and conspicuous visitors to the meadow will be the birds and butterflies. The number and kind that will frequent your area will depend on the region in which you live, the types of flowers and plants that you have chosen, and the type of vegetation that surrounds the meadow area. If you want permanent visitors, you must provide some sort of water. A pond or stream is best, but just a bird bath will do. Part Two includes lists of plants for each region that will attract birds and butterflies.

Meadows afford opportunity to study phases of botany, horticulture, ornithology, entomology, and ecology. Because the plants are the most important and outstanding part of the meadow, learning about them is the first step in learning about the meadow. Studying the plants need not be an intense examination of their physiology or a careful scrutiny of their taxonomy. There are aspects of plant study that are suitable for a wide variety of ages and temperaments. Preschoolers can explore the meadow with all of their senses. Smelling the fragrances, feeling how the textures of leaves and blossoms differ from one plant to another, tasting the succulent leaves and roots of the edible plants, and listening to all the critters living in the meadow are wonderful exercises for young people, often resulting in an increased awareness and perhaps the beginning of a real love for the natural world. Older children will find the meadow to be a treasure house for observing the relationships between plants and insects, discovering how the same plant changes from one season to another, and perhaps how weather and climate effect different plants. The basis of conservation is education.

Now if you will take any flower you please and look it carefully all over and turn it about, and smell it and feel it and try and find out all its little secrets; not of flower only but of leaf, bud, and stem as well, you will discover many wonderful things. This is how to make friends with plants, and very good friends you will find them to the end of your lives. — Gertrude Jekyll, Children and Gardens

WILDFLOWER FOLKLORE

One fun way for people of any age to learn about the plants is to learn a little of their folklore. Many of the plants found in meadow areas have been used for centuries. Many were valued for their medicinal qualities, and others were used for food. Learning what the different plants were used for and where they got their names can be fascinating. Discovering a plant's place of origin and how it spread from one area to another might lead to better understanding of the risk of bringing non-native plants into a new region. As you learn the stories of the different plants, it becomes clear that these wildflowers and grasses played a very important part in the lives of the people who first settled in all parts of the United States. These plants provided medicines when they were ill, food when they were hungry, and perhaps most importantly beauty to uplift the spirits.

Here are just a few folklore facts to spark your interest.

Butterfly weed *(Asclepias tuberosa)* was used by the early pioneers to cure pleurisy and is sometimes referred to as pleurisy root. The soft, downy seeds were often used to stuff mattresses or pillows.

Bee balm *(Monarda didyma)* leaves can be dried and brewed for an excellent tea. A member of the mint family, bee balm has a strong flavor that made it useful for cooking, for cooling fevers, and for soothing a stomachache.

The phloxes were not used in cultivation until they were taken from the wild in North America, grown in the gardens of Europe, and then reintroduced to American gardens. According to the Victorian language of flowers, phlox sends a message of sweet dreams and a proposal of love.

The leaves of fireweed *(Epilobium angustifolium)* were dried and made into a tasty tea. The young shoots can be picked and boiled and taste somewhat like asparagus.

Many people know of the many culinary uses of the sunflower *(Helianthus annuus)*. What is not so widely known is that American settlers in the nineteenth century planted the sunflower outside their homes as protection against malaria.

The botanical name for goldenrod is *Solidago,* from Latin words meaning "to heal" or "to make whole." The American Indians held great belief in the healing power of goldenrod and included it in steam baths, designed to steam pain out of an ailing person. Folktales tell us that he who carries a piece of the goldenrod will soon find treasure.

Milkweeds *(Asclepias* species) have been used for a variety of purposes. The Delaware Indian name for milkweed boiled with dumplings is *pee-too-can-oh-uk.* The Quebec Indians used the plant as a contraceptive (of questionable efficacy), and the Shawnee Indians used the milky sap to take away warts.

Asters *(Aster* species) are known and loved in many parts of the world. During Roman times, asters were considered sacred and were placed in the temples of all the gods. People of that time believed that asters were created out of star dust. Several unusual powers have been attributed to the asters, including the ability to cure the bite of a mad dog, to clear the complexion, and to drive away snakes.

SUGGESTED REFERENCES

Brown, Lauren. *The Audubon Society Nature Guide to Grasslands.* Alfred A. Knopf, New York, 1985.

Forte, Imogene, and Marjorie Frank. *Puddles and Wings and Grapevine Swings: Things to Make and Do with Nature's Treasures.* Incentive Publications, Nashville, Tenn., 1982.

Martin, Laura. *Wildflower Folklore.* The East Woods Press, Charlotte, N.C., 1984.

National Wildlife Federation, The. *Gardening with Wildlife.* The National Wildlife Federation, Washington, D.C., 1974.

Schofield, Eileen K. *Botanical Crafts: An Annotated List of References.* The New York Botanical Garden, Bronx, New York; The Council on Botanical and Horticultural Libraries, Inc., 1983.

CHAPTER SEVEN

The Meadow
As A
Community Garden

Meadow gardening by yourself is a very satisfying experience. Putting in a meadow with a group of friends or co-workers is not only satisfying, it is a lot of fun and a downright uplifting experience. With the fast-paced lifestyles that seem to be here to stay, it is often difficult to obtain a sense of community in our lives. The very word community means people interacting with one another, but this interaction, especially in a large city, is often limited to a particular place or time. The people we work with, we see only at work. The people who are our neighbors, we all too often do not see at all except to wave across the driveway. Community gardening, people working together to plant and care for a garden, has proven to be a very effective way of getting people together who live within the same community. Although traditionally community gardens have been vegetable gardens, the idea of establishing a meadow as a community project is one that is gaining in popularity. Working together to create a place of beauty will go a long way in promoting friendships among members of a neighborhood or organization.

There are many kinds of meadow gardens that a group can establish and many reasons for putting in a garden. Although beauty is reason enough to put in a meadow garden, such areas can also serve as an unsurpassed educational tool. Located at a school or nature center, a meadow can provide an outdoor classroom that is an excellent place to study a dozen different disciplines including botany, horticulture, zoology, ornithology, entomology, geology, climatology, and perhaps most importantly, ecology. In short, it is a great place to study all parts of an active natural community and how they interact. As the seasons progress and the light green covering of early spring changes to the lush growth of summer and eventually to the stark stalks of dried seed heads in the winter, there is a succession of birds and butterflies enjoying the fruits of the field. In a wilderness condensed into an area right outside the door, it is possible to study and learn all year long.

I have a garden of my own, shining with flowers of every hue. I loved it dearly while alone, But I shall love it more with you. — Thomas More

You work that you may keep pace with the earth and the soul of the earth. For to be idle is to become a stranger unto the seasons, and to step out of life's procession, that marches in majesty and proud submission towards the infinite. — Kahlil Gibran, The Prophet

There are many other reasons for creating a meadow. For groups of bird enthusiasts, the establishment of a meadow is a natural step in attracting certain birds to a particular area. For neighbors tired of looking at an unkempt empty lot down the street, planting a meadow can turn a defect into a real asset.

Planting and maintaining a meadow area is a perfect civic project for a garden club. It even fits into the schedule that most clubs keep, for the majority of the work will be done in spring and fall and not during the summer months when most garden clubs do not meet. With a minimal amount of money and by sharing the workload, a garden club can make a real contribution to its community.

DETERMINING INTEREST

The first step in developing a community meadow garden is to determine how much interest there really is in carrying out this project. Naturally the larger the group or organization you are involved with, the more elaborate will be your initial interest probes. Within a small office, casual conversation over lunch can give you an instant opinion poll. If you are involved with a botanical garden or arboretum with a large membership, a notice in the newsletter might be the best way to alert people to your idea. Within a neighborhood, fliers in the mailboxes are a possibility, and if you are involved with a school, a brief discussion at the next parent's meeting might let you know of potential support.

You give but little when you give of your possessions. It is when you give of yourself that you truly give.
— Kahlil Gibran, The Prophet

Don't overlook support from the county or city government. Maintaining a meadow involves much less time and money than maintaining a lawn. The department of parks and recreation in your area might be delighted to work with your group in establishing a meadow of wildflowers on a public site.

Once sufficient interest has been shown in the idea, form a core group to make the major decisions involving the project.

FINDING LAND

The best place for a meadow is as close as possible to the people who are going to use it. Unless it is to be used strictly for study purposes or a display area, it does not make sense to buy or lease land far from your center of activity.

Within a neighborhood an overgrown empty lot is a natural spot to put a meadow. Consider the possibility of converting a lot in the inner city or around public housing. What a wonderful gift a field of wildflowers would be to an otherwise drab or run-down neighborhood. Community vegetable gardening in the inner city has enjoyed a great deal of popularity. The same concepts can be applied to meadow gardening, and though it will not supply food for the body, it will supply food for the soul and flowers for the table.

If your office building or place of business includes land that is conducive to a naturalized planting, talk to your boss about it. Many establishments have back lots that are infrequently used and are usually not planted or managed. What a pleasant change it would be to look out the back window onto a meadow full of flowers rather than a lot full of weeds and stubble.

Remember that meadows do not necessarily need to cover large areas. A side yard or the back portion of the playground at a school can be converted into a meadow. A parking lot strip at a local shopping center can be made into a small meadow area. A small grassy spot at a hospital, filled with wildflowers, will lift the spirits of the patients and of staff and visitors as well. The creation of a bit of wilderness within your city will be a unique and well-loved gift.

LEGALITIES

Before you put the first shovel into the first piece of ground, make sure that you have legal rights to plant that ground. Unless the land belongs to you or your organization, get permission in writing to put in a meadow. Sketch out what your plans are. Be honest and realistic with people: let them know that the land you are borrowing will look spectacular some of the time and very good most of the time, but that the natural cycle of seasons is going to bring on changes in the meadow that some might consider untidy. Even if you are a part of a nature center or botanical garden and are using a portion of their land, permission in writing from the director might prevent confrontation with another group of enthusiastic gardeners who had very different plans for the same spot of land.

Noxious weed laws for every state list the plant species that are considered potential or very real problems within the state. Get a list of these species, and respect this list when you are choosing your plants and seeds. Plenty of native and non-aggressive species are available to create a spectacular display in any region of the country.

In addition to noxious weed lists, many communities have "lawn laws" that regulate the height and general overall condition of plantings within neighborhoods. Find out what these laws are in your area and abide by them to the best of your ability. If your plan cannot be changed to meet the requirements of these laws, go to the proper authorities and explain what you are planning to do and your purposes in doing so. With the recent popularity of meadow gardening, government agencies are getting a quick education. If you present your plans and purposes in a professional manner, chances are that you will receive special permission to carry on. If you are establishing a meadow for educational purposes at a school or nature center, you should have no problem at all. However, find out about any possible problems before you start rather than half way through your project.

If legalities tend to be a problem in your area, incorporate structures within the meadow that make it look carefully planned. Create paths through some areas; strategically place a bench or two; include stepping stones; or place a fence at one end of the area. Such structures create the effect of a carefully designed landscape. Make sure that you put up a sign giving your group credit for creating this wonderful display.

PLANNING THE MEADOW

Your initial decision should be what kind of meadow you want to plant. If you have unlimited resources and unlimited use of your land, your plans will be quite different from the plans of a group that has the use of a plot of land for a single year and is working on a shoe-string budget. Both groups can have beautiful meadows, but your approaches need to be different.

SHORT-TERM MEADOW PROJECTS

It is often easier to lease or borrow a plot of land on a year-to-year basis than it is to obtain permission to use it for an unlimited amount of time. Sometimes, too, you might be asked to go through a one-year "probation" period in which the success of the first year's meadow determines your ability to use the land for subsequent years. Under these conditions, you might choose to plant an annual meadow, for a meadow full of carefully chosen annual flowers can almost be guaranteed to give you wonderful color and diversity. Your best display from an annual mixture will be in mid to late summer. If you obtain permission to use the area for another year, collect or purchase seeds and reseed the entire area. If you receive permission to use the area for many years, plan to incorporate perennials within your area as soon as possible to give a more balanced and natural look. Include within your mixture as many annuals native to your region and to the United States as possible, and use non-native species sparingly.

LONG-TERM MEADOW PROJECTS

If you are lucky enough to have the use of a piece of property for several years, you can take your time about establishing a meadow area. Depending on the resources available to you, obtain plants or seeds that include both annuals, biennials, and perennials. Particularly if you plan to use the meadow as an outdoor laboratory, you might want to include birdhouses or nesting boxes and try to incorporate water into the meadow area in order to attract more birds and wildlife.

OBTAINING RESOURCES

Although you can establish a meadow on a low budget, you can't create something out of nothing. Shovels, rakes, scythes, and weed eaters can probably be borrowed from members of your group, but a tractor or plow (for large areas) or a rototiller (for small areas) might need to be rented. If you spray the area to get rid of weeds, both the herbicide and a sprayer will be needed. If possible, water should be close at hand to supply the plants with enough moisture to become established, so hoses and sprinklers will be necessary.

One part of obtaining resources will be a lot of fun, and that is gathering seeds from the wild. This is not only an inexpensive way to get the seeds, but it will also be a very valuable learning experience. Seeing the plants growing in their native habitat gives you an idea of what to expect from them in your own meadow. If your meadow is quite different from the natural habitat of certain plants, don't try to use these species in your area. Start deciding what you want early in the season while the plants are still in bloom. Take an expert along with you to help you identify desirable wildflowers. Tag the plants that you want to gather seeds from, and check these plants frequently during the remainder of the growing season. Some plants are quite impatient to rid themselves of seeds once they are ripe, and they might not wait for you to come and gather.

There are only two kinds of money — no money and not quite enough. — John Steinbeck, The Winter of Our Discontent

If you are unable to gather seeds from the wild, you will need funds to purchase plants and seeds. If you are on a tight budget, you will probably choose to use only seeds. If you have green thumbs among your group, however, let them start some of these seeds indoors to get established plants to put into the meadow at the appropriate times.

There are several ways to obtain the necessary funds. If it is a civic project, talk to the correct government agencies. Even if they are unable to give you money, they might be willing to loan you equipment or perhaps even share in the workload by offering to plow the area or to be responsible for watering until the plants get established.

The use of money is all the advantage there is in having money. — Benjamin Franklin

If you are working with a nature center or botanical garden, you might get at least partial funds from their operating expenses, although these organizations always seem to have more places to spend their money than they have money.

If you are planning to put a meadow next to a school, let the children help raise the money. Have a bake sale or a car wash, or better yet, a plant sale! Funds for a school meadow also might be obtained from the parent's association or the school auxiliary or maybe even from the school board.

SHARING THE WORKLOAD

One great joy of community gardening is sharing the workload. When you are with a group of congenial people, the work seems to go faster. Just as much work is involved in planting a meadow as in planting a vegetable garden. After the planting is done and the seedlings are established, however, the maintenance of a meadow is quite low as compared to that of a vegetable plot.

To everything there is a season,
and a time to every purpose under
the heaven. — Ecclesiastes

The greatest concentration of work is in preparing the soil for planting. Depending on your schedules and on how you can best prepare your area (see Chapter Two), this can be done either in the fall or the spring. You might choose to have one or two "work days" and ask that the entire group participate so that this part of the work can be done quickly. The rest of the work schedule should consist of periodic watering (if necessary) and some hand weeding to keep the undesirable plants in check. The group could be split up into pairs and assigned a few days each to accomplish these tasks. Another work day should be scheduled in the fall to mow and clean up any excess plant litter.

If your meadow is at a school or nature center, part of the workload could be taking children on nature walks through the meadow. There is sure to be a variety of expertise in your group, so let each expert talk about what he or she loves best. The bird watcher, the butterfly collector, and the wildflower enthusiast should all be encouraged to share their knowledge. For other ideas on how to use your meadow see Chapter Six.

In a Nutshell:

(1) Determine interest within your organization or neighborhood for creating a meadow garden.

(2) Find a piece of land close to your center of activity.

(3) Check out all the legal ramifications. Get written permission allowing you to garden on your selected spot. Stay within the legal planting guidelines of your area.

(4) Determine the purpose of your meadow and choose plants accordingly.

(5) Plan your meadow well and include structures to create the effect of a well designed part of the landscape.

(6) Decide how you will obtain the resources necessary to plant the meadow.

(7) Share the workload with the entire group. Take advantage of expertise and knowledge found in your group.

CASE STUDIES

(1) One of the most successful community meadows in the country is in New York City's South Bronx. The project was initiated by the Bronx Frontier Development Corporation and was designed to take city-owned vacant lots of one acre or more and plant wildflower meadows on them. Bronx Frontier leveled the rubble on these lots, and volunteers from the neighborhood removed the litter and helped prepare the soil for planting. Seeds, donated by Applewood Seed Company, were hydroseeded onto

the soil. The wildflower seed mixture included annuals, biennials, and perennials that were chosen for their adaptability and their ability to withstand drought. Cornflowers, white yarrow, ox-eye daisies, larkspur, and poppies now grow in these empty lots, delighting the children and land developers, too — land values in the area are said to have greatly increased.

(2) The Virginia Wildflower Preservation Society has initiated an exciting wildflower project at Great Meadow, a steeplechase racecourse and the site of the prestigious Virginia Gold Cup. The Society put in the meadow area at the racecourse to create a dramatic and spectacular display of wildflowers for the thousands of spectators and visitors to Great Meadow. By showcasing the beauty of the wildflowers in a high-use area, the Society hopes that a great many people will realize the horticultural value of using native plants in a landscape plan. Members of the Wildflower Society were responsible for choosing the twenty-six plant species used in the meadow. They were careful to select only those wildflowers native to or naturalized within the Fauquier County area. Great attention was paid to correctly matching particular species to areas within the meadow providing their necessary growing requirements. Society members obtained permission from local property owners to collect some of the seed used in this project. Most seed was derived from their own gardens or from fellow plant societies. Thousands of individually potted first year seedlings were planted at the project site by volunteer members in September. Because peak visitation to the area corresponds with the running of two steeplechase meets (the Virginia Gold Cup the first Saturday in May and the Great Meadow Races the third Saturday in October), wildflowers were chosen that would give the greatest display during these times. Consequently the area is a sea of gold from wild mustard in the spring, and it glows with the hues of goldenrods and asters in the fall.

CHAPTER EIGHT

Organizations
Working With
Cultivating Wildflowers

The science and art of cultivating wildflowers is a relatively new one. Many outstanding organizations throughout the country are involved in or are enthusiastically supporting and encouraging the research necessary to make this science better understood and practiced. Botanical gardens and arboretums, landscape design schools, and horticulture and botany departments of universities all over the country are learning that the enthusiasm shown by native plant gardeners is not the result of a passing fad but is the fruit of the realization that gardening in America must change to meet the need to conserve the nation's national resources. Water and energy conservation should be the concern of every gardener, and this concern can best be exemplified by using the native plants in their own landscape plan. There is a great need for research on using the native plants in every part of this country.

Three national organizations deserve special support and attention for their work on landscaping with the native plants. These are the National Wildflower Research Center headquartered in Austin, Texas; the American Horticultural Society, with headquarters in Mount Vernon, Virginia; and Operation Wildflower, co-sponsored by the National Federation of State Garden Clubs and the Federal Highway Administration. These organizations, and others like them, need both our moral and financial support. Membership in a local botanical garden or arboretum or one of these national organizations provides for an interchange of ideas between gardeners sharing similar interests as well as an opportunity to support much-needed work and research.

THE NATIONAL WILDFLOWER RESEARCH CENTER

The National Wildflower Research Center was founded in December, 1982, with a gift of land and a pledge of $125,000 from Lady Bird Johnson. Its goal is to promote the use of native plants, to raise the level of knowledge about these plants, and to disseminate this knowledge to the general public. Basic to these goals is a dedication to the conservation of native plants and their natural habitats.

Research on many aspects of growing wildflowers and other native plants is being conducted at the Center in Austin, Texas. In addition, the Center has established a Scientific Advisory Board, and the beginning of a network of universities, arboretums, botanical gardens, government agencies, and knowledgeable individuals who will conduct cooperative and contract research in many other parts of the country. There are currently seventy-two test plots on the grounds of the Center, on which the effects of different growing conditions for various commercial wildflower seed mixtures, native grasses, and stands of individual wildflower species are being investigated. Various planting techniques used for establishing a meadow area are being tested including sowing seeds by hand, sowing with a grain drill, and spreading of wildflower mulch (a mixture of cut wildflowers and their seed). Ground preparation methods include mowing to varied heights, surface scarification with a flail mower, and tilling. This type of research needs to be done in every part of the nation to determine the best ground preparation methods, best planting techniques, best types of seeds and plants, and most efficient maintenance methods needed for different regions.

Within a few weeks now Draba, the smallest flower that blows, will sprinkle every sandy place with small blooms ... Draba plucks no heartstrings. Its perfume, if there is any, is lost in the gusty winds. Its color is plain white. Its leaves wear a sensible wooly coat. Nothing eats it; it is too small. No poets sing of it. Some botanist gave it a Latin name, and then forgot it. Altogether it is of no importance — just a small creature that does a small job quickly and well. — Aldo Leopold, A Sand County Almanac

The Center hopes to act as a catalyst to stimulate interest in using wildflowers. By educating the public they hope to get people to accept the wildflowers, appreciate their natural beauty, and realize that wildflowers can be used in their own home or business landscape.

A major effort of the Center is the establishment of an information clearing-house. In this clearing-house they have lists of organizations and resource people who are knowledgeable about growing the native plants in different regions. They also have a list of seed companies and nurseries who specialize in native plants suitable for each area. Research from different regions will provide information on growing conditions and cultural requirements for different plants, and this too will be on file. They will also have an annotated bibliography of the best resource materials available.

For membership application or information write to:
The National Wildflower Research Center, 2600 FM 973 North, Austin, Texas 78725

THE AMERICAN HORTICULTURAL SOCIETY

The American Horticultural Society has been a source of information and inspiration for American gardeners since 1922. AHS has served as a central resource for both amateur and professional gardeners in the country and has placed special emphasis on its educational programs and materials. Membership in the organization includes an annual subscription to *The American Horticulturist* magazine, the American Horticulturist News Edition, free seeds, a gardeners' information service, and a book buyers' service.

Over the past few years the Society has become increasingly concerned over the loss of many plant species and has dedicated itself to plant conservation. In this effort they have established two programs designed to encourage wise plant conservation. The first is the annual publication of the Endangered Wildflowers Calendar, which is designed to spark public interest in endangered plant species. The second is the Wildflower Rediscovery Project, which awards individuals who discover new populations of species thought to be extinct or known to be extremely threatened. In connection with this, they have taken great interest in using native plants in landscape design. Their national headquarters at River Farms, Mount Vernon, Virginia, boasts an outstanding meadow garden. Covering six acres of gently rolling hillside meandering down to the banks of the Potomac River, the meadow has proven that horticultural beauty without intensive maintenance can be accomplished and that the native plants can fill both an aesthetic and an economic need.

Charles Huckins, director of the American Horticultural Society expressed the goals of the Society as he wrote "Let us work together in the knowledge that even though vast portions of our landscape are forever altered or gone, we may still surround ourselves with the remnants, understand the richness and diversity of the plants left to us, and reconstruct some of nature's beauty in harmony with man's other needs."

For information or a membership application write:
The American Horticultural Society, P.O. Box 0105, Mount Vernon, Virginia 22121

OPERATION WILDFLOWER

Operation Wildflower is a national cooperative program involving the National Council of State Garden Clubs, the state highway agencies, and the Federal Highway Administration. It is designed to promote the propagation and the use of wildflowers along Federal-aid highways. The program encourages local garden clubs to work with the highway departments in their state to help beautify the roadsides by planting wildflowers. The garden clubs may pay for (or furnish) seeds, plants, or bulbs of suitable wildflowers native to their region and may offer expertise in the area of cultivation or propagation of the donated plant material. The state highway agency must determine the best areas to use the donated materials and is responsible for planting and maintaining the wildflowers. The agency may use Federal-aid highway funds to help pay for planting costs.

In addition to working closely with the appropriate highway agencies, the National Council of State Garden Clubs in cooperation with

Operation Wildflower publishes a newsletter describing wildflower projects and future plans of garden clubs from all over the nation. The National Council, in conjunction with state garden clubs' educational efforts, also helps to plan and sponsor wildflower workshops in different regions. These workshops are designed to teach people in the area about the wild plants indigenous to their region.

The benefits of using native plants along the roadsides are many. The native plants are generally better suited to the local environment than are non-native plants, and this reduces the need for watering and intensive maintenance. The establishment of natural wildflower plantings will provide habitats for many different types of wildlife and birds. Carefully chosen combinations of wildflowers will provide for seasonal color and can be a great help to erosion control.

If you or your garden club are interested in becoming a part of Operation Wildflower, contact your state council of garden clubs or your state highway agency.

Part Two

Introduction

All of the American wildflowers are special to people across the country, but each part of the nation seems to have certain wildflowers that are particularly loved and are a source of regional pride. Californians have their poppy, Texans have their bluebonnet, and Midwesterners love their prairie flowers. While there are some wildflowers such as butterfly weed *(Asclepias tuberosa)* or black-eyed Susan *(Rudbeckia hirta)* that will grow in nearly every region of the country, there are other wildflowers with environmental needs so exacting that they will grow in only a very small range. This diversity of wildflowers and wide range of habitats in which our native wildflowers can be found is part of what makes meadow gardening so exciting and rewarding. There are hundreds of species of native wildflowers that are of horticultural value, and there are species suitable for nearly every meadow environment possible — from wet to dry, alkaline to acidic, flat to steeply sloping.

Most of our native wildflowers adhere to a geographic range rather than horticultural zones decided upon by scientists. The areas included within each region listed in this book are based on the delineation of regions used by Applewood Seed Company in Arvada, Colorado. However, any such delineation of regions or zones is chosen arbitrarily, and there will be an overlapping of growing regions, just as there is overlapping of horticultural zones. Ecosystems and the vegetation found within them do not always stay within set boundaries, and growing conditions can be very similar in distinctly different regions. For example, growing conditions for the eastern part of the Southwest region are very similar to those of the Great Plains, so gardeners living in this area might want to refer to the Midwest section as well as to that of their own region. This will be true for many areas of the country. For this reason, use the regional chapters as guidelines, but be flexible enough to adapt them to your own individual situation. Regions are listed alphabetically.

Within each regional section there is discussion of general growing conditions, the best time to plant, a list of weeds that are particularly troublesome for that area, and other information pertinent to each individual region. Lists of grasses and wildflower species well suited for different kinds of meadow situations are included. Of particular value will be information from actual meadow projects listed in each region. Individuals and institutions from all over the country shared their experiences with me and offered advice for conditions specific to their region. This collection of data is proof that meadow gardening is a very real landscape alternative in every region of the country.

Both native species (those plants that grew in an area naturally before the intervention of man) as well as many introduced plants (those brought in by man) are listed. It is strongly recommended that the meadow gardener primarily use those plants native to his own region. Non-native species often do not compete well with the native vegetation. Some species adapt to a new region so poorly that they require a great deal of pampering even to get them to live. Other species adapt so readily to a new region that they outcompete the existing vegetation for space and nutrients and become a real pest. There are plenty of native species to choose from that are well suited to many different kinds of environments.

However, there are non-native species that will grow well in different regions without becoming invasive. Many of these are included within wildflower seed mixtures. As long as they can be controlled and do not pose a threat to the balance of an existing plant community, these can be used and will add great beauty to the meadow.

The areas included within each region are as follows:

Midwest: Illinois, Indiana, Iowa, eastern Kansas, Kentucky, Michigan, Minnesota, Missouri, eastern Nebraska, Ohio, Wisconsin

Northeast: Connecticut, Delaware, Maine, Maryland, Massachusetts, New Hampshire, New Jersey, New York, Pennsylvania, Rhode Island, Vermont, West Virginia

Pacific Northwest: northern California, western Oregon, western Washington

Southeast: Alabama, Arkansas, Florida, Georgia, Louisiana, Mississippi, North Carolina, eastern Oklahoma, Tennessee, eastern Texas, South Carolina, Virginia, Washington, D.C.

Southwest: Arizona, southern California, southern Nevada, New Mexico

Texas-Oklahoma: all but the eastern edge of these two states

West: Colorado, Idaho, western Kansas, Montana, western Nebraska, northern Nevada, North Dakota, eastern Oregon, South Dakota, Utah, eastern Washington, Wyoming

CHAPTER NINE

The Midwest

Illinois, Indiana, Iowa, eastern Kansas, Kentucky, Michigan, Minnesota, Missouri, eastern Nebraska, Ohio, Wisconsin

Much has been written about the beauty of the prairies, which at one time covered hundreds of thousands of square miles on this continent. The tall-grass prairie has been described as an awe-inspiring landscape, and a delicate, vulnerable one. The vulnerability and delicate balance of the prairie community is due to a myriad of factors influencing the ecosystem. Although the overall community may appear to be static, there are many, many fluctuations of plant life within smaller segments of the prairie due, in part, to newly formed mounds made by burrowing animals and subsequent changes in the number and types of plants present.

Fires have always played an important part in maintaining the dominance of grasses and forbs and have been found to be beneficial to the prairie plants for many reasons. Experiments have shown that these fires move so quickly that the basal shoots of the plants are not killed. Though the soil temperatures can reach up to 400° F. for a few minutes during these fires, the temperature of the ground at lower levels does not change. Growth after a fire seems to be much stronger, as more light gets to new grass shoots and nutrients are released from dead plant material.

Why all this talk of prairies in a meadow book? It was the popularity of restoring prairie areas that first caught the public's eye, and most work on establishing meadows has been based on careful and thorough research on prairie restoration — for which we can thank the botanists, horticulturists, and gardeners of the Midwest. Although the basic principles are the same — planting a naturalized area within the landscape for both aesthetic reasons and for reduced maintenance — there are major differences between prairies and meadow gardens. A prairie is a naturally balanced plant community; a meadow is a manmade and man-maintained part of the landscape. Although we should try to use plants native to our own regions in meadow gardens, introduced or alien species can be used to accent or provide a special effect, as long as they are kept under control. This is not possible in a prairie, because the very presence of alien species is a threat to the natural balance of these areas. When alien or introduced species are brought in, they spread vegetatively or through seed dispersal, and they eventually destroy the balance of a restored or naturally occurring prairie area. Seed mixtures that include non-native species should not be used in a meadow garden in an area in which they would pose a threat to a prairie.

There are many ways to establish prairie gardens, and many excellent books tell how to do it. One of the best source books is *The Prairie Propagation Handbook,* published by Wehr Nature Center. For information about this book and others on the subject, see the list of books at the end of this chapter.

CONDITIONS TO CONSIDER IN THE MIDWEST

NATURALLY OCCURRING PLANT COMMUNITIES

The dominant plant community of the Midwest is a tall-grass prairie, bounded by a deciduous forest in the southern and eastern parts of this region and a mixed forest in the northern parts. Within the tall-grass prairies one of the more abundant grasses is big bluestem. Though it usually grows to a height of 4 to 9 feet, it sometimes can grow as tall as 12 feet. Other prairie grasses that can be found here include Indian grass (in the same habitat), prairie cordgrass (in moister areas), switchgrass, and little bluestem. Cool-season grasses growing and blooming in the early spring include needlegrass, Junegrass, and prairie dropseed. The forbs (wildflowers), although not dominant in number, certainly claim their share of attention. Two main families are represented — the legumes and the composites. Trees do occur in this area, though they are found chiefly along riverbanks where extra moisture makes their growth possible. The most prevalent tree is bur oak, which has adapted to conditions in the prairie by having leathery leaves (which reduce water loss) and by developing a very deep taproot that can take advantage of moisture deep in the soil during periods of drought. Winters in this area tend to be very cold and summers very hot. Rainfall varies from almost 40 inches in the east to 15 inches toward the western borders. Precipitation is unevenly distributed, usually coming in the form of summer rains.

Where the prairie meets the forest there are alternating belts of grasses and trees. This transition zone is called a prairie parkland, and trees in this region include oak, hickory, and aspen.

The eastern deciduous forest, found in southern Missouri, Kentucky, Indiana, Ohio, Wisconsin, and Michigan, has a very rich and diversified flora, consisting of many species of deciduous trees and an understory of shrubs, small trees, ferns, and wildflowers. Rainfall is generally well distributed throughout the year and averages 40 inches annually. The growing season lasts from four to six months.

The northern mixed forests of Wisconsin and Michigan are primarily composed of coniferous trees (pines, spruce, red cedar, and hemlock) interspersed with stands of deciduous trees (beech, sugar maple, basswood).

The winters are very harsh and the growing season short. Rainfall averages between 24 and 45 inches annually.

NOXIOUS WEEDS

Some of the biggest problems with weeds in the Midwest are caused by aggressive perennial grasses and from the introduction of potentially invasive European weedy species. Some of the most troublesome include dandelions, thistles, quack grass, and turf grasses.

WHEN TO PLANT

Where ample amounts of moisture are available, repeated shallow tilling of the soil during the spring months will help rid the area of aggressive weeds and grasses. Plow as early as possible, and do repeated shallow tilling until you plant — usually by mid-June. If you can work the ground in late fall before winter sets in, you'll have a headstart on dealing with the weeds, and the optimum planting time will be mid-March to mid-May. Except in the extreme northern reaches of this region, planting can also be done in the fall (October and November) after active plant growth has stopped.

MAINTENANCE

Weed control is essential to retain the balance of plants in a meadow garden. Traditionally, fire has been used to maintain prairies, and within the Midwestern states this still proves to be the most effective control measure for prairies and, presumably, for meadows as well. Fires should be undertaken with extreme care and caution, only after the second year of growth, and only after contacting the local fire department and following their instructions. After the first burning, fires are generally necessary only every two to three years. Hand-weeding of undesirable species will help during the first two years.

PROBLEM WILDFLOWERS

Where prairies are prevalent use only species that are native to your particular region. Many non-native species become overly aggressive, and they can do real harm to the balance of the prairie community. Some of the native plants are also considered invasive, so be careful with these species. Some commercially available seed mixtures contain seeds of both alien and native species that are particularly troublesome, so be wary of these as well. The following plants are some of the worst offenders. Native species are marked with a *.

Achillea millefolium	yarrow
Asclepias syriaca	common milkweed
Campanula rapunculoides	bluebell
Centaurea cyanus	bachelor's button
Chrysanthemum leucanthemum	ox-eye daisy

Cichorium intybus	chicory
Daucus carota	Queen Anne's lace
*Helianthus annuus	sunflower
*Helianthus grosseserratus	sunflower
*Helianthus mollis	downy sunflower
Lathyrus latifolius	sweet pea
Linaria vulgaris	butter and eggs
Mirabilis jalapa	four o'clock

MEADOW PLANTS THAT GROW IN THE MIDWEST

In the Midwest, even more than elsewhere in the country, you should use species native to the region (and if possible, native to your particular area). The wonderful diversity of flora in the prairies makes it possible for you to use hundreds of different wildflowers that are native to these states. This is not to say that only these species should be used. On the contrary, you should learn about the flora of your immediate vicinity and collect seeds from the wild so that your meadow or prairie area will look as authentic as possible. You have a responsibility to retain the character of your local vegetation. Choose your plants wisely.

Although cultural requirements for the following species will vary greatly, all of the species listed below will grow somewhere within the Midwestern region. This list was based on the commercial availability of these seeds, on their beauty, and on their ability to grow in this area. In this list, and in all the lists that follow, native species are marked with a *; invasive species are marked with an X; and plants that are not marked are non-native species that usually are non-invasive.

Achillea millefolium	yarrow
Anagallis arvensis	pimpernel
*Aquilegia canadensis	columbine
Argemone hispida	white prickly poppy
*Asclepias incarnata	swamp milkweed
*Asclepias syriaca X	common milkweed
*Asclepias tuberosa	butterfly weed
*Aster azyreus	blue aster
*Aster laevis	smooth aster
*Aster lineariifolius	aster
*Aster novae-angliae	New England aster
*Baptisia australis	false indigo
*Baptisia leucantha	wild white indigo
*Baptisia leucophaea	false indigo
Belamcanda chinensis	blackberry lily
*Bidens aristosa	tickseed sunflower
*Bidens polylepis	tickseed sunflower
Campanula rapunculoides X	bluebell
*Campanula rotundifolia	bluebell

Centaurea cyanus X	bachelor's button
Chrysanthemum leucanthemum X	ox-eye daisy
Cichorium intybus X	chicory
*Claytonia virginica	spring beauty
Consolida orientalis (same as *Delphinium ajacis*)	rocket larkspur
*Coreopsis lanceolata	lance-leaved coreopsis
Coreopsis tinctoria	annual coreopsis
Cosmos bipinnatus	cosmos
Daucus carota X	Queen Anne's lace
Dianthus barbatus	sweet William
Dianthus deltoides	maiden pinks
Digitalis purpurea	foxglove
*Dodecatheon meadia	shooting star
*Dracopis amplexicaulis (same as *Rudbeckia amplexicaulis*)	coneflower
Echinacea angustifolia	black Samson
Echinacea pallida	pale purple coneflower
*Echinacea purpurea	purple coneflower
Epilobium angustifolium	fireweed
Erigeron speciosus	Oregon fleabane
*Erythronium americanum	fawn lily
Eschscholzia californica	California poppy
Eupatorium maculatum	Joe-pye weed
Eupatorium perfoliatum	boneset
Gaillardia aristata	perennial Indian blanket
Gaillardia pulchella	annual Indian blanket
*Geranium maculatum	wild geranium
*Geum triflorum	prairie smoke
Gypsophila paniculata	baby's breath
*Helenium autumnale	sneezeweed
*Helianthus angustifolius X	swamp sunflower
*Helianthus annuus X	sunflower
*Helianthus grosseserratus	sunflower
Iberis umbellata	candytuft
Iris cristata	dwarf crested iris
Lathyrus latifolius X	sweet pea
*Liatris aspera	rough blazing star
*Liatris pycnostachya	blazing star
*Liatris scariosa	blazing star
*Liatris spicata	blazing star
*Linum perenne lewisii	blue flax
*Lupinus perennis	lupine
Lychnis chalcedonica	Maltese cross
Machaeranthera tanacetifolia	prairie aster

Mirabilis jalapa X	four o'clock
Monarda didyma	bee balm
Monarda fistulosa	bergamot
Myosotis sylvatica	forget me not
Nemophila menziesii	baby blue eyes
Oenothera biennis X	evening primrose
Oenothera missouriensis	sundrops
Penstemon digitalis	beard tongue
Penstemon grandiflorus	beard tongue
Petalostemon purpureum	prairie clover
Phlox divaricata	blue phlox
Phlox drummondii	annual phlox
Phlox pilosa	western phlox
Ratibida columnaris	prairie coneflower
Rudbeckia fulgida	coneflower
Rudbeckia hirta	black-eyed Susan
Sisyrinchium angustifolium	blue-eyed grass
Solidago juncea	goldenrod
Solidago nemoralis	gray goldenrod
Solidago odora	scented goldenrod
Thymus serpyllum	creeping thyme
Tradescantia virginiana	spiderwort
Trifolium incarnatum	crimson clover
Verbena stricta	hoary vervain
Vernonia altissima	ironweed
Vernonia fasciculata	western ironweed
Viola cornuta	Johnny-jump-up

THE TOP TEN

The following list is not designed as a balanced mixture of wildflowers and should not be used as such. The flowers included within this list are noted for their adaptability and reliability. They are all generally hardy and easy to grow from seed in this region.

Asclepias tuberosa	butterfly weed
Coreopsis lanceolata	lance-leaved coreopsis
Dracopis amplexicaulis	
(same as *Rudbeckia amplexicaulis*)	coneflower
Echinacea purpurea	purple coneflower
Helenium autumnale	sneezeweed
Helianthus angustifolius	swamp sunflower
Helianthus grosseserratus	sunflower
Oenothera missouriensis	sundrops
Ratibida columnaris	prairie coneflower
Rudbeckia hirta	black-eyed Susan

GRASSES

Grass is as necessary to a meadow garden as it is to a restored prairie, and the Midwest is lucky to have a number of native grass species borrowed from the prairie that will thrive in a meadow environment. Grasses are important to fill niches within the meadow that the wildflowers might be unable to fill. The use of grasses also helps to create the feeling of openness that is basic to the charm of a meadow or prairie. The following species of native grasses should thrive within the Midwestern region.

Andropogon gerardii	big bluestem
Bouteloua curtipendula	side oats grama
Panicum virgatum	switchgrass
Scizachyrium scoparium	
(same as *Andropogon scoparius*)	
Sorghastrum nutans	Indian grass
Stipa spartea	needlegrass

PLANTS FOR CUTTING

To many people, the best part of having a naturalized area is the number of cut flowers that it makes readily available. Even a small area can yield an abundant supply of cut flowers throughout the growing season. The following list includes flowers that are best suited for bringing inside as cut flowers. For extra tips on treating cut flowers, refer to Chapter 6.

Achillea millefolium X	yarrow
Anagallis arvensis	pimpernel
*Aquilegia canadensis	columbine
*Asclepias tuberosa	butterfly weed
*Aster species	asters
Centaurea cyanus X	bachelor's button
Chrysanthemum leucanthemum X	ox-eye daisy
Consolida orientalis	
(same as *Delphinium ajacis*)	rocket larkspur
*Coreopsis lanceolata	coreopsis
Coreopsis tinctoria	annual coreopsis
Cosmos bipinnatus	cosmos
Daucus carota X	Queen Anne's lace
Dianthus barbatus	sweet William
*Dracopis amplexicaulis	
(same as *Rudbeckia amplexicaulis*)	coneflower
*Echinacea purpurea	purple coneflower
Erigeron speciosus	Oregon fleabane
Gaillardia pulchella	annual Indian blanket
Gypsophila paniculata	baby's breath
*Helianthus species	sunflowers
*Liatris pycnostachya	blazing star

Lupinus perennis	lupine
Phlox species	phlox
Solidago juncea	goldenrod

SEASONAL BLOOM

You can have good color in your meadow during all parts of the growing season if you pay some attention to the blooming times for different species. The following lists should help you find some favorites for each season. There will be great variation as to the actual time of bloom depending on growing conditions, local weather, and when the seeds were sown or the plants set out. These are general guidelines. As always, use as many native species (marked with a *) as possible.

SPRING: Many of the spring-blooming plants are woodland border plants.

Achillea millefolium X	yarrow
Aquilegia canadensis	columbine
Chrysanthemum leucanthemum X	ox-eye daisy
Claytonia virginica	spring beauty
Dianthus barbatus	sweet William
Dodecatheon meadia	shooting star
Eschscholzia californica	California poppy
Geranium maculatum	wild geranium
Iris cristata	dwarf crested iris
Lupinus perennis	lupine
Nemophila menziesii	baby blue eyes
Penstemon grandiflorus	beard tongue
Phlox divaricata	blue phlox
Sisyrinchium angustifolium	blue-eyed grass
Viola cornuta	Johnny-jump-up

SUMMER:

Anagallis arvensis	pimpernel
Argemone hispida	white prickly poppy
Asclepias tuberosa	butterfly weed
Baptisia australis	false indigo
Belamcanda chinensis	blackberry lily
Centaurea cyanus X	bachelor's button
Cichorium intybus X	chicory
Consolida orientalis (same as *Delphinium ajacis*)	rocket larkspur
Coreopsis lanceolata	coreopsis
Coreopsis tinctoria	annual coreopsis
Cosmos bipinnatus	cosmos
Daucus carota X	Queen Anne's lace
Dracopis amplexicaulis (same as *Rudbeckia amplexicaulis*)	coneflower

*Echinacea purpurea	purple coneflower
Epilobium angustifolium	fireweed
Erigeron speciosus	Oregon fleabane
Gaillardia aristata	Indian blanket
Gaillardia pulchella	annual Indian blanket
*Helenium autumnale	sneezeweed
*Helianthus annuus	common sunflower
Iberis umbellata	candytuft
Lathyrus latifolius X	sweet pea
Liatris pycnostachya	blazing star
Linum perenne lewisii	blue flax
Lychnis chalcedonica	Maltese cross
Machaeranthera tanacetifolia	prairie aster
Mirabilis jalapa	four o'clock
Monarda fistulosa	bergamot
Myosotis sylvatica	forget me not
*Oenothera biennis	evening primrose
*Petalostemon purpureum	prairie clover
Phlox drummondii	annual phlox
*Ratibida columnaris	prairie coneflower
Rudbeckia hirta	black-eyed Susan
Thymus serpyllum	creeping thyme
Tradescantia virginiana	spiderwort
Trifolium incarnatum	crimson clover
*Verbena stricta	hoary vervain

FALL:

*Asclepias incarnata	swamp milkweed
*Aster novae-angliae	New England aster
*Bidens aristosa	tickseed sunflower
*Eupatorium maculatum	Joe-pye weed
*Helianthus angustifolius	swamp sunflower
Machaeranthera tanacetifolia	prairie aster
Oenothera biennis	evening primrose
*Solidago species	goldenrods
*Vernonia altissima	ironweed

PLANTS TO ATTRACT BIRDS AND BUTTERFLIES

Birds and butterflies will find your meadow, just as they do any area with a profusion of flowers. However, if you would like to plant a few extra species that are especially attractive to birds and butterflies, choose some of the following:

*Asclepias species	milkweeds
*Asclepias tuberosa	butterfly weed
*Aster species	asters
Aurinia saxatilis	basket of gold

Chrysanthemum leucanthemum X	ox-eye daisy
*Coreopsis species	coreopsis
Cosmos species	cosmos
Daucus carota X	Queen Anne's lace
Dianthus barbatus	sweet William
*Helianthus species	sunflowers
Monarda species	bee balms
*Phlox species	phlox

EROSION CONTROL

If you need help with erosion control, choose plants that establish quickly, that are low growing, and that have mat-forming roots to better hold the soil. Some of the following species might be helpful.

Achillea millefolium	yarrow
*Baptisia australis	false indigo
Eschscholzia californica	California poppy
*Oenothera missouriensis	sundrops
*Penstemon strictus	penstemon
Trifolium incarnatum	crimson clover

DATA FROM PRAIRIE RESTORATIONS AND MEADOW PROJECTS

(1) Location: Minnesota

Description: Approximately 2,000 square feet of neutral soils with average moisture were planted on a slight slope.

Soil preparation: Existing weeds were sprayed with herbicide; soil was then tilled; resulting grass and forb seedlings were sprayed again. No fertilizer was applied.

Planting: A combination of commercial seed mixture and hand-collected seeds was used at a rate of two ounces of wildflower seeds and one and a half pounds of native grass seed per 1,000 square feet.

Maintenance: The area was watered to establish the seedlings. The first year the area was cut three or four times, and occasional hand-weeding was also necessary, especially for thistles. The second year it was cut twice, and the third year and subsequent years, an annual mowing in April was all that was needed.

Dominant flowers: ox-eye daisy, black-eyed Susan, coneflowers, asters, blazing star.

Comments: Be sure to establish desired forbs when you do the initial planting for it is nearly impossible to introduce them later without disturbing many of the existing plants.

(2) Location: Minnesota

Description: 4,000 square feet of dry, neutral soil on a flat area was planted.

Soil preparation: The area was sprayed with a general herbicide, then resprayed where necessary. It was then disked, or harrowed, and raked smooth.

Planting: A commercial mixture of prairie grasses and forbs was sown at the rate of one pound per 1,000 square feet. After the seeds were broadcast, they were raked lightly into the soil.

Maintenance: Selective weeding was done as necessary, requiring ten hours the first year and three hours per year afterwards. The area is burned annually.

Dominant flowers: All the grasses and forbs are indigenous to central Minnesota. The grasses dominate. Some of the showier forbs include prairie smoke, golden Alexander, black-eyed Susan, purple coneflower, prairie clover, prairie phlox, sunflowers, wild bergamot, goldenrods, asters, and the downy gentian.

(3) Location: Illinois

Description: Fifteen acres of both dry and wet areas with both alkaline and neutral soils were planted.

Soil preparation: The soil was disked two or three times the year before planting to let weeds germinate; then the weeds were turned under.

Planting: Seeds were collected in local prairie remnants, stratified, planted in the greenhouse, and then transplanted into 1-foot grids.

Maintenance: Intensive weeding was necessary the first two years, and then the area was burned once a year. There is no maintenance other than an annual burning, which takes about four hours a year.

Dominant flowers: About fifteen to thirty species of flowers are in bloom from June 1 to October 1 and only two to ten species bloom before the first of June or after the first of October.

Comments: Perhaps using an herbicide the year or two before planting would help eliminate many weeds. It would also be nice to have more spring-blooming plants.

(4) Location: Michigan

Description: Three acres of dry, slightly acidic soils were planted.

Soil preparation: A general herbicide was used on the quack grass. The area was then plowed and disked.

Planting: Seeds were collected from nearby prairie remnants. These were started in the greenhouse, and forb and grass plugs were put into the ground in rows to make weeding easier.

Maintenance: New plants were watered, as conditions demanded. A great deal of hand weeding was necessary to help get the plants established. The area is burned every other year to stop woody growth and weeds and to improve the vigor of the prairie plants.

Dominant flowers: violets, prairie smoke, shooting stars, composites and grasses, asters, goldenrods, gentians.

Comments: The grasses have become quite thick. A reduction of the amount of grass seed planted should help this problem.

RESOURCES

INSTITUTIONS AND ORGANIZATIONS

The following organizations and institutions might be able to give you more information about establishing prairies or meadows and about growing plants native to your region. In addition, you can contact your county extension agent, state government offices, local garden clubs, and local chapters of the Soil Conservation Society.

Illinois

Chicago Botanic Garden
P. O. Box 433
Glencoe, Illinois 60022

The Morton Arboretum
Route 53
Lisle, Illinois 60532

Iowa

Bickelhaupt Arboretum
340 South 14th St.
Clinton, Iowa 52732

Michigan

Fernwood Nature Center
1720 Range Line Rd.
Niles, Michigan 49120

Michigan Botanical Club
Department of Botany and Plant Pathology
Michigan State University
East Lansing, Michigan 48824

Minnesota

University of Minnesota Landscape Arboretum
3675 Arboretum Dr.
Chanhassen, Minnesota 55318

Missouri

The Missouri Botanical Garden
P. O. Box 299
St. Louis, Missouri 63166

Missouri Native Plant Society
Missouri Department of Conservation
Box 180
Jefferson City, Missouri 65102

Wisconsin

Boerner Botanical Gardens
5879 South 92nd St.
Hales Corners, Wisconsin 53130

University of Wisconsin Arboretum
1207 Seminole Highway
Madison, Wisconsin 53711

Wehr National Center
9701 W. College Avenue
Franklin, Wisconsin 53132

NURSERIES AND SEED COMPANIES

Seed companies and nurseries selling native plants and seeds in the Midwest are listed below. These are not recommendations — merely possible sources. No attempt has been made to determine the quality of seeds and plants available from these sources.

Richard R. Clinebell
1874 Church St.
San Francisco, California 94131
(collecting source is native prairie plantings in Stark County, Illinois)

Dutch Mountain Nursery
7984 North 48th St.
Augusta, Michigan 49012

Great Lakes Wildflowers
Box 1923
Milwaukee, Wisconsin 53201

Hi-Mountain Farm
Route 1, Box 662
Seligman, Missouri 65745

Horizon Seeds, Inc.
1600 Cornhusker Highway
P. O. Box 81823
Lincoln, Nebraska 68501

Illini Gardens
Box 125
Oakford, Illinois 62673

LaFayette House Nursery
RR 1, Box 1A
LaFayette, Illinois 61449

Little Valley Farm
RR 1, Box 287
Richland Center, Wisconsin 53581

Midwest Wildflowers
Box 64
Rockton, Illinois 61072

Natural Habitat Nursery
4818 Terminal Rd.
McFarland, Wisconsin 53558

Prairie Associates
6328 Piping Rock Rd.
Madison, Wisconsin 53711

Prairie Nursery
Route 1, Box 365
Westfield, Wisconsin 53711

Prairie Restorations
P. O. Box 327
Princeton, Minnesota 55371

Prairie Ridge Nursery
RR 2, 9738
Overland Road
Mount Horeb, Wisconsin 53572

Prairie Seed Source
P. O. Box 83
North Lake, Wisconsin 53064

Wehr Nature Center
5879 South 92nd St.
Hales Corner, Wisconsin 53130

Windrift Prairie Nursery
RD 2
Oregon, Illinois 61061

Wildlife Nursery
P. O. Box 2724
Oshkosh, Wisconsin 54903

SELECTED READING

Barr, Claude A. *Jewels of the Plains: Wildflowers of the Great Plains*. University of Minnesota Press, Minneapolis, Minnesota; 1983.

Costello, David. *The Prairie World*. University of Minnesota Press, Minneapolis, Minnesota; 1969.

Courtenay, and Zimmerman. *Wildflowers and Weeds* (Great Lakes Region). Van Nostrand, Reinhold, New York; 1972.

Currah, Smreciu, and Van Dyk. *Prairie Wildflowers*.

Klimas, John E., and James A. Cunningham. *Wildflowers of Eastern America*. Alfred A. Knopf, Inc., New York; 1974.

Peterson, R. T., and Margaret McKenny. *Field Guide to Wildflowers of Northeastern and North Central North America*. Houghton Mifflin, Boston; 1968.

Niering, William A., and Nancy C. Olmstead. *The Audubon Society Field Guide to North American Wildflowers* (Eastern). Alfred A. Knopf, New York; 1979.

Robert, J. and B. S. Smith. *The Prairie Garden*. University of Wisconsin Press, Madison, Wisconsin; 1980.

Rock, Harold W. *The Prairie Propagation Handbook*. Milwaukee County Park System, Milwaukee, Wisconsin; 1977.

Van Bruggen, *Wildflowers, Grasses and Other Plants of the Northern Plains and Black Hills*.

CHAPTER TEN

The Northeast

Connecticut, Delaware, Maine, Maryland, Massachusetts, New Hampshire, New Jersey, New York, Pennsylvania, Rhode Island, Vermont, West Virginia

CONDITIONS TO CONSIDER IN THE NORTHEAST

NATURALLY OCCURRING PLANT COMMUNITIES

Two major native plant communities are found within the Northeast: northern mixed forests and eastern deciduous forests. The northern mixed forests are found in northern New England and are composed primarily of coniferous trees. The climate of this area is characterized by long, hard winters and a short growing season. Rainfall is ample and evenly distributed, averaging 24 to 25 inches annually. The eastern deciduous forest is found south of the Great Lakes and is made up of beech, maple, elm, and basswood. The growing season generally lasts four to six months, and the average annual rainfall is 40 inches.

In almost all parts of this region, natural succession would cause a cleared field to eventually turn into a forest, though the rate of succession is much slower than in the Southeast. In northern areas the first tree to appear in a cleared field is white spruce. In southern New England the first species is red cedar. Other species that will invade depend on the existing vegetation — how close it is and how successfully the invading seeds are dispersed.

NOXIOUS WEEDS

As in other areas of the country, establishing a meadow garden will be made more difficult by the invasion of uninvited weeds. Some of the worst offenders in the Northeast are honeysuckle, poison ivy, Canadian thistle, and wild garlic.

WHEN TO PLANT

Planting is possible in either fall or spring, and each season has its benefits. You eliminate the need to pretreat many of the species by planting in fall. However, although natural weather conditions will break the dormancy of many seeds, it is not as reliable a process as stratifying or scarifying the seeds and treating each species separately depending on its individual requirements. Seeds sown in the fall are sometimes buried by mud or winter rains, eaten by birds and small mammals, or choked out by weeds before they have a chance to grow. If you sow in the fall, you'll get the best results by sowing perennials in early fall (late September) and sowing annuals in late fall (late November). If you use a seed mixture, compromise and sow in October. Seeds sown in the spring will not have the advantage of early germination and root growth that fall-sown seeds will have. You might base your decision about when to sow on how and when you prepared your meadow area and when it will be ready for seeds. Either a fall or a spring planting can give good results.

MAINTENANCE

Watering to get the seedlings or plants established will be necessary. And you must mow the area annually to help keep the weeds in check and open up the meadow. Hand weeding and selective spraying of undesirable species during the first year or two will be beneficial.

PROBLEM SOILS

New England is famous, or infamous, for its rocky soils. Although it's often difficult to work around, this well-drained soil creates very good environmental conditions for growing many of the meadow plants. However, *A Sierra Club Naturalists's Guide to Southern New England* (Sierra Club Books, 1978) suggests that most soils in the southern part of this region are too sandy, stony, thin, or wet to support agriculture on a large scale. Perhaps planting on a very small scale, such as a backyard meadow, is just the thing to maintain ecological and species diversity in an area that is presently seventy-five percent woodland.

PROBLEM WILDFLOWERS

The following wildflowers might be included in some wildflower seed mixtures and might become invasive within some areas of the Northeast. They can be used, but be aware of their potentially aggressive character and use them judiciously.

Achillea millefolium	yarrow
Chrysanthemum leucanthemum	ox-eye daisy
Daucus carota	Queen Anne's lace
Eupatorium maculatum	Joe-pye weed
Lythrum salicaria	loosestrife
Tradescantia virginiana	spiderwort
Verbascum thapsus	mullein

MEADOW PLANTS THAT GROW IN THE NORTHEAST

Creating a combination of wildflowers and native grasses that will thrive and be compatible involves knowing the conditions present in your own meadow area. The first step, of course, is to choose plants that do grow in your region. Even this is not easy, however, for the wonderful diversity and variety of growing conditions presented in our country make it impossible to know exactly what will grow where. Your own backyard might contain just the right conditions to grow a plant that does not normally do well in your area. For this reason, use the following lists as guidelines, but don't hesitate to experiment and try to grow some favorites, even if they are not on these lists. The lists were based on recommendations from botanists and horticulturists from universities, botanical gardens, arboretums, and native plant societies, as well as the sage advice of many "dirt gardeners" who live in the Northeast.

Growth requirements will vary enormously from one species to another, but all of the species listed below are reported as growing well in at least some part of the northeastern region. In the list below and other lists that follow, the species native to this region are marked with an *. Species with an invasive tendency are marked with an X. Species that are non-native, but generally non-invasive, are unmarked.

*Achillea millefolium X	yarrow
Ammi majus	bishop's flower
Anagallis arvensis	pimpernel
*Aquilegia canadensis	columbine
Arabis alpina	rock cress
*Asclepias incarnata	swamp milkweed
*Asclepias syriaca	common milkweed
*Asclepias tuberosa	butterfly weed
*Aster azureus	blue aster
*Aster cordifolius	aster
*Aster novae-angliae	New England aster
*Aster spectabilis	aster
*Baptisia australis	false indigo
*Baptisia leucantha	wild indigo
Belamcanda chinensis	blackberry lily
*Bidens aristosa X	tickseed sunflower
Campanula rotundifolia	bluebell
Centaurea cyanus X	bachelor's button
Cerastium bierbersteinii	snow in summer
Cheiranthus cheiri	wallflower
Chrysanthemum leucanthemum X	ox-eye daisy
Cichorium intybus X	chicory
*Claytonia virginica	spring beauty
Consolida orientalis	
(same as Delphinium ajacis)	rocket larkspur

*Coreopsis lanceolata	lance-leaved coreopsis
Coreopsis tinctoria	annual coreopsis
Cosmos bipinnatus	cosmos
Daucus carota X	Queen Anne's lace
Dianthus barbatus	sweet William
Dianthus deltoides	maiden pink
Digitalis purpurea	foxglove
*Dodecatheon meadia	shooting star
Dracopis amplexicaulis	
(same as Rudbeckia amplexicaulis)	coneflower
*Echinacea purpurea	purple coneflower
Epilobium angustifolium	fireweed
Erigeron speciosus	Oregon fleabane
Erythronium americanum	fawn lily
Eschscholzia californica	California poppy
*Eupatorium maculatum X	Joe-pye weed
*Eupatorium perfoliatum	boneset
Gaillardia aristata	Indian blanket
Gaillardia pulchella	annual Indian blanket
*Geranium maculatum	wild geranium
*Geum triflorum	prairie smoke
Gypsophila paniculata	baby's breath
*Helenium autumnale	sneezeweed
*Helianthus angustifolius	swamp sunflower
*Helianthus annuus	sunflower
Iberis umbellata	candytuft
*Iris cristata	dwarf crested iris
Lathyrus latifolius	sweet pea
*Liatris pycnostachya	prairie blazing star
*Liatris scariosa	blazing star
*Liatris spicata	blazing star
*Lilium canadense	Turk's cap lily
*Lobelia cardinalis	cardinal flower
Lobularia maritima	sweet alyssum
*Lupinus perennis	lupine
Mirabilis jalapa	four o'clock
*Monarda didyma	bee balm
*Monarda fistulosa	bergamot
Myosotis sylvatica	forget me not
Nemophila menziesii	baby blue eyes
*Oenothera biennis	evening primrose
Oenothera missouriensis	sundrops
Papaver rhoeas	corn poppy
*Penstemon digitalis	beard tongue
*Phlox divaricata	blue phlox

Phlox drummondii	annual phlox
Ratibida columnaris	prairie coneflower
Rudbeckia fulgida	coneflower
*Rudbeckia hirta	black-eyed Susan
Silene armeria	catchfly
*Sisyrinchium angustifolium	blue-eyed grass
*Solidago canadensis	meadow goldenrod
*Solidago juncea	goldenrod
*Solidago nemoralis	gray goldenrod
*Solidago odora	scented goldenrod
Stokesia laevis	Stoke's aster
Thymus serpyllum	creeping thyme
*Tradescantia virginiana X	spiderwort
Verbena stricta	hoary vervain
*Vernonia altissima	ironweed
*Vernonia noveboracensis	New York ironweed
Viola cornuta	Johnny-jump-up

THE TOP TEN

The following list is not designed as a balanced mixture of wildflowers and should not be used as such. The flowers included within this list are noted for their adaptability and reliability. They are generally hardy and easy to grow from seed in this region. Native species are marked with a *.

*Asclepias tuberosa	butterfly weed
*Aster novae-angliae	New England aster
Chrysanthemum leucanthemum	ox-eye daisy
*Coreopsis lanceolata	lance-leaved coreopsis
Coreopsis tinctoria	annual coreopsis
*Echinacea purpurea	purple coneflower
Gaillardia pulchella	annual Indian blanket
*Helianthus angustifolius	swamp sunflower
*Oenothera biennis	evening primrose
*Rudbeckia hirta	black-eyed Susan

GRASSES

When planting sunny, naturalized areas, it is important to include some non-spreading grasses to fill in niches that the wildflowers cannot fill. This will create the open feeling that is part of the basic charm of a meadow. Several clumping grasses, including some of the fescues, will grow in the Northeast. They help to bind the soil and give interesting texture to the meadow, yet they spread in moderation, thus making them desirable as meadow grasses. Watch out for grasses such as Kentucky bluegrass that will spread rapidly and hurt the wildflowers in the competition for space in the meadow. Some of the best native grasses to use in this area are:

Andropogon virginicus	broomsedge
Bouteloua curtipendula	side oats grama
Chasmanthium latifolium	wild oats
Festuca elatior	meadow fescue
Koeleria cristata	June grass
Panicum virgatum	switchgrass
Scizachyrium scoparium (same as *Andropogon scoparius*)	little bluestem

SEASONAL BLOOM

You can have good color in your meadow during all parts of the growing season if you pay attention to the time of bloom of the different species. The following lists should help you find some favorites for each season. There will be great variation as to actual time of bloom, for this depends on the growing conditions, local weather, and when the seeds were sown or the plants set out. These are general guidelines. As always, use as many native species as possible. These are marked with an *.

SPRING:

*Aquilegia canadensis	columbine
*Baptisia australis	false indigo
Centaurea cyanus X	bachelor's button
Cheiranthus cheiri	wallflower
*Claytonia virginica	spring beauty
Consolida orientalis (same as *Delphinium ajacis*)	rocket larkspur
Dianthus barbatus	sweet William
*Erythronium americanum	fawn lily
Eschscholzia californica	California poppy
*Geranium maculatum	wild geranium
*Iris cristata	dwarf crested iris
Nemophila menziesii	baby blue eyes
*Penstemon digitalis	beard tongue
Penstemon smallii	beard tongue
*Phlox divaricata	blue phlox
*Sisyrinchium angustifolium	blue-eyed grass
Stokesia laevis	Stoke's aster
Viola cornuta	Johnny-jump-up

SUMMER:

*Achillea millefolium X	yarrow
Ammi majus	bishop's flower
Anagallis arvensis	pimpernel
*Asclepias incarnata	swamp milkweed
*Asclepias tuberosa	butterfly weed
*Baptisia australis	false indigo

Belamcanda chinensis	blackberry lily
*Bidens aristosa	tickseed sunflower
*Campanula rotundifolia	bluebell
*Castilleja coccinea	Indian paintbrush
Centaurea cyanus	bachelor's button
Chrysanthemum leucanthemum X	ox-eye daisy
Cichorium intybus	chicory
Consolida orientalis (same as *Delphinium ajacis*)	rocket larkspur
*Coreopsis lanceolata	lance-leaved coreopsis
Coreopsis tinctoria	annual coreopsis
Cosmos bipinnatus	cosmos
Daucus carota	Queen Anne's lace
*Dodecatheon meadia	shooting star
*Echinacea purpurea	purple coneflower
*Epilobium angustifolium	fireweed
Erigeron speciosus	Oregon fleabane
Eschscholzia californica	California poppy
*Eupatorium maculatum X	Joe-pye weed
Gaillardia aristata	Indian blanket
Gaillardia pulchella	annual Indian blanket
*Helenium autumnale	sneezeweed
*Helianthus angustifolius	swamp sunflower
*Helianthus annuus	sunflower
Lathyrus latifolius	sweet pea
*Liatris pycnostachya	prairie blazing star
*Liatris scariosa	blazing star
*Liatris spicata	blazing star
*Lilium canadense	Turk's cap lily
*Lupinus perennis	lupine
*Monarda didyma	bee balm
*Monarda fistulosa	bergamot
Myosotis sylvatica	forget-me-not
*Oenothera biennis	evening primrose
Oenothera missouriensis	sundrops
Papaver rhoeas	corn poppy
Phlox drummondii	annual phlox
Ratibida columnaris	prairie coneflower
*Rudbeckia hirta	black-eyed Susan
Silene armeria	catchfly
*Solidago odora	scented goldenrod
*Tradescantia virginiana X	spiderwort
*Vernonia altissima	ironweed

FALL:

Achillea millefolium	yarrow
Asclepias incarnata	swamp milkweed
Aster azureus	blue aster
Aster cordifolius	aster
Aster novae-angliae	New England aster
Belamcanda chinensis	blackberry lily
Bidens aristosa	tickseed sunflower
Echinacea purpurea	purple coneflower
Helianthus annuus	sunflower
Oenothera biennis	evening primrose
Solidago nemoralis	gray goldenrod
Solidago odora	scented goldenrod
Solidago sempervirens	seaside goldenrod
Vernonia noveboracensis	New York ironweed

SHORT MEADOW PLANTS

When you live in an area that has strict lawn laws based on height, you might consider using dwarf or naturally low-growing plants. In appropriate areas, alpine plants are great to use. Small and low-growing plants are also useful for very small meadow areas. Heights will vary depending on growth conditions, but generally these species and varieties grow no more than 24 inches high. Native plants are marked with an *.

Achillea millefolium rubra	12-24 in. yarrow
Anagallis arvensis	6-12 in. pimpernel
Aurinia saxatilis	
(same as *Alyssum saxatile*)	6-12 in. basket of gold
Baptisia leucophaea	12-18 in. wild indigo
Campanula rotundifolia	10-15 in. bluebell
Cerastium bierbersteinii	8 in. snow in summer
Cheiranthus cheiri	24 in. wallflower
Chrysanthemum leucanthemum	24 in. ox-eye daisy
Claytonia virginica	4-6 in. spring beauty
Coreopsis lanceolata	12-14 in. lance-leaved coreopsis
Dianthus barbatus	24 in. sweet William
Dianthus deltoides	6-8 in. maiden pink
Dodecatheon meadia	10-12 in. shooting star
Erysimum hieraciifolium	18 in. Siberian wallflower
Erythronium americanum	4-10 in. fawn lily
Eschscholzia californica	12 in. California poppy
Gaillardia pulchella	12-24 in. annual Indian blanket
Geranium maculatum	12-24 in. wild geranium
Geum triflorum	12-18 in. prairie smoke
Iberis umbellata	16 in. candytuft

*Iris cristata	4-9 in. dwarf crested iris
Lathyrus latifolius	trailing vine, sweet pea
Lobularia maritima	24 in. sweet alyssum
Myosotis sylvatica	6-15 in. forget me not
Nemophila menziesii	10 in. baby blue eyes
*Oenothera missouriensis	20 in. sundrops
Papaver nudicaule	24 in. Iceland poppy
Phlox drummondii	20 in. annual phlox
*Phlox divaricata	8-12 in. blue phlox
Salvia coccinea	24 in. scarlet sage
Sisyrinchium angustifolium	6-10 in. blue-eyed grass
Stokesia laevis	24 in. Stoke's aster
Thymus serpyllum	3 in. creeping thyme
*Tradescantia virginiana X	24 in. spiderwort
Viola cornuta	5-8 in. Johnny-jump-up

ALL-ANNUAL SPECIES

For those who love color and want to replant yearly, a mixture of annuals will fill a meadow with a riot of color from spring until fall. Although many species will reseed, you should collect or purchase seeds and replant each year to be assured of a good display. This is the least natural kind of meadow, but in some circumstances it is a good way to have a naturalized look. By sowing seeds annually, you can be assured of good color and diversity in the meadow every year without having to wait for the sometimes slower perennial plants to get established. Because the Northeastern section does not have many common species of annual meadow flowers, a good alternative would be to use species native to Texas and the Midwest such as *Coreopsis tinctoria, Gaillardia pulchella, Dracopis amplexicaulis,* or *Phlox drummondii.*

Ammi majus	bishop's flower
Anagallis arvensis	pimpernel
*Bidens aristosa	tickseed sunflower
Centaurea cyanus X	bachelor's button
Consolida orientalis	
(same as Delphinium ajacis)	rocket larkspur
Coreopsis tinctoria	annual coreopsis
Cosmos bipinnatus	cosmos
Dracopis amplexicaulis	
(same as Rudbeckia amplexicaulis)	coneflower
Eschscholzia californica	California poppy
Gaillardia pulchella	annual Indian blanket
*Helianthus annuus	sunflower
Lavatera trimestris	tree mallow
Myosotis sylvatica	forget me not
Nemophila menziesii	baby blue eyes

Papaver rhoeas	corn poppy
Phlox drummondii	annual phlox

PLANTS FOR SHADY AREAS

Although a meadow area is by definition sunny, many of us have shady areas that we would like to naturalize so that they look like a meadow. Many plants will bloom in semi-shade, but blossoms will usually be much smaller and not as abundant as those on plants grown in sunny locations. The woodland plants generally are more exacting in their environmental requirements and are more difficult to propagate, but there are some easy-to-grow and easy-to-propagate plants as well. When using a mixture designed for the shade, watch out for differences in plant heights. Quite a few of the shade plants are very low growing and could be lost among taller varieties. The following species will do well in partial shade and might do well in a transition area between the meadow and a woodland. Cultural requirements will vary greatly, so check on each species's needs before you plant. Native species are marked with an *.

Anagallis arvensis	pimpernel
Aquilegia canadensis	columbine
Aster cordifolius	aster
Aster divaricata	aster
Aurinia saxatilis	basket of gold
Baptisia australis	false indigo
Centaurea cyanus X	bachelor's button
Cerastium bierbersteinii	snow in summer
Claytonia virginica	spring beauty
Consolida orientalis	
(same as *Delphinium ajacis*)	rocket larkspur
Coreopsis lanceolata	lance-leaved coreopsis
Dianthus barbatus	sweet William
Digitalis purpurea	foxglove
Dodecatheon meadia	shooting star
Erigeron speciosus	Oregon fleabane
Erythronium americanum	fawn lily
Eupatorium maculatum X	Joe-pye weed
Geranium maculatum	wild geranium
Iris cristata	dwarf crested iris
Lathyrus latifolius	sweet pea
Lilium canadense	Turk's cap lily
Lobularia maritima	sweet alyssum
Monarda didyma	bee balm
Monarda fistulosa	bergamot
Nemophila menziesii	baby blue eyes
Oenothera lamarckiana	evening primrose
Papaver rhoeas	corn poppy

Penstemon digitalis   beard tongue
Rudbeckia laciniata   coneflower

PLANTS FOR CUTTING

One of the best parts of having a meadow is the abundant supply of fresh cut flowers it supplies during the growing season. Plant some of the following to use as cut flowers.

Achillea millefolium X	yarrow
Ammi majus	bishop's flower
Aquilegia canadensis	columbine
Asclepias tuberosa	butterfly weed
Centaurea cyanus X	bachelor's button
Chrysanthemum leucanthemum X	ox-eye daisy
Coreopsis lanceolata	lance-leaved coreopsis
Coreopsis tinctoria	annual coreopsis
Cosmos bipinnatus	cosmos
Cosmos sulphureus	orange cosmos
Daucus carota X	Queen Anne's lace
Dianthus barbatus	sweet William
Echinacea purpurea	purple coneflower
Erigeron speciosus	Oregon fleabane
Gaillardia aristata	Indian blanket
Gaillardia pulchella	annual Indian blanket
Helianthus annuus	sunflower
Liatris pycnostachya	blazing star
Lupinus perennis	lupine
Phlox species	phlox
Rudbeckia hirta	black-eyed Susan

PLANTS TO ATTRACT BIRDS AND BUTTERFLIES.

Birds and butterflies will find your meadow, just as they do any area with a profusion of flowers. However, if you would like to plant a few extra species that birds (particularly hummingbirds) and butterflies are especially attracted to, choose some of the following

Asclepias species	milkweeds
Asclepias tuberosa	butterfly weed
Aster species	aster
Aurinea saxatilis	basket of gold
Chrysanthemum leucanthemum X	ox-eye daisy
Coreopsis lanceolata	lance-leaved coreopsis
Cosmos bipinnatus	cosmos
Daucus carota X	Queen Anne's lace
Dianthus barbatus	sweet William
Helianthus annuus	sunflower

Lobularia maritima	sweet alyssum
*Monarda didyma	bee balm
Phlox species	phlox

HILLSIDE PLANTS

For those who have a steep hillside that is hard to mow, perhaps the planting of a few hardy wildflowers suited to erosion control will be the answer. Although many plants will do well on a hillside, the following were chosen for their ability to establish themselves quickly and control erosion.

Achillea millefolium	yarrow
*Baptisia australis	false indigo
*Oenothera missouriensis	sundrops

DATA FROM MEADOW PROJECTS

(1) Location: New York

Description: ¼ acres of dry, acidic soils.

Soil preparation: The entire area was rototilled. A 10-6-4 fertilizer was added to amend the soil.

Planting: Large quantities of seeds were collected from the wild.

Maintenance: The area is mowed twice a year and hand weeding is done when possible (at the average rate of two hours per month).

Dominant flowers: violets, butterfly weed, goldenrods and asters, andropogons (beard grasses).

Comments: Concentrate on one or two species of plants that you know will be successful under these conditions.

(2) Location: Massachusetts

Description: ¼ acre of moist, acidic to neutral soil in an area that is flat and rolling.

Soil preparation: The area was fumigated with methyl bromide.

Planting: Thirty species of container-grown plants were plugged into the area. Thirteen pounds of native grass seed was sown.

Maintenance: The garden was watered during the first year to establish the plants during a dry period. Annual mowing and some hand weeding is done to maintain the area.

Dominant flowers: black-eyed Susan, blazing star, asters, goldenrods, gentians.

(3) Location: Pennsylvania

Description: 20,000 square feet of moist, rolling hillside with neutral soils.

Soil preparation: The entire area was rototilled.

Planting: Several different kinds of commercial seed mixtures were used at a rate of ½ pound per 1,000 square feet.

Maintenance: The area was watered when seeded to aid germination and help establish seedlings. It is mowed in early spring to a 4- to 6-inch height to help scatter the seed.

Dominant flowers: black-eyed Susan, poppies, flax, tree mallow.

(4) Location: Maryland

Description: ¼ acre of dry, acidic soils on a rolling hillside.

Soil preparation: Sod on part of the area was removed with a sod-cutting machine. The remaining area was tilled. Fertilizer was added to the soil.

Planting: Twenty-five pounds of three different commercial mixtures were sown with a seed spreader.

Maintenance: The area is watered in spring. Hand weeding is done to eliminate pokeweed and lamb's quarters. Some reseeding is done each year.

Dominant flowers: coreopsis, mustard, black-eyed Susan, chicory, ox-eye daisy, goldenrod, white yarrow, evening primrose, purple coneflower

(5) Location: New York

Description: ten acres of dry, acidic soils.

Soil preparation: Paths were created by rototilling manure into them and then seeding them with a sun-tolerant bluegrass mix.

Planting: Established plants were plugged into existing vegetation.

Maintenance: Paths are mowed regularly. The entire meadow is mowed to a height of 4 inches with tractor-drawn sickle bar in early to mid-June to give optimum growth conditions for the little bluestem grass that dominates the area. No watering or hand weeding is done.

Dominant flowers: butterfly weed, coreopsis, purple coneflower, wild bergamot, blazing star, black-eyed Susan.

(6) Location: Southeastern Pennsylvania

Description: ¼ acre of slightly sloping ground; slightly acidic soil.

Soil preparation: None. Existing vegetation was primarily fine fescue grass, mowed as lawn for the previous twenty years. Meadow mode was established by ceasing mowing in 1979. No soil amendments.

Planting: Seeds of native species were hand broadcast, with no success. Inserting transplants has proven satisfactory; early fall is the best time.

Maintenance: Meadow is mowed annually at 4 to 6 inches, preferably in early winter. Early spring is an alternative time. Paths are fertilized and mowed regularly all summer at 2 inches. Wild garlic, poison ivy seedlings, and honeysuckle are removed by hand. Wild strawberries are hand pulled where they become overpowering. Invading brambles, sassafras, ash, and grey dogwood are removed chemically with brushkiller concentrate brushed on fresh-cut stubs.

Dominant flowers: lythrum, butterfly weed, goldenrod, New England and heath asters, blazing star, purple coneflower, yarrow, evening primrose, cardinal flower, grape hyacinth, cyclamineus narcissi, Canada lilies.

Comments: Defining the meadow's limit with a split-rail fence and adding bayberry and gray birch by a large rock added considerable interest. A neighbor has copied these procedures, thus increasing the apparent extent of each area.

RESOURCES

INSTITUTIONS AND ORGANIZATIONS

The following list includes institutions and organizations within the Northeast that might be able to give you additional horticultural advice on growing native plants. In addition, check with your county extension agencies, state governments, and local Soil Conservation Society chapters.

Delaware

Mt. Cuba Center
P. O. Box 3570
Greenville, Delaware 19807

Winterthur Museum Gardens and Grounds Division
Winterthur, Delaware 19735

Massachusetts

The New England Wildflower Society
Garden in the Woods
Hemenway Road
Framingham, Massachusetts 01701

New York

The Brooklyn Botanic Garden
1000 Washington Ave.
Brooklyn, New York 11225

Cornell Plantations
One Plantations Road
Ithaca, New York 14850

The New York Botanical Garden
Bronx, New York 10458

Pennsylvania

Bowman's Hill State Wildflower Preserve
Historic Park
Washington Crossing, Pennsylvania 18977

Longwood Gardens
Kennett Square, Pennsylvania 19348

The Morris Arboretum
9414 Meadowbrook Road
Philadelphia, Pennsylvania 19118

Pennsylvania Horticultural Society
325 Walnut St.
Philadelphia, Pennsylvania 19106

NURSERIES AND SEED COMPANIES

The nurseries and seed companies listed below sell wildflower plants
and/or seeds. These are not recommendations — merely possible sources.
No attempt has been made to determine the quality of seeds or plants
sold.

A. E. Allgrove Nursery
281 Woburn St.
Wilmington, Massachusetts 01887

Appalachian Wildflower Nursery
Route 1, Box 275 A
Reedsville, Pennsylvania 17084

Beachley Hardy Seed Co.
P. O. Box 336
Camp Hill, Pennsylvania 17011

Blackthorne Gardens
48 Quincy St.
Holbrook, Massachusetts 02343

Bluemont Nurseries, Inc.
2103 Bluemont Rd.
Worthton, Maryland 21111

Carino Nurseries
P. O. Box 538
Indiana, Pennsylvania 15701

Church's Greenhouse and Nursery
522 Seashore Rd.
Cape May, New Jersey 08204

CMS
Box 535-HW
Washington, West Virginia 26181

Comstock, Ferre and Co.
263 Main St.
Wethersfield, Connecticut 06109

Conley Tree Surgeons and
Garden Center, Inc.
145 Townsend Ave.
Boothbay Harbor, Maine 04538

Timothy D. Field
395 Newington Rd.
Newington, New Hampshire 03801

Joseph Harris Co., Inc.
3670 Buffalo Rd.
Rochester, New York 14624

Herbst Brothers Seedsmen, Inc.
1000 N. Main St.
Brewster, New York 10509

Lakeland Nurseries Sales
340 Poplar St.
Hanover, Pennsylvania 17331

Lexington Gardens
93 Hancock St.
Lexington, Massachusetts 02173

Loft's Inc.
Chimney Rock Road
Bound Brook, New Jersey 08805

McGregor Nurseries Sales
340 Poplar St.
Hanover, Pennsylvania 17331

Musser Forests
Box 340
Indiana, Pennsylvania 15701

Native Seeds, Inc.
14590 Triadelphia Mill Rd.
Dayton, Maryland 210368

Painted Meadows Seed Co.
Dept. AH
P. O. Box 1865
Kingston, Pennsylvania 18704

Panfield Nurseries, Inc.
322 Southdown Rd.
Huntington, West Virginia 11743

Princeton Nurseries
P. O. Box 191
Princeton, New Jersey 08540

Putney Nursery, Inc.
Putney, Vermont 05346

Strathmeyer Forests, Inc.
RD 1, Ziegler Rd.
Dover, Pennsylvania 17315

K. Van Bourgondien and Sons, Inc.
245 Farmingdale Rd.
P. O. Box A
Babylon, New York 11702

Vick's Wildgarden's, Inc.
Box 115
Gladwyne, Pennsylvania 19035

Weston Nurseries, Inc.
P. O. Box 186, E. Main St.
Hopkinton, Massachusetts 01748

White Flower Farm
Route 63
Litchfield, Connecticut 06759

SELECTED READING

Bruce, Hal. *How to Grow Wildflowers and Wild Shrubs in Your Garden*. Alfred A. Knopf, Boston; 1976.

DuPont, Elizabeth. *Landscaping with Native Plants in the Middle Atlantic Region*. Brandywine Conservancy; 1978.

Gleason, Henry A. *The New Britton and Brown Illustrated Flora of the Northeastern United States and Adjacent Canada*. New York Botanical Gardens, New York; 1958.

Gill, John D., and W. M. Healy. *Shrubs and Vines for Northeastern Wildlife*. U.S.D.A. Forest Service, Gen. Tech. Report NE-9.

McHarg, Ian L. *Design With Nature*. Natural History Press; 1969.

Miles, Bebe. *Bluebells and Bittersweet: Gardening with Native American Plants*. Van Nostrand Reinhold Co., New York; 1970.

Miles, Bebe. *Wildflower Perennials for Your Garden*, Hawthorne Books, Inc.; 1976.

Newcomb, Lawrence. *Newcomb's Wildflower Guide*. Little, Brown and Co.; 1977.

Niering, William A., and Nancy C. Olmstead. *The Audubon Society Field Guide to North American Wildflowers* (Eastern). Alfred A. Knopf, New York; 1979.

Penn, Cordelia. *Landscaping with Native Plants.* John F. Blair; 1982.

Peterson, R. T., and Margaret McKenny. *Field Guide to Wildflowers of Northeastern and North Central North America.* Houghton Mifflin Co., Boston; 1968.

Rickett, H. W. *Wildflowers of the United States* (Volume I, Northeast States). McGraw Hill, New York; 1966.

Sperka, Marie, *Growing Wildflowers: A Gardener's Guide.* Charles Scribner's Sons, New York; 1984.

Steffek, Edwin, *The New Wildflowers and How to Grow Them.* Timber Press, Portland, Oregon; 1983.

Taylor, Kathryn, and Stephen Hamblin. *Handbook of Wildflower Cultivation.* Macmillan, New York; 1963.

Watts, May T. *Reading the Landscape of America.* Collier Books; 1975.

CHAPTER ELEVEN

The Pacific Northwest

Northern California, western Oregon, western Washington

CONDITIONS TO CONSIDER IN THE PACIFIC NORTHWEST

NATURALLY OCCURRING PLANT COMMUNITIES

To the west of the arid Great Basin lies one of the wettest areas of the country. The Cascade Mountains of western Oregon and Washington and the California North Coast ranges are covered by dense forests called the Pacific Forest. These forests are made up of Douglas fir and species of true fir, hemlocks, western red cedar, and California's redwoods. Rainfall is plentiful, particularly in the Washington Olympic Peninsula, where annual precipitation is sometimes as much as 300 inches. Because of the abundant rainfall, vegetative growth is lush, resulting in unusually tall trees and a rich and diversified undergrowth of rhododendrons and other shrubs, ferns, mosses, and wildflowers. The climate of the coastal areas is very mild with moderate temperatures in both summer and winter. The blooming season along the Pacific Coastal strip is from January to October. During the summer, this entire area is covered by a band of fog that produces up to 15 inches of precipitation from "fog drip." Within the Cascade range, naturally occurring meadows are common in the alpine and subalpine zones. The blooming season peaks in the alpine zone in July and August.

NOXIOUS WEEDS

The good growing conditions that produce lush growth of wildflowers, also produce lush weeds. In planting a meadow in the Pacific Northwest the biggest problem is competition from perennial grasses. Other weeds that might invade the meadow are plantains, dandelions, chickweed, quackgrass, blackberries, annual bluegrass, Canada thistle, and ragweed.

WHEN TO PLANT

The mild temperatures of the Pacific Northwest make it possible to plant either in the fall or the spring. Seeds sown in the fall will be subjected to winter weather conditions that might help to break the dormancy of many types of seeds. If sown in the spring, seeds of many species will need pretreating (stratification or scarification) to break the seed coat.

MAINTENANCE

Hand weeding or selective spraying during the first two years will help keep undesirable species in check. A late fall or early winter mowing will be necessary.

PROBLEM WILDFLOWERS

The following wildflowers — which might be included in some wildflower seed mixtures — might become invasive in the Pacific Northwest. They can be used, but be aware of their potentially aggressive character and use them judiciously.

Centaurea cyanus	bachelor's button
Chrysanthemum carinatum	painted daisy
Chrysanthemum coronarium	garland chrysanthemum
Chrysanthemum leucanthemum	ox-eye daisy
Cichorium intybus	chicory
Daucus carota	Queen Anne's lace
Lathyrus latifolius	sweet pea
Linaria maroccana	spurred snapdragon
Linaria vulgaris	butter and eggs
Lobularia maritima	sweet alyssum
Prunella vulgaris	heal all
Rudbeckia hirta	black-eyed Susan
Verbascum thapsus	mullein

MEADOW PLANTS THAT GROW IN THE NORTHWEST

Creating a combination of wildflowers and native grasses that will thrive in the climate of the Pacific Northwest involves knowing the conditions of your own meadow area. The first step, of course, is to know what will grow in your area, but even this is difficult. Peterson's *Field Guide to Pacific States Wildflowers* says that the Pacific states have the greatest number of flowering plant species in the country because of the number of different ecosystems in the region. However, the wonderful diversity and variety of growing conditions found in this region make it impossible to know exactly what will grow where. Your own backyard might contain just the right conditions to grow a plant that does not normally do well in your area. For this reason, use the following lists as guidelines, but don't hesitate to experiment and try to grow some favorites that might not be on these lists.

We should all strive to use as many of the plants native to our own regions as possible. Not only are native plants better suited to the particular climate and environmental conditions found within that region, but using them will help to preserve the character of the local vegetation. Although many of the introduced species are flashier and showier, these should be used for accent only. Let the backbone of the meadow be the plants indigenous to the area. Check cultural requirements for each species before planting.

Growth requirements will vary enormously from one species to another, but all of the species listed below are reported as growing well in at least some part of this region. In the list below and the other lists that follow, the species native to this region are marked with an *. Species that have a tendency to become invasive are marked with an X.

Achillea filipendulina	gold yarrow
Achillea millefolium	yarrow
Achillea millefolium rubra	red yarrow
Ammi majus	bishop's flower
Anagallis arvensis	pimpernel
Aquilegia caerulea	blue columbine
Aquilegia canadensis	columbine
Arabis alpina	rock cress
Asclepias tuberosa	butterfly weed
Aster lineariifolius	aster
Aster novae-angliae	New England aster
Aurinia saxatilis	basket of gold
Camassia quamash	bluebell
Campanula carpaticaa	harebell
Campanula rotundifolia	camas
Centaurea cyanus X	bachelor's button
Cerastium tomentosum	snow in summer
Cheiranthus cheiri	wallflower
Chrysanthemum carinatum X	painted daisy
Chrysanthemum coronarium X	garland chrysanthemum
Chrysanthemum leucanthemum X	ox-eye daisy
Cichorium intybus X	chicory
Clarkia amoena	farewell to spring
Clarkia concinna	red ribbons
Clarkia pulchella	deerhorn clarkia
Clarkia unguiculata	elegant clarkia
Claytonia lanceolata	spring beauty
Collinsia heterophylla	Chinese houses
Consolida orientalis (same as *Delphinium ajacis*)	rocket larkspur
Coreopsis lanceolata	lance-leaved coreopsis
Coreopsis tinctoria	annual coreopsis

Cosmos bipinnatus	cosmos
Daucus carota X	Queen Anne's lace
*Delphinium cardinale	scarlet larkspur
Dianthus barbatus	sweet William
Dianthus deltoides	maiden pink
Digitalis purpurea	foxglove
Dodecatheon meadia	shooting star
*Dodecatheon pulchellum	western shooting star
Dracopis amplexicaulis	
(same as *Rudbeckia amplexicaulis*)	coneflower
Echinacea purpurea	purple coneflower
*Epilobium angustifolium	fireweed
*Erigeron speciosus	Oregon fleabane
Erysimum hieraciifolium	Siberian wallflower
*Erythronium grandiflorum	fawn lily
*Eschscholzia californica	California poppy
Eupatorium maculatum	Joe-pye weed
*Fritillaria pudica	yellow bell
*Gaillardia aristata	Indian blanket
Gaillardia pulchella	annual Indian blanket
Gazania rigens	treasure flower
*Geum triflorum	prairie smoke
*Gilia capitata	blue thimble flower
*Gilia tricolor	bird's eye gilia
Gypsophila elegans	annual baby's breath
Gypsophila paniculata	baby's breath
*Helenium autumnale	sneezeweed
*Helianthus annuus	sunflower
Iberis umbellata	candytuft
Ipomopsis rubra	standing cypress
Iris cristata	dwarf crested iris
*Iris tenax	tough leaf iris
Lathyrus latifolius X	sweet pea
Liatris spicata	blazing star
*Linanthus grandiflorus	mountain phlox
Linaria maroccana X	spurred snapdragon
Linaria vulgaris X	butter and eggs
Linum grandiflorum rubrum	red flax
*Linum perenne lewisii	blue flax
Lobularia maritima X	sweet alyssum
*Lupinus densiflorus	golden lupine
Lupinus perennis	lupine
Lupinus succulentus	succulent lupine
Lupinus texensis	bluebonnet
Lychnis chalcedonica	Maltese cross

Mentzelia lindleyi	blazing star
Mirabilis jalapa	four o'clock
Monarda didyma	bee balm
Myosotis sylvatica	forget me not
Nemophila maculata	five spot
Nemophila menziesii	baby blue eyes
Oenothera biennis	evening primrose
Oenothera caespitosa	gumbo lily
Oenothera speciosus	evening primrose
Papaver nudicaule	Iceland poppy
Papaver rhoeas	corn poppy
Phacelia tanacetifolia	tansy phacelia
Phlox drummondii	annual phlox
Prunella vulgaris	heal all
Ratibida columnaris	prairie coneflower
Rudbeckia hirta	black-eyed Susan
Salvia coccinea	scarlet sage
Silene armeria	catchfly
Sisyrinchium bellum	blue-eyed grass
Solidago californica	California goldenrod
Solidago sempervirens	seaside goldenrod
Stylomecon heterophylla	wind poppy
Thymus serpyllum	creeping thyme
Tradescantia virginiana	spiderwort
Trifolium incarnatum	crimson clover
Viola cornuta	Johnny-jump-up

THE TOP TEN

The following list is not designed as a balanced mixture of wildflowers and should not be used as such. The flowers included in this list are noted for their adaptability and reliability. They are all generally hardy and easy to grow from seed in the Pacific Northwest.

Collinsia heterophylla	Chinese houses
Coreopsis lanceolata	lance-leaved coreopsis
Coreopsis tinctoria	annual coreopsis
Eschscholzia californica	California poppy
Helenium autumnale	sneezeweed
Linanthus grandiflorus	mountain phlox
Nemophila maculata	five spot
Oenothera caespitosa	gumbo lily
Ratibida columnaris	prairie coneflower
Stylomecon heterophylla	wind poppy

GRASSES

When planting sunny, naturalized areas, it is important to include some non-spreading grasses to fill in niches that the wildflowers cannot fill. Non-spreading fescues, such as sheep and tall fescue, help to bind the soil and provide food for many species of birds, yet they reproduce in moderation, making them desirable meadow grasses. Though they are generally slow growing and take a while to get established, many of the native grasses, such as big bluestem and little bluestem, are non-spreading and attractive.

SEASONAL BLOOM

You can have a good color in your meadow during all parts of the growing season if you pay attention to the time of bloom of the different species. The following lists should help you find some favorites for each season. There will be great variation as to actual time of bloom depending on growing conditions, local weather, and when the seeds were sown or when the plants were set out. These are general guidelines. As always, use as many native species as possible (marked with an *).

SPRING:

Aquilegia caerulea	blue columbine
Aquilegia canadensis	columbine
Arabis alpina	rock cress
Aurinia saxatilis	basket of gold
*Camassia quamash	camas
Centaurea cyanus	bachelor's button
Cerastium tomentosum	snow in summer
Cheiranthus cheiri	wallflower
*Claytonia lanceolata	spring beauty
*Collinsia heterophylla	Chinese houses
*Delphinium cardinale	scarlet larkspur
Dianthus barbatus	sweet William
Erysimum hieraciifolium	Siberian wallflower
*Erythronium grandiflorum	fawn lily
*Eschscholzia californica	California poppy
*Iris missouriensis	blue flag iris
*Iris tenax	tough leaf iris
*Linanthus grandiflorus	mountain phlox
Linaria maroccana X	spurred snapdragon
*Linum perenne lewisii	blue flax
Lobularia maritima X	sweet alyssum
*Lupinus perennis	lupine
Lupinus succulentus	succulent lupine
Lupinus texensis	bluebonnet
Mentzelia lindleyi	blazing star

Papaver rhoeas	corn poppy
*Sisyrinchium bellum	blue eyed grass
Viola cornuta	Johnny-jump-up

SUMMER:

Achillea millefolium X	yarrow
Ammi majus	bishop's flower
Anagallis arvensis	pimpernel
Arabis alpina	rock cress
*Asclepias tuberosa	butterfly weed
Campanula rotundifolia	bluebell
*Castilleja miniata	giant red paintbrush
Centaurea cyanus X	bachelor's button
Cerastium tomentosum	snow in summer
Chrysanthemum carinatum X	painted daisy
Chrysanthemum coronarium X	garland chrysanthemum
Chrysanthemum leucanthemum X	ox-eye daisy
Cichorium intybus X	chicory
*Clarkia amoena	farewell to spring
*Clarkia concinna	red ribbons
Clarkia pulchella	deerhorn clarkia
*Clarkia unguiculata	elegant clarkia
*Collinsia heterophylla	Chinese houses
Consolida orientalis (same as *Delphinium ajacis*)	rocket larkspur
Coreopsis lanceolata	lance-leaved coreopsis
Coreopsis tinctoria	annual coreopsis
Cosmos bipinnatus	cosmos
Daucus carota X	Queen Anne's lace
*Delphinium cardinale	scarlet larkspur
Dianthus barbatus	sweet William
Dodecatheon pulchellum	western shooting star
Echinacea purpureum	purple coneflower
*Epilobium angustifolium	fireweed
*Erigeron speciosus	Oregon fleabane
*Eriogonum umbellatum	sulphur flower
*Eschscholzia californica	California poppy
Gaillardia aristata	Indian blanket
Gaillardia pulchellum	annual Indian blanket
Gazania rigens	treasure flower
Gypsophila elegans	annual baby's breath
Gypsophila paniculata	baby's breath
*Helenium autumnale	sneezeweed
*Helianthus annuus	sunflower
Iberis umbellata	candytuft

Ipomopsis rubra	standing cypress
Lathyrus latifolius X	sweet pea
Liatris spicata	blazing star
*Linanthus grandiflorus	mountain phlox
Linaria maroccana X	spurred snapdragon
Linum grandiflorum rubrum	red flax
Lobularia maritima X	sweet alyssum
Lupinus perennis X	lupine
Lupinus succulentus	succulent lupine
Lychnis chalcedonica	Maltese cross
Mirabilis jalapa	four o'clock
Monarda didyma	bee balm
Myosotis sylvatica	forget me not
Oenothera biennis	evening primrose
*Oenothera caespitosa	gumbo lily
Oenothera speciosa	evening primrose
Papaver rhoeas	corn poppy
Phlox drummondii	annual phlox
Ratibida columnaris	prairie coneflower
Rudbeckia hirta X	black-eyed Susan
Salvia coccinea	scarlet sage
Silene armeria	catchfly
Solidago sempervirens	seaside goldenrod
Thymus serpyllum	creeping thyme
Tradescantia virginiana	spiderwort
Trifolium incarnatum	crimson clover
Viola cornuta	Johnny-jump-up

FALL:

Achillea millefolium X	yarrow
Aster lineariifolius	aster
Aster novae-angliae	New England aster
Echinacea purpurea	purple coneflower
Gypsophila paniculata	baby's breath
*Helianthus annuus	sunflower
Oenothera biennis	evening primrose
*Solidago californica	California goldenrod
Solidago sempervirens	seaside goldenrod

SHORT MEADOW PLANTS

If you live in an area that has strict lawn laws based on height, you might consider using low-growing plants. In appropriate areas, alpine plants are wonderful to use. Small and low-growing plants are also useful for very small meadow areas. Heights will vary depending on growing conditions, but on the whole these species grow 24 inches tall or less.

Achillea millefolium rubra	12-24 in.	red yarrow
Anagallis arvensis	6-2 in.	pimpernel
Arabis alpina	16 in.	rock cress
Aurinia saxatilis	6-12 in.	basket of gold
Campanula carpatica	12-24 in.	harebell
*Campanula rotundifolia	10-15 in.	bluebell
Cerastium tomentosum	8 in.	snow in summer
Chrysanthemum leucanthemum X	12-24 in.	ox-eye daisy
*Clarkia concinna	18 in.	red ribbons
Clarkia pulchella	18 in.	deerhorn clarkia
*Collinsia heterophylla	24 in.	Chinese houses
Coreopsis lanceolata	24 in.	lance-leaved coreopsis
Dianthus barbatus	24 in.	sweet William
Dianthus deltoides	6-18 in.	maiden pinks
Dodecatheon meadia	10-12 in.	shooting star
*Erigeron speciosus	24 in.	Oregon fleabane
*Eschscholzia californica	12 in.	California poppy
*Fritillaria pudica	6-16 in.	yellow bell
Gaillardia aristata	18-24 in.	Indian blanket
Gaillardia pulchella	12-24 in.	annual Indian blanket
Gazania rigens	12 in.	treasure flower
*Geum triflorum	18 in.	prairie smoke
*Gilia capitata	24 in.	blue thimble flower
*Gilia tricolor	10-20 in.	bird's eye gilia
Gypsophila elegans	12-20 in.	annual baby's breath
Iberis umbellata	16 in.	candytuft
Iris cristata	4-9 in.	dwarf crested iris
Iris tenax	16 in.	tough leaf iris
Lathyrus latifolius	trailing vine,	sweet pea
*Linanthus grandiflorus	4-20 in.	mountain phlox
Linum grandiflorum rubrum	14 in.	red flax
*Linum perenne lewisii	24 in.	blue flax
Lobularia maritima	12 in.	sweet alyssum
Lupinus perennis	24 in.	lupine
Lupinus texensis	12 in.	bluebonnet
Lychnis chalcedonica	24 in.	Maltese cross
Myosotis sylvatica	6-15 in.	forget me not
*Nemophila maculata	6 in.	five spot
*Oenothera caespitosa	8 in.	gumbo lily
Papaver nudicaule	24 in.	Iceland poppy
Phlox drummondii	20 in.	annual phlox
Salvia coccinea	24 in.	scarlet sage
Silene armeria	24 in.	catchfly
Sisyrinchium bellum	24 in.	blue-eyed grass

*Stylomecon heterophylla	24 in. wind poppy
Thymus serpyllum	3 in. creeping thyme
Tradescantia virginiana	24 in. spiderwort
Trifolium incarnatum	8-14 in. crimson clover
Viola cornuta	4-6 in. Johnny-jump-up

ALL-ANNUAL MIXTURE

For those who love color and want to replant yearly, a mixture of annuals will fill a meadow with a riot of color from spring until fall. Many species will reseed, but to be assured of a good display, you should collect or purchase seed and replant every year. This is the least natural kind of meadow, but in some circumstances it is a good way to have a naturalized look. By sowing seeds annually, you can be assured of good color and diversity in the meadow every year without having to wait for the slower perennial plants to become established. This type of meadow is particularly useful for short-term landscaping, such as in an empty lot that you have access to for only a year or two.

Ammi majus	bishop's flower
Anagallis arvensis	pimpernel
Centaurea cyanus	bachelor's button
Chrysanthemum carinatum	painted daisy
Chrysanthemum coronarium	garland chrysanthemum
*Clarkia amoena	farewell to spring
*Clarkia concinna	red ribbons
*Clarkia pulchella	deerhorn clarkia
*Clarkia unguiculata	elegant clarkia
*Collinsia heterophylla	Chinese houses
Consolida orientalis (same as Delphinium ajacis)	rocket larkspur
*Coreopsis tinctoria	annual coreopsis
Cosmos bipinnatus	cosmos
Dracopis amplexicaulis (same as Rudbeckia amplexicaulis)	coneflower
*Eschscholzia californica	California poppy
Gaillardia pulchella	annual Indian blanket
*Gilia capitata	blue thimble flower
*Gilia tricolor	bird's eye gilia
Gypsophila elegans	annual baby's breath
*Helianthus annuus	sunflower
Liatris spicata	blazing star
*Linanthus grandiflorus	mountain phlox
Linaria marocanna	spurred snapdragon
Linum grandiflorum rubrum	red flax
Lobularia maritima	sweet alyssum
Lupinus succulentus	succulent lupine

Lupinus texensis	bluebonnet
Mentzelia lindleyi	blazing star
Myosotis sylvatica	forget me not
*Nemophila maculata	five spot
*Nemophila menziesii	baby blue eyes
Papaver rhoeas	corn poppy
Phacelia tanacetifolia	tansy phacelia
Phlox drummondii	annual phlox
Silene armeria	catchfly
*Stylomecon heterophylla	wind poppy
Trifolium incarnatum	crimson clover

PLANTS TO ATTRACT BIRDS AND BUTTERFLIES

Birds and butterflies will find your meadow, just as they do any area with a profusion of flowers. However, if you would like to plant a few extra species that are especially attractive to birds (particularly hummingbirds) and butterflies, choose some of the following.

Asclepias tuberosa	butterfly weed
Aster species	asters
Aurinia saxatilis	basket of gold
Chrysanthemum species	daisies
*Coreopsis species	coreopsis
Cosmos bipinnatus	cosmos
Daucus carota X	Queen Anne's lace
Dianthus barbatus	sweet William
Gaillardia species	Indian blankets
*Gilia capitata	blue thimble flower
*Helianthus annuus	sunflower
Ipomopsis rubra	standing cypress
Lobularia maritima	sweet alyssum
Monarda didyma	bee balm
Phlox species	phlox
Salvia coccinea	scarlet sage

PLANTS FOR CUTTING

To some people the best aspect of having a meadow area is the number of cut flowers that it makes readily available. Even a small area can yield an abundant supply of cut flowers throughout the growing season. The following flowers are well suited for bringing indoors as cut flowers. For further tips on treating these cut flowers see Chapter 6.

Achillea millefolium	yarrow
Ammi majus	bishop's flower
Aquilegia caerulea	blue columbine
Aquilegia canadensis	columbine
Asclepias tuberosa	butterfly weed

Aster novae-angliae	New England aster
Centaurea cyanus X	bachelor's button
Chrysanthemum carinatum X	painted daisy
Chrysanthemum leucanthemum X	ox-eye daisy
*Clarkia amoena	farewell to spring
*Clarkia unguiculata	elegant clarkia
*Collinsia heterophylla	Chinese houses
Coreopsis lanceolata	lance-leaved coreopsis
*Coreopsis tinctoria	annual coreopsis
Cosmos bipinnatus	cosmos
Daucus carota	Queen Anne's lace
Echinacea purpurea	purple coneflower
*Erigeron speciosus	Oregon fleabane
Gaillardia aristata	Indian blanket
Gaillardia pulchella	annual Indian blanket
*Gilia capitata	blue thimble flower
*Gilia tricolor	bird's eye gilia
Gypsophila elegans	annual baby's breath
Gypsophila paniculata	baby's breath
*Helianthus annuus	sunflower
Liatris spicata	blazing star
Lupinus species	lupines
*Phacelia tanacetifolia	tansy phacelia
Rudbeckia hirta X	black-eyed Susan

PLANTS FOR SHADY AREAS

Although a meadow area is by definition sunny, many of us have shady areas that we would like to naturalize so that they look like a meadow. Many plants will bloom in partial shade, but on the whole, blossoms will be smaller and not as abundant as in sunny locations. Many of these plants make excellent specimens to use in a woody area bordering the meadow. Most of these plants adapt well to partial shade; few of them do well in full shade. Cultural requirements will vary greatly, so check on each species's needs before you plant.

Anagallis arvensis	pimpernel
Aquilegia caerulea	blue columbine
Aquilegia canadensis	columbine
Aurinia saxatilis	basket of gold
Centaurea cyanus	bachelor's button
*Clarkia concinna	red ribbons
*Collinsia heterophylla	Chinese houses
Consolida orientalis	
(same as *Delphinium ajacis*)	rocket larkspur
Coreopsis lanceolata	lance-leaved coreopsis
*Coreopsis tinctoria	annual coreopsis

Dodecatheon meadia	shooting star
*Erigeron speciosus	Oregon fleabane
Erysimum hieraciifolium	Siberian wallflower
Gaillardia aristata	Indian blanket
*Gilia capitata	blue thimble flower
Ipomopsis rubra	standing cypress
Lathyrus latifolius	sweet pea
*Linanthus grandiflorus	mountain phlox
Linaria maroccana	spurred snapdragon
Linaria vulgaris	butter and eggs
Linum grandiflorum rubrum	red flax
Monarda didyma	bee balm
*Nemophila maculata	five spot
Papaver rhoeas	corn poppy
Rudbeckia hirta X	black-eyed Susan
Silene armeria	catchfly
*Sisyrinchium bellum	blue-eyed grass
*Stylomecon heterophylla	wind poppy
Tradescantia virginiana	spiderwort
Trifolium incarnatum	crimson clover
Viola cornuta	Johnny-jump-up

MOISTURE-LOVING PLANTS

The generous rainfall and high humidity of the Pacific Northwest often create moist meadows where some very beautiful moisture-loving species will grow. These plants like a moist environment, but most of them also require well-drained soil.

*Camassia quamash	camas
*Claytonia lanceolata	spring beauty
Digitalis purpurea	foxglove
Echinacea purpurea	purple coneflower
*Epilobium angustifolium	fireweed
Eupatorium maculatum	Joe-pye weed
*Helenium autumnale	sneezeweed
Monarda didyma	bee balm
Myosotis sylvatica	forget me not
Viola cornuta	Johnny-jump-up

DATA FROM MEADOW PROJECTS

(1) Location: Western Washington

Description: roadside planting ½ block long, ¼ block wide on wet, acidic, flat soils.

Soil preparation: Disturbed soil on construction sites was raked smooth. In grassy areas, holes were dug for transplants.

Planting: Seeds from a regional seed company were purchased and added to those collected by local garden club members to total approximately one pound. Some were sown directly into the top soil, and others were started in styroblocks until the seedlings were large enough to transplant. Individual species were kept separate and were planted in groups of fifteen to twenty-five plants in a large oval to allow better control.

Maintenance: No maintenance was done on this planting.

Dominant flowers: lupines, ox-eye daisy, foxglove, pearly everlasting, asters.

Comments: Lupines were most successful. Care was taken not to plant any lupines that appear on noxious weed lists. Every effort was made to use species indigenous to the area.

RESOURCES

INSTITUTIONS AND ORGANIZATIONS

California

California Native Plant Society
2380 Ellsworth St. Suite D
Berkeley, California 94704

Pacific Horticultural Foundation
P. O. Box 100
Mill Valley, California 94942

San Mateo Arboretum Society
P. O. Box 1523
San Mateo, California 94401

Oregon

Berry Botanic Garden
11505 Southwest Summerville Ave.
Portland, Oregon 97219

Hoyte Arboretum
4000 Southwest Fairview Blvd.
Portland, Oregon 97221

Mount Pisgah Arboretum
P. O. Box 5621
Eugene, Oregon 97405

Native Plant Society of Oregon
Department of Biology
University of Oregon
Eugene, Oregon 97403

Peavy Arboretum
School of Forestry
Oregon State College
Corvallis, Oregon 97331

Washington

Bloedel Reserve
7571 Northeast Dolphin Dr.
Brianbridge Island, Washington 98110

Finch Arboretum
West 3404 Woodland Blvd.
Spokane, Washington 98195

Washington Native Plant Society
Department of Botany
University of Washington
Seattle, Washington 98195

Wild River Arboretum
U.S. Forest Service
Carson, Washington 98610

NURSERIES AND SEED COMPANIES

Nurseries and seed companies in the Pacific Northwest that sell wildflowers are listed below. These are not recommendations; they are merely possible sources.

Browning's Nursery
P. O. Box 243
Sixes, Oregon 97476

Callahan Seeds
6045 Foley Lane
Central Point, Oregon 97502

Clyde Robin Seed Co.
P. O. Box 2366
Castro Valley, California 94546

Forest Farm
990 Tethernow Rd.
Williams, Oregon 97544

Great Western Seed Co.
4030 Eagle Crest Rd.
Salem, Oregon 97304

Edgar L. Kline
17495 Southwest Briant Rd.
Lake Grove, Oregon 97034

McLaughlin's Seeds
Buttercup's Acre
Mead, Washington 99021

MSK Nursery
20066 15th Ave. Northwest
Seattle, Washington 98177

Northwest Biological Enterprises
23351 Southwest Boxky Dell Lane
West Linn, Oregon 97068

Northwest Ground Covers and Nursery
14461 Northeast 190
P. O. Box 248
Woodinville, Washington 98072

Plants of the Wild
P. O. Box 866
Tekoa, Washington 99033

Russel Graham
4030 Eagle Crest Rd. Northwest
Salem, Oregon 97304

Siskiyou Rare Plant Nursery
2825 Cummings Rd.
Medford, Oregon 97501

SELECTED READING

Hitchcock, C. L., and Arthur Cronquist. *Flora of the Pacific Northwest*. University of Washington Press, Seattle, Washington; 1973.

Kruckeberg, Arthur R. *Gardening with Native Plants of the Pacific Northwest, an Illustrated Guide*. University of Washington Press, Seattle, Washington, and London, England; 1982.

Niehaus, Theodore F., and Charles L. Ripper. *A Field Guide to Pacific States Wildflowers*. Houghton Mifflin Co., Boston; 1976.

Rickett, Harold W. *Wildflowers of the United States* (Volume V, Northwest States). McGraw Hill, New York; 1966.

Santa Barbara Botanic Garden. *Seed Propagation of Native California Plants*.

Spellenberg, Richard. *The Audubon Society Field Guide to North American Wildflowers* (Western). Alfred A. Knopf, Inc., New York; 1979.

Sunset Magazine and Book Editors. *New Western Garden Book*. Sunset-Lane; 1979.

CHAPTER TWELVE

The Southeast

Alabama, Arkansas, Florida, Georgia, Louisiana, Mississippi, North Carolina, eastern Oklahoma, Tennessee, eastern Texas, South Carolina, Virginia, Washington, D.C.

CONDITIONS TO CONSIDER IN THE SOUTHEAST

NATURALLY OCCURRING PLANT COMMUNITIES

The Southeastern region of the United States has excellent growing conditions for a variety of plants, and several different native plant communities occur within the Southeast. Ranging from a dry pine forest to a moist, rich, deciduous forest, these plant communities contain quite a diversity of flora. A grassland community within this area is in a constant state of change, and unless it is maintained by mechanical or chemical means, it will soon change from grassland to a shrub community and eventually to a forest community.

The entire region is characterized by mild winters, abundant rainfall, and hot, humid summers. Precipitation is evenly distributed throughout the year and ranges from 50 to 60 inches per year. The soils are rich within the mountain and deciduous forest areas but tend to be nutrient poor and acidic in the plains. Part of the reason for this is cultural: much of the area that was once rich agricultural land has been severely damaged by overuse. Part of the reason is that the abundant rainfall leaches many of the nutrients out of the soil, particularly in the sandy coastal plain.

Growing conditions are generally quite good so long as gardeners choose plants that can take the hot, muggy summers and that do not need long periods of cold. The same conditions that cause the meadow plants to become established and grow with ease are also a boon to the many weeds that will find their way into the meadow garden. It is important, for this reason, to be aware of the invasive weeds that grow in this region and to be careful not to plant species that might take over the meadow.

PROBLEM SOILS

Although many areas in the Southeast have sandy, well-drained soils, much of the soil in this region is mostly clay and drains poorly. Most meadow plants aren't picky about the amount of nutrients in the soil, but they do require good drainage. For this reason, the Southern gardener must either choose species whose roots do not mind poorly drained soil or add sand and/or humus to the soil before planting. The high acidity characteristic of southern soils might also be a problem. If a species is sensitive to the amount of acidity in the soil, you may need to add lime.

WHEN TO PLANT

Mild Southern temperatures make either a fall or spring planting a possibility. If you're planting individual species, check Part Three for the best time to plant each species, and be sure to pretreat the seeds if necessary. If you're plugging in plants, be certain that they get plenty of water to establish themselves well, no matter whether you plant in fall or spring. The time of planting seeds or plants may depend on how and when you prepared the area for planting (see Chapter 2). If you use a wildflower seed mixture, the following guidelines will be helpful.

Spring: Although precipitation seems to be spread out evenly throughout the year, there is generally more rainfall in spring than in fall. For this reason, a spring planting lessens the need for extra watering. However, many wildflower seeds need a period of cold before they will germinate, and you might have to pretreat the seeds before planting. A spring planting should take place after the last frost and before the weather gets too hot for the delicate seedlings. Generally, between the end of March and the end of April is a good time.

Fall: Unless you live in a very mild area within the South, a fall planting will eliminate the need to pretreat many of the seeds. A fall planting allows the seeds to be exposed to the cold temperatures that are necessary for germination. Plant after the weather cools and while the soil is still easy to work with — generally sometime during October or early November.

MAINTENANCE

Until the seedlings are established, you must water unless Mother Nature provides sufficient rain. Once the plants are established, water only if the plants show stress. During the first few years do some selective spraying and weeding to rid the area of aggressive weeds and pests. An annual cutting of the entire meadow is necessary: it opens up the area and keeps woody species from invading and taking over. The area may be cut in the fall after the seeds have ripened (October or November) or, if you want to leave the plants for bird food and winter interest, the meadow may be cut in late winter. If you have groupings of individual species within the meadow, these can be cut as they set seed.

NOXIOUS WEEDS

The king of Southern weeds has to be kudzu. It can grow 80 to 100 feet in a single growing season, so a stand of uncontrolled kudzu could reduce your meadow to a field or large-lobed leaves in very short order. Fortunately, kudzu can be controlled with a combination of pulling up roots and spraying. The best control, of course, is prevention. It's possible to create a meadow out of an area covered with kudzu, but allow a full growing season to rid the area of the pest before you spend the first dime on plants or seeds, and be sure to immediately attack and eliminate the first sign of kudzu that appears from then on.

Other weeds that will give you particular problems in this area are fescue and other "lawn" grasses that will want to choke out the wildflower seedlings. Johnson grass, knotweed, ground cherry, and honeysuckle might be problems, and pokeweed, blackberries, and elderberries might also invade your meadow, thanks mainly to bird droppings.

PROBLEM WILDFLOWERS

The following wildflowers might be included in some wildflower seed mixtures and *might* become invasive in the Southeastern region. They can be used, but be aware of their potentially aggressive character and use them judiciously.

Achillea millefolium	yarrow
Bidens aristosa	tickseed sunflower
Bidens polylepis	tickseed sunflower
Centaurea cyanus	bachelor's button
Cichorium intybus	chicory
Daucus carota	Queen Anne's lace
Linaria vulgaris	butter and eggs
Mirabilis jalapa	four o'clock
Prunella vulgaris	heal all
Salvia lyrata	lyre-leafed sage
Saponaria officinalis	soapwort
Verbascum thapsus	mullein

MEADOW PLANTS THAT GROW IN THE SOUTHEAST

Creating a combination of wildflowers and native grasses that will thrive and be compatible involves knowing the conditions of your own meadow area. The first step, of course, is to choose plants that do grow in your region. Even this is not easy, however, for the wonderful diversity and variety of growing conditions presented in our country make it impossible to know exactly what will grow where. Your own backyard might contain just the right conditions to grow a plant that does not normally do well in your area. For this reason, use the following lists as guidelines, but don't hesitate to experiment and try to grow some favorties that might not be on these lists.

The following lists were based on recommendations from botanists and horticulturists from universities, botanical gardens, arboretums, and native plant societies, as well as the sage advice of many "dirt gardeners" who live in the Southeast.

Although cultural requirements for the following species will vary tremendously, it is possible to grow each of these species somewhere within this region. Many of these are not native or naturalized within this area but will grow under cultivation with some degree of success. Species that are endangered or threatened or are difficult to obtain are not included. In this list and those that follow, species native to this area are marked with an *; species that have a tendency to become invasive are marked with an X; and unmarked species are non-native but generally non-invasive.

Achillea filipendulina	gold yarrow
Achillea millefolium X	yarrow
Achillea millefolium rubra	red yarrow
Ammi majus	bishop's flower
Anagallis arvensis	pimpernel
Aquilegia canadensis	columbine
Asclepias incarnata	swamp milkweed
Asclepias syriaca	common milkweed
Asclepias tuberosa	butterfly weed
Aster laevis	smooth aster
Aster lateriflorus	calico aster
Aster lineariifolius	aster
Aster novae-angliae	New England aster
Aurinia saxatilis	basket of gold
Baptisia australis	false indigo
Baptisia leucantha	wild white indigo
Baptisia leucophaea	false indigo
Baptisia pendula	wild indigo
Baptisia tinctoria	wild white indigo
Belamcanda chinensis	blackberry lily
Bidens aristosa X	tickseed sunflower
Campanula rapunculoides	bluebell
Campanula rotundifolia	bellflower
Castilleja coccinea	Indian paintbrush
Centaurea cyanus X	bachelor's button
Cerastium bierbersteinii	snow in summer
Cheiranthus cheiri	wallflower

Chrysanthemum carinatum	painted daisy
Chrysanthemum leucanthemum X	ox-eye daisy
Cichorium intybus X	chicory
Claytonia virginica	spring beauty
Consolida orientalis (same as *Delphinium ajacis*)	rocket larkspur
Coreopsis lanceolata	lance-leaved coreopsis
Coreopsis tintoria	annual coreopsis
Cosmos bipinnatus	cosmos
Cosmos sulphureus	orange cosmos
Daucus carota X	Queen Anne's lace
Delphinium tricorne	spring larkspur
Dianthus barbatus	sweet William
Dianthus deltoides	maiden pink
Digitalis purpurea	foxglove
Dimorphotheca aurantiaca	African daisy
Dodecatheon meadia	shooting star
Dracopis amplexicaulis (same as *Rudbeckia amplexicaulis*)	coneflower
Echinacea purpurea	purple coneflower
Epilobium angustifolium	fireweed
Erigeron speciosus	Oregon fleabane
Erysimum hieraciifolium	Siberian wallflower
Erythronium americanum	fawn lily
Eschscholzia californica	California poppy
Eupatorium maculatum	Joe-pye weed
Eupatorium perfoliatum	boneset
Gaillardia aristata	Indian blanket
Gaillardia pulchella	annual Indian blanket
Gazania rigens	treasure flower
Geranium maculatum	wild geranium
Geum triflorum	prairie smoke
Gypsophila paniculata	baby's breath
Helenium autumnale	sneezeweed
Helianthus angustifolius	swamp sunflower
Helianthus annuus	sunflower
Hesperis matronalis	dame's rocket
Iberis umbellata	candytuft
Ipomopsis rubra	standing cypress
Iris cristata	dwarf crested iris
Lathyrus latifolius	sweet pea
Lavatera trimestris	tree mallow
Liatris aspera	rough blazing star
Liatris pycnostachya	blazing star
Liatris scariosa	blazing star

Liatris spicata	blazing star
Lilium canadense	Turk's cap lily
Linaria maroccana	spurred snapdragon
Linum grandiflorum rubrum	red flax
Linum perenne lewisii	blue flax
Lobularia maritima	sweet alyssum
Lupinus perennis	lupine
Lychnis chalcedonica	Maltese cross
Mirabilis jalapa X	four o'clock
Monarda didyma	bee balm
Monarda fistulosa	bergamot
Myosotis sylvatica	forget me not
Nemophila menziesii	baby blue eyes
Oenothera biennis	evening primrose
Oenothera missouriensis	sundrops
Oenothera speciosa	evening primrose
Papaver nudicaule	Iceland poppy
Papaver rhoeas	corn poppy
Penstemon digitalis	beard tongue
Penstemon grandiflorus	beard tongue
Penstemon smallii	beard tongue
Petalostemon purpureum	prairie clover
Phlox divaricata	blue phlox
Phlox drummondii	annual phlox
Phlox pilosa	western phlox
Ratibida columnaris	prairie coneflower
Rudbeckia fulgida	coneflower
Rudbeckia hirta	black-eyed Susan
Salvia coccinea	scarlet sage
Silene armeria	catchfly
Sisyrinchium angustifolium	blue-eyed grass
Solidago juncea	goldenrod
Solidago nemoralis	gray goldenrod
Solidago odora	scented goldenrod
Solidago sempervirens	seaside goldenrod
Stokesia laevis	Stoke's aster
Thymus serpyllum	creeping thyme
Tradescantia virginiana	spiderwort
Trifolium incarnatum	crimson clover
Verbena stricta	hoary vervain
Vernonia altissima	ironweed
Vernonia noveboracensis	New York ironweed
Viola cornuta	Johnny-jump-up

THE TOP TEN

The following list is not designed as a balanced mixture of wildflowers and should not be used as such. The flowers included within this list are noted for their adaptability and reliability. They are generally hardy and easy to grow from seed in this region.

*Asclepias tuberosa	butterfly weed
Centaurea cyanus	bachelor's button
Chrysanthemum leucanthemum	ox-eye daisy
*Coreopsis lanceolata	lance-leaved coreopsis
Coreopsis tinctoria	annual coreopsis
*Dracopis amplexicaulis	coneflower
*Echinacea purpurea	purple coneflower
*Gaillardia pulchella	annual Indian blanket
*Ipomopsis rubra	Texas plume
*Rudbeckia hirta	black-eyed Susan

GRASSES

When you plant sunny, naturalized areas, you should include some non-spreading grasses to fill in niches that the wildflowers cannot fill. Grasses serve as a foil for the colorful wildflowers and help to create the feeling of openness that is basic to the charm of a meadow. Several clumping-type grasses, including some of the fescues, will grow in the Southeast. They help to bind the soil and give interesting texture to the meadow, yet they spread in moderation, which makes them desirable as meadow grasses. Watch out for grasses that outcompete the wildflowers for space in the meadow. DO not use any lawn or turf grasses. Some of the best native grasses to use in this area are:

Andropogon virginicus	broomsedge
Festuca ovina glauca	sheep fescue
Miscanthus floridulus	Asian grass
Miscanthus sinensis gracillimus	zebra grass
Panicum virgatum	switchgrass
Schizachyrium scoparium (same as Andropogon scoparius)	little bluestem

ALL-ANNUAL MIXTURE

For those who love color and want to replant yearly, a mixture of annuals will present a riot of color from spring until fall. The advantage to an all-annual mixture is that once the meadow has been prepared correctly the first time, you can surface till the ground and broadcast seed annually without having to worry about damaging perennial plants. By broadcasting seeds annually you can be assured of good diversity every year. An all-annual mixture should be planted in spring. Although you should try to use as many native species as possible, few showy meadow annuals are native to the Southeast. A good alternative is to use some of the Texas native annuals such as *Coreopsis tinctoria* or *Phlox drummondii*.

Ammi majus	bishop's flower
Anagallis arvensis	pimpernel
Bidens aristosa X	tickseed sunflower
Centaurea cyanus X	bachelor's button
Chrysanthemum carinatum	painted daisy
Coreopsis tinctoria	annual coreopsis
Cosmos bipinnatus	cosmos
Cosmos sulphureus	orange cosmos
Dimorphotheca sinuata	African daisy
Dracopis amplexicaulis (same as *Rudbeckia amplexicaulis*)	coneflower
Eschscholzia californica	California poppy
Gaillardia pulchella	annual gaillardia
Helianthus annuus	sunflower
Linaria maroccana	spurred snapdragon
Linum grandiflorum rubrum	red flax
Lobularia maritima	sweet alyssum
Myosotis sylvatica	forget me not
Nemophila maculata	five spot
Nemophila menziesii	baby blue eyes
Papaver rhoeas	corn poppy
Phlox drummondii	annual phlox
Silene armeria	catchfly
Trifolium incarnatum	crimson clover

SEASONAL BLOOM

You can have good color in your meadow during all parts of the growing season if you pay some attention to the blooming times of the different species. The following lists should help you find some favorites for each season. There will be great variation as to actual time of bloom depending on growing conditions, local weather, and when the seeds were sown or when the plants were set out. These are general guidelines. As always, use as many native species (marked with an *) as possible.

SPRING:

Aquilegia canadensis	columbine
Arabis alpina	rock cress
Aurinia saxatilis	basket of gold
Baptisia australis	false indigo
Centaurea cyanus	bachelor's button
Cerastium bierbersteinii	snow in summer
Cheiranthus cheiri	wallflower

*Claytonia virginica	spring beauty
Consolida orientalis	
(same as Delphinium ajacis)	rocket larkspur
*Delphinium tricorne	spring larkspur
Dianthus barbatus	sweet William
Erysimum hieraciifolium	Siberian wallflower
*Erythronium americanum	fawn lily
Eschscholzia californica	California poppy
*Geranium maculatum	wild geranium
*Iris cristata	dwarf crested iris
Linaria maroccana	spurred snapdragon
Linum grandiflorum rubrum	red flax
*Linum perenne lewisii	blue flax
Lobularia maritima	sweet alyssum
Nemophila menziesii	baby blue eyes
Papaver rhoeas	corn poppy
*Penstemon digitalis	beard tongue
*Penstemon smallii	beard tongue
*Phlox divaricata	blue phlox
*Sisyrinchium angustifolium	blue-eyed grass
*Stokesia laevis	Stoke's aster
Viola cornuta	Johnny-jump-up

SUMMER:

Achillea millefolium X	yarrow
Ammi majus	bishop's flower
Anagallis arvensis	pimpernel
*Asclepias incarnata	swamp milkweed
*Asclepias tuberosa	butterfly weed
*Baptisia australis	false indigo
Belamcanda chinensis	blackberry lily
*Bidens aristosa X	tickseed sunflower
*Campanula rotundifolia	bluebell
*Castilleja coccinea	Indian paintbrush
Centaurea cyanus X	bachelor's button
Chrysanthemum carinatum	painted daisy
Chrysanthemum leucanthemum	ox-eye daisy
Cichorium intybus X	chicory
Consolida orientalis	
(same as Delphinium ajacis)	rocket larkspur
*Coreopsis lanceolata	lance-leaved coreopsis
Coreopsis tinctoria	annual coreopsis
Cosmos bipinnatus	cosmos
Daucus carota X	Queen Anne's lace
*Dodecatheon meadia	shooting star

*Echinacea purpurea	purple coneflower
*Epilobium angustifolium	fireweed
Erigeron speciosus	Oregon fleabane
Eschscholzia californica	California poppy
*Eupatorium maculatum	Joe-pye weed
Gaillardia aristata	Indian blanket
*Gaillardia pulchella	annual Indian blanket
Gazania rigens	treasure flower
Gypsophila paniculata	baby's breath
*Helenium autumnale	sneezeweed
*Helianthus annuus	sunflower
*Ipomopsis rubra	standing cypress
Lathyrus latifolius	sweet pea
Lavatera trimestris	tree mallow
*Liatris pycnostachya	blazing star
*Lilium canadense	Turk's cap lily
Linaria maroccana	spurred snapdragon
Linum grandiflorum rubrum	red flax
*Lupinus perennis	lupine
*Monarda didyma	bee balm
*Monarda fistulosa	bergamot
Myosotis sylvatica	forget me not
*Oenothera biennis	evening primrose
Oenothera missouriensis	sundrops
*Oenothera speciosa	evening primrose
*Phlox drummondii	annual phlox
Ratibida columnaris	prairie coneflower
*Rudbeckia hirta	black-eyed Susan
*Rudbeckia laciniata	coneflower
*Salvia coccinea	scarlet sage
Silene armeria	catchfly
*Solidago odora	scented goldenrod
Thymus serpyllum	creeping thyme
*Tradescantia virginiana	spiderwort
Trifolium incarnatum	crimson clover
Venidium fastuosum	African daisy
*Vernonia altissima	ironweed

FALL:

Achillea millefolium X	yarrow
*Asclepias incarnata	swamp milkweed
*Aster laevis	smooth aster
*Aster lateriflorus	calico aster
*Aster lineariifolius	aster
*Aster novae-angliae	New England aster

Belamcanda chinensis	blackberry lily
*Bidens aristosa	tickseed sunflower
*Echinacea purpurea	purple coneflower
Gypsophila paniculata	baby's breath
*Helianthus annuus	sunflower
*Oenothera biennis	evening primrose
*Solidago nemoralis	gray goldenrod
*Solidago odora	scented goldenrod
*Solidago sempervirens	seaside goldenrod
*Vernonia altissima	ironweed
*Vernonia noveboracensis	New York ironweed

SHORT MEADOW PLANTS

For small areas and places where "lawn laws" restrict the height of plants growing in a meadow or lawn, one answer is to choose plants that do not exceed a certain height. Although the heights of plants vary enormously from one area to another due to differences in growing conditions, the following plants generally grow no more than 24 inches tall.

Achillea millefolium rubra	12-24 in. red yarrow
Anagallis arvensis	6-12 in. pimpernel
Aurinia saxatilis	6-12 in. basket of gold
*Baptisia leucophaea	12-18 in. false indigo
*Campanula rotundifolia	10-15 in. bluebell
*Castilleja coccinea	12-24 in. Indian paintbrush
Chrysanthemum leucanthemum	24 in. ox-eye daisy
*Claytonia virginica	4-6 in. spring beauty
*Coreopsis lanceolata	12-24 in. lance-leaved coreopsis
Dianthus barbatus	24 in. sweet William
Dianthus deltoides	6-18 in. maiden pink
Dimorphotheca sinuata	6-12 in. African daisy
*Dodecatheon meadia	10-12 in. shooting star
Erigeron speciosus	24 in. Oregon fleabane
Erysimum hieraciifolium	18 in. Siberian wallflower
*Erythronium americanum	4-10 in. fawn lily
Eschscholzia californica	12 in. California poppy
Gaillardia pulchella	12-24 in. annual Indian blanket
Gazania rigens	12 in. treasure flower
*Geranium maculatum	12-24 in. wild geranium
Geum triflorum	12-18 in. prairie smoke
Iberis umbellata	16 in. candytuft
*Iris cristata	4-10 in. dwarf crested iris
Lathyrus latifolius	vine, sweet pea
Linum grandiflorum rubrum	14 in. red flax

Linum perenne lewisii	24 in.	blue flax
Lobularia maritima	12 in.	sweet aslyssum
*Lupinus perennis	12-24 in.	lupine
Lychnis chalcedonica	24 in.	Maltese cross
Myostis sylvatica	6-15 in.	forget me not
Nemophila menziesii	10 in.	baby blue eyes
*Oenothera missouriensis	20 in.	sundrops
Papaver nudicaule	24 in.	Iceland poppy
*Phlox divaricata	8-12 in.	blue phlox
Phlox drummondii	20 in.	annual phlox
Salvia coccinea	24 in.	scarlet sage
*Sisyrinchium angustifolium	6-10 in.	blue-eyed grass
*Solidago nemoralis	24 in.	gray goldenrod
*Stokesia laevis	24 in.	Stoke's aster
Thymus serpyllum	3 in.	creeping thyme
*Tradescantia virginiana	24 in.	spiderwort
Trifolium incarnatum	8-14 in.	crimson clover
Viola cornuta	5-8 in.	Johnny-jump-up

PLANTS FOR SHADY AREAS

Although most meadow areas are sunny, many of us have shady areas that we would like to naturalize so that they look like a meadow. Many sun-loving plants will bloom in the shade, but on the whole, blossoms will be much smaller and not as abundant as in sunny locations. The woodland plants generally have more exacting environmental requirements and are more difficult to propagate, but there are some easy-to-grow and easy-to-propagate woodland plants as well. When using a mixture designed for the shade, watch out for differences in plant heights. Quite a few of the shade plants are very low growing and could be easily lost among taller varieties. The following species will do well in partial shade and might be useful for a low-maintenance open area under trees or in a woody border next to a meadow.

Anagallis arvensis	pimpernel
*Aquilegia canadensis	columbine
*Aster cordifolius	aster
*Aster divaricata	aster
*Aurinia saxatilis	basket of gold
*Baptisia australis	false indigo
Centaurea cyanus	bachelor's button
Cerastium bierbersteinii	snow in summer
*Claytonia virginica	spring beauty
Consolida orientalis	
(same as *Delphinium ajacis*)	rocket larkspur
*Coreopsis lanceolata	lance-leaved coreopsis
Dianthus barbatus	sweet William
Digitalis purpurea	foxglove

*Dodecatheon meadia	shooting star
Erigeron speciosus	Oregon fleabane
Erysimum hieraciifolium	Siberian wallflower
*Erythronium americanum	fawn lily
*Eupatorium maculatum	Joe-pye weed
*Geranium maculatum	wild geranium
*Impomopsis rubra	standing cypress
*Iris cristata	dwarf crested iris
Lathyrus latifolius	sweet pea
*Lilium canadense	Turk's cap lily
Linum grandiflorum rubrum	red flax
Lobularia maritima	sweet alyssum
*Monarda didyma	bee balm
*Monarda fistulosa	bergamot
Nemophila menziesii	baby blue eyes
Oenothera lamarckiana	evening primrose
Papaver rhoeas	corn poppy
*Penstemon digitalis	beard tongue
*Phlox divaricata	blue phlox
*Rudbeckia laciniata	coneflower
Silene armeria	catchfly
*Stokesia laevis	Stoke's aster
Thymus serpyllum	creeping thyme
Viola cornuta	Johnny-jump-up

PLANTS FOR POORLY DRAINED AREAS

Many locations in the Southeast have soils with a high clay content and are poorly drained. Although this is usually a very poor growing medium, some plants are not particular about their soil and will do just fine in soil that stays dried out during dry times and stays soggy during wet times. The following plants are suited for such areas.

Ammi majus	bishop's flower
Anagallis arvensis	pimpernel
*Asclepias incarnata	swamp milkweed
Daucus carota X	Queen Anne's lace
*Helianthus annuus	sunflower
Lathyrus latifolius	sweet pea
*Penstemon digitalis	beard tongue
*Rudbeckia hirta	black-eyed Susan
Silene armeria	catchfly
*Solidago sempervirens	seaside goldenrod
*Tradescantia virginiana	spiderwort
Venidium fastuosum	African daisy

PLANTS FOR CUTTING

One of the best side effects of having a natural area right outside the doorstep is the profusion of cut flowers that will be available. The following list includes some of the best species to plant for cut flowers. For tips on treating cut flowers, refer to Chapter 6.

Achillea millefolium	yarrow
Ammi majus	bishop's flower
*Aquilegia canadensis	columbine
*Asclepias tuberosa	butterfly weed
*Aster novae-angliae	New England aster
Centaurea cyanus	bachelor's button
Chrysanthemum leucanthemum	ox-eye daisy
*Coreopsis lanceolata	lance-leaved coreopsis
*Coreopsis tinctoria	annual coreopsis
Cosmos bipinnatus	cosmos
Cosmos sulphureus	orange cosmos
Daucus carota X	Queen Anne's lace
Dianthus barbatus	sweet William
*Echinacea purpurea	purple coneflower
Erigeron speciosus	Oregon fleabane
Gaillardia aristata	Indian blanket
*Gaillardia pulchella	annual Indian blanket
Gypsophila paniculata	baby's breath
*Helianthus annuus	sunflower
*Liatris pycnostachya	blazing star
*Lupinus species	lupines
Phlox series	phlox
*Rudbeckia hirta	black-eyed Susan
Venidium fastuosum	African daisy

HILLSIDE PLANTS

For those who have a steep hillside that they hate to mow, perhaps planting a few hardy wildflowers suited to erosion control is the answer. Although many plants will do well on a hillside, the following were chosen for their ability to get established quickly and to control erosion.

Achillea millefolium X	yarrow
*Baptisia australis	false indigo
*Oenothera missouriensis	sundrops
*Penstemon strictus	beard tongue
Trifolium incarnatum	crimson clover

PLANTS TO ATTRACT BIRDS AND BUTTERFLIES

Birds and butterflies will find your meadow, just as they do any area with a profusion of flowers. However, if you would like to plant a few extra species that birds (particularly hummingbirds) and butterflies are especially attracted to, choose some of the following species listed below.

*Asclepias species	milkweeds
*Asclepias tuberosa	butterfly weed
Aster species	asters
Aurinia saxatilis	basket of gold
Chrysanthemum species	daisies
*Coreopsis species	coreopsis
Cosmos species	cosmos
Daucus carota X	Queen Anne's lace
Dianthus barbatus	sweet William
*Helianthus species	sunflowers
*Ipomopsis rubra	standing cypress
Lobularia maritima	sweet alyssum
*Monarda species	bee balms
*Phlox species	phlox
Salvia coccinea	scarlet sage

MOISTURE-LOVING PLANTS

The generous rainfall and high humidity in the Southeast often create moist meadows where you can grow some very beautiful moisture-loving species. These plants like a moist environment, but most also require well-drained soils.

*Asclepias incarnata	swamp milkweed
*Bidens aristosa	tickseed sunflower
*Claytonia virginica	spring beauty
Digitalis purpurea	foxglove
*Echinacea purpurea	purple coneflower
*Epilobium angustifolium	fireweed
*Erythronium americanum	fawn lily
*Eupatorium maculatum	Joe-pye weed
*Helenium autumnale	sneezeweed
*Iris cristata	dwarf crested iris
*Lilium canadense	Turk's cap lily
*Monarda didyma	bee balm
Myosotis sylvatica	forget me not
*Stokesia laevis	Stoke's aster
*Vernonia altissima	ironweed
Viola cornuta	Johnny-jump-up

DATA FROM MEADOW PROJECTS

(1) Location: North Carolina

Description: 1½ acres of dry rolling area with acidic soil.

Soil preparation: Surface was cultivated and weeds sprayed with a general herbicide. Limestone and small amounts of 8-8-8 fertilizer were added.

Planting: Direct seeding was done using six to seven pounds of a commercial wildflower seed mixture.

Dominant flowers: Queen Anne's lace, purple coneflower, bur marigold.

Comments: There was a great deal of competition from fescue and Queen Anne's lace.

(2) Location: Georgia

Description: a ¾-acre hillside (which serves as a dam). Some areas very wet, others very dry. Acidic soil.

Soil preparation: Since this site was also a dam, only limited cultivation of the soil was possible because of the potential for erosion. A sod-dethatcher was used for better soil/seed contact.

Planting: Only three species of plants were used, all perennials: *Rudbeckia hirta* (black-eyed Susan), *Coreopsis lanceolata* (perennial coreopsis), and *Solidago* (goldenrod). Each species was seeded separately, using a cyclone spreader. Four pounds of seed were used.

Maintenance: The area was mowed twice, once at the end of June and once in early November.

Dominant flowers: black-eyed Susan, coreopsis, goldenrod.

Comments: Because only perennial species were used, there was very little bloom during the first season. There was a nice show of color by the second year.

(3) Location: Tennessee

Description: dry, slightly acidic on a rolling hillside.

Soil preparation: The area was spot fertilized with a 14-14-14 fertilizer.

Planting: Established plants were plugged into one area, and another area was directly seeded on fairly recent grade with only light grass cover. Approximately one pound of seed was collected and broadcast.

Maintenance: The areas were mowed at the end of the growing season, after seeds were dispersed.

Dominant flowers: blue-eyed grass, ox-eye daisy, butterfly weed, black-eyed Susan, bee balm, goldenrods, heal-all, asters, sunflowers.

Comments: Direct seeding requires a two-year lag time to see blossoms from the perennials.

(4) Location: Georgia

Description: 2,200-square-foot flat area with a drainage ditch through the center. Slightly acidic soil.

Soil preparation: The area was tilled in early spring; weeds were allowed to grow for five weeks and then were sprayed with a general herbicide. After ten days the area was planted.

Planting: A combination of direct seeding and plugging of established plants was done. One pound of commercial seed mixture was used, containing perennials and annuals suitable for growing in the Southeast. Approximately sixty perennial plants were placed in groups throughout the area.

Maintenance: The area was mowed at the end of October and many annuals were reseeded then, using seed collected during the growing season.

Dominant flowers: annual coreopsis, bachelor's button, black-eyed Susan, Queen Anne's lace, annual phlox, chicory, New England aster, ox-eye daisy, evening primrose, toadflax, butterfly weed.

Comments: Grasses were the biggest problem, and they began to crowd out many wildflower seedlings. A late fall spot spraying of the worst areas helped alleviate the problem.

(5) Location: Virginia

Description: five acres of dry, slightly acidic soil on a gentle slope.

Soil preparation: The area was plowed, double disked, and smoothed out.

Planting: Fifty pounds of a commercial seed mixture was sown with hand cyclone spreader.

Maintenance: The area was not fertilized or watered. It is mowed at the end of winter. During the growing season, approximately fifty man-hours were spent hand weeding invasive weeds and woody plants. A general herbicide was applied when needed.

Dominant flowers: ox-eye daisy, purple coneflower, black-eyed Susan, coreopsis, bachelor's button, chicory, columbine, evening primrose, toadflax, yarrow, phlox, asters.

Comments: If they were to do it again, they would not plow but would disturb only the top 1 inch of soil. Additionally, they would acquire seeds of individual species and would not use a ready-made mix.

RESOURCES

The following list includes institutions and organizations within the Southeast that might be able to give you additional advice on establishing meadow areas or growing native plants. In addition, check with your county extension agencies, state governments, local Soil Conservation Society chapters, and local garden clubs.

INSTITUTIONS AND ORGANIZATIONS
Southeast

Annual Southeastern Conference on Landscaping with Native Plants. For information contact: Dr. Joseph L. Collins, Tennessee Valley Authority, Natural Resources Building, Norris, Tennessee 37828, (615) 494-9800

Alabama

Alabama Wildflower Society
P. O. Box 508
Tuscaloosa, Alabama 36803-0508

The Birmingham Botanical Gardens
2612 Lane Park Rd.
Birmingham, Alabama 35223

Florida

Florida Native Plant Society
1203 Orange Ave.
Winter Park, Florida 32789

Georgia

The Atlanta Botanical Gardens
P. O. Box 77246
Atlanta, Georgia 30357

Callaway Gardens Education Department
U.S. Highway 27
Pine Mountain, Georgia 31822

The Cherokee Library
Atlanta Historical Society
3101 Andrews Dr.
Atlanta, Georgia 30327

The Georgia Botanical Society
Route 1
Tiger, Georgia 30576

State Botanical Gardens
2450 South Milledge Ave.
Athens, Georgia 30605

Mississippi

The Crosby Arboretum
P. O. Box 190
Picayune, Mississippi 39466

North Carolina

North Carolina Botanical Garden
University of North Carolina
Totten Center
Chapel Hill, North Carolina 27514

North Carolina State Museum of Natural History
P. O. Box 27647
102 North Salisbury St.
Raleigh, North Carolina 27611

North Carolina Wildflower Preservation Society
c/o North Carolina Botanical Garden
Totten Center 457-A
Chapel Hill, North Carolina 27514

Tennessee

Cheekwood Botanical Garden
Forest Park Drive
Nashville, Tennessee 37205

Memphis Pink Palace Museum
Memphis, Tennessee 38111

Tennessee Native Plant Society
Department of Botany
University of Tennessee
Knoxville, Tennessee 37916

Virginia

The American Horticultural Society
P. O. Box 0105
Mount Vernon, Virginia 22121

The Virginia Wildflower Preservation Society
Box 844
Annandale, Virginia 22003

NURSERIES AND SEED COMPANIES

The following Southeastern nurseries and seed companies sell native plants and seeds. This is only a partial list, however, and no attempt has been made to determine the quality of seeds and plants from these companies. These are not recommendations, but merely possible sources.

Byer Nursery Co., Inc.
6001 Moores Mill Rd.
Huntsville, Alabama 35811

Horticultural Systems, Inc.
P. O. Box 70
Parrish, Florida 33564

Mountain Ornamental Nursery
P. O. Box 83
Altamont, Tennessee 37301

Native Nurseries
Route 5, Box 229A
Covington, Louisiana 70433

Passiflora
Rt. 1, Box 190A
Germanton, North Carolina 27019

Plant/Flower Locators, Inc.
998 Pelican Lane, Drawer 1000
Del Ray Beach, Florida 33447

Shadow Nursery
Route 1
Winchester, Tennessee 37398

Sunlight Gardens, Inc.
Route 3, Box 286-B
Loudon, Tennessee 37774

Tom Dodd Nurseries, Inc.
Post Office Drawer 45
Semmes, Alabama 36575

Triangle Nursery, Inc.
Route 2
McMinnville, Tennessee 37110

Wayside Gardens
Hodges, South Carolina 29647

We-du Nurseries
Route 5, Box 724
Marion, North Carolina 28752

Woodlanders
1128 Colleton Ave.
Aiken, South Carolina 29801

Natural Gardens
113 Jasper Lane
Oak Ridge, Tennessee 37830

SELECTED READING

Batson, Wade T. *Wild Flowers of South Carolina.* University of South Carolina Press, Columbia, S.C.; 1964.

Bell, C. Ritchie, and William S. Justice. *Wildflowers of North Carolina.* University of North Carolina Press, Chapel Hill, N.C.; 1968.

Dormon, Caroline. *Flowers Native to the Deep South.* J. Horace McFarland Co.; 1958.

Duncan, Wilbur, and L. Foote. *Wildflowers of the Southeastern United States.* University of Georgia Press, Athens, Ga.; 1975.

Gupton, Oscar W., and Fred C. Swope. *Wildflowers of the Shenandoah Valley and Blue Ridge Mountains.* University Press of Virginia, Charlottesville, Va.; 1979.

Gupton, Oscar W., and Fred C. Swope. *Wildflowers of Tidewater Virginia.* University Press of Virginia, Charlottesville, Va.; 1982.

Hunt, Lanier William. *Southern Gardens, Southern Gardening.* Duke University Press, Durham, N.C.; 1982.

Krochmal, Arnold and Connie. *Gardening in the Carolinas.* Doubleday and Co., Inc., Garden City, N.Y.; 1975.

Niering, William A., and Nancy C. Olmstead. *The Audubon Society Field Guide to North American Wildflowers* (Eastern). Alfred A. Knopf, New York; 1979.

North Carolina Wild Flower Preservation Society, Inc. *North Carolina Native Plant Propagation Handbook.* Chapel Hill, N.C.; 1977.

Parker, Lucille. *Mississippi Wildflowers.* Pelican Publishing Co.; 1981.

Phillips, Harry R. *Growing and Propagating Wildflowers.* University of North Carolina Press, Chapel Hill, N.C.; 1985.

Radford, Albert E., Harry E. Ahles, and C. Ritchie Bell. *Manual of the Vascular Flora of the Carolinas.* University of North Carolina Press, Chapel Hill, N.C.; 1968.

Rickett, William. *Wildflowers of America* (Volume 2, Eastern United States). McGraw Hill, New York; 1966.

Small, John Kunkel. *Manual of the Southeastern Flora.* Hafner Publishing Co.; 1972.

Smith, Arlo I. *A Guide to Wildflowers of the Mid-South.* Memphis State University Press; 1979.

CHAPTER THIRTEEN

The Southwest

Arizona, southern California, southern Nevada, New Mexico

CONDITIONS TO CONSIDER IN THE SOUTHWEST

NATURALLY OCCURRING PLANT COMMUNITIES

Several different kinds of plant communities can be found in the Southwest. These include a desert grassland and warm desert in the southern parts of Arizona, New Mexico, Nevada, and California; a pinyon-juniper woodland in northern Arizona and New Mexico; a coastal chaparral along the southern California coast; a tall-grass prairie in central southern California; and forests in the mountain areas.

The elevation of the pinyon-juniper woodland is between 5,000 and 7,000 feet. The soils are poor and the trees (pinyon pine and several species of junipers) rarely grow taller than 30 feet. Shrubs that grow in this area include serviceberry and cliffrose. Generally, winters are cold and the summers are hot with cool nights. Though it varies from one location to another, rainfall averages 20 inches annually.

Much of the region is made up of desert grassland, found at elevations just above the warm desert (between 4,000 and 7,000 feet). Sometimes considered a transition between the desert and the mountain forests, these grasslands seem to be a distinct ecosystem, for they still exist even though they have been periodically severely altered. Annual rainfall is between 8 and 17 inches, and although rain falls in both summer and winter, the months of April, May, and June are completely dry. This grassland is primarily composed of species of grama grasses (genus Bouteloua), succulents (cacti), and semi-succulents (such as yucca).

At lower elevations, three deserts, each with its own unique climate, make up this area. The Mojave in southeastern California is composed of creosote bush and the Joshua tree. The Sonoran of Arizona is composed of saguaro cactus, ocotillo, and creosote bush. The Chihuahuan of southern New Mexico and eastern Texas is composed of creosote bush, tarbush, whitethorn acacia, yucca, mesquite, ocotillo, and cacti.

The coastal chaparral in California is made up of evergreen shrubs and trees producing small, leathery leaves. The precipitation almost always comes in the form of winter rains and averages between 12 and 40 inches. The summer months are hot and dry.

There is one small sliver of tall-grass prairie in central southern California. It supports grasses such as big bluestem and Indian grass, as well as several different species of wildflowers.

Vegetation in the mountain regions varies according to the elevation and may consist of spruce, timber pines, Douglas fir, ponderosa and lodgepole pines, and aspen.

PROBLEM SOILS AND GROWING CONDITIONS

Whether or not you can establish a meadow in this region usually depends on the availability of moisture. The soils are very poor and are extremely dry, for there is little rainfall and very high evaporation. At lower elevations the area known as warm desert contains soils that are finely textured, heavy, and highly alkaline, and these soils have excessive accumulations of salts. There is often a very hard subsoil, or caliche, formed by the accumulated salts. This makes it very difficult for plants to grow.

WHEN TO PLANT

If you use a premixed blend of seeds, planting in late September or October, just before the seasonal rains, is most practical. In very cold areas where snow cover is light, the area may be prepared in the fall but planted in March or April. However, best results can be obtained by treating each species separately and giving each type of seed the pretreatment and conditions that suit it best. Many seeds need a period of stratification or scarification to break seed dormancy. Other seeds are sensitive to the temperature of the soil into which they are planted. To naturally stratify seeds, plant them in November or December. Seeds that were pretreated indoors can be sown in March or April, and seeds that benefit from warm soil temperatures should be planted in May. Established plants should be set out in late fall to take advantage of the natural rainfall. Be sure to provide additional water if rainfall is insufficient.

MAINTENANCE

Watering to get the seedlings and plants established is very important. Once they are established, watering should be necessary only when the plants show stress. Hand weeding and/or selective spraying is necessary to keep the undesirable species under control.

NOXIOUS WEEDS

Many of the plant communities look very different than they did in the days before the white man settled this area. Extensive use of fire and overgrazing has resulted in the invasion of junipers, creosote bushes, acacia, and mesquites. Annuals such as kochia and tumbleweed and perennials such as bermuda grass, Johnson grass, and bindweed are other invaders that might cause problems in a meadow garden.

PROBLEM WILDFLOWERS

The following wildflowers are sometimes included within a seed mixture, but they have the tendency to become invasive and overly aggressive and might outgrow their welcome.

Achillea millefolium	yarrow
Anagallis arvensis	pimpernel
Chrysanthemum coronarium	garland chrysanthemum
Chrysanthemum leucanthemum	ox-eye daisy
Cichorium intybus	chicory
Eschscholzia californica	California poppy
Helianthus annuus	sunflower
Lobularia maritima	sweet alyssum
Saponaria officinalis	soapwort
Verbascum thapsus	mullein

MEADOW PLANTS THAT GROW IN THE SOUTHWEST

The gardener in the Southwest must deal with many variables and with growing conditions that can change drastically within a very small area. In most areas irrigation is needed for all but the most drought tolerant plants. This is due to the combination of scarce rainfall and hot, drying winds. For this reason, windbreaks of tamarisk, Russian olive, or pussy willows are useful bordering the meadow areas. Deep infrequent watering during the summer will result in a longer blooming cycle and a more lush "garden" look. Take care not to overwater, however, for the result will be a profusion of leaves but fewer flowers. The quality of the soil in the Southwest is poor, and it generally lacks humus.

Creating a combination of wildflowers and native grasses that will thrive and grow together compatibly involves knowing the conditions of your own meadow area. The first step, of course, is to choose plants that do grow in your region. However, even this is difficult because the wonderful diversity and variety of growing conditions presented in our country make it impossible to know exactly what will grow where. Your own backyard might contain just the right conditions to grow a plant that does not normally do well in your area. For this reason, use the following lists as guidelines, but don't hesitate to experiment and try some favorites that might not be on these lists. The lists were based on recommendations from botanists and horticulturists from universities, botanical gardens, arboretums, and native plant societies, as well as the sage advice of many "dirt gardeners" who live in the Southwest.

Although cultural requirements for the following species will vary greatly, it should be possible to grow these species somewhere within the Southwestern region. These species were chosen on the basis of their availability and their presence in many commercial premixed blends of seeds. Many of the species are not native to this region, some are considered cultivated varieties instead of wildflowers, and some have the tendency to become invasive. In the list below and those that follow, native species are marked with an *, invasive species with an X, and unmarked species are non-native but generally non-invasive.

Achillea millefolium X	yarrow
Ammi majus	bishop's flower
Anagallis arvensis X	pimpernel
Aquilegia caerulea	blue columbine
Aquilegia formosa	scarlet columbine
Arabis alpina	rock cress
Argemone hispida	white prickly poppy
Asclepias curassavica	sunset flower
Asclepias incarnata	swamp milkweed
Asclepias tuberosa	butterfly weed
Baptisia australis	false indigo
Belamcanda chinensis	blackberry lily
Campanula rotundifolia	bluebell
Castilleja miniata	giant red paintbrush
Centaurea cyanus X	bachelor's button
Cerastium bierbersteinii	snow in summer
Chrysanthemum coronarium X	garland chrysanthemum
Chrysanthemum leucanthemum X	ox-eye daisy
Cichorium intybus X	chicory
Clarkia amoena	farewell to spring
Clarkia concinna	red ribbons
Clarkia pulchella	deerhorn clarkia
Clarkia unguiculata	elegant clarkia
Collinsia heterophylla	Chinese houses
Consolida orientalis (same as *Delphinium ajacis*)	rocket larkspur
Coreopsis lanceolata	lance-leaved coreopsis
Coreopsis tinctoria	annual coreopsis
Cosmos bipinnatus	cosmos
Cosmos sulphureus	orange cosmos
Dianthus barbatus	sweet William
Dimorphotheca sinuata	African daisy
Echinacea purpurea	purple coneflower
Epilobium angustifolium	fireweed
Erigeron speciosus	Oregon fleabane
Eriogonum umbellatum	sulphur flower
Erysimum hieraciifolium	wallflower
Eschscholzia californica X	California poppy
Fritillaria pudica	yellow bell
Gaillardia aristata	Indian blanket

*Gaillardia pulchella	annual Indian blanket
Gazania rigens	treasure flower
*Geum triflorum	prairie smoke
*Gilia capitata	blue thimble flower
Gilia leptantha	blue gilia
Gypsophila elegans	annual baby's breath
Gypsophila paniculata	baby's breath
enium autumnale	sneezeweed
Helenium autumnale	sneezeweed
*Helianthus annuus X	sunflower
Iberis umbellata	candytuft
Ipomopsis rubra	standing cypress
Lathyrus latifolius	sweet pea
Lavatera trimestris	tree mallow
*Layia platyglossa	tidy tips
Liatris pycnostachya	blazing star
*Linanthus grandiflorus	mountain phlox
Linaria maroccana	spurred snapdragon
Linum grandiflorum rubrum	red flax
Lobularia maritima X	sweet alyssum
*Lupinus densiflorus	golden lupine
Lupinus perennis	lupine
*Lupinus succulentus	succulent lupine
Lychnis chalcedonica	Maltese cross
*Machaeranthera tanacetifolia	prairie aster
*Mentzelia lindleyi	blazing star
*Mirabilis multiflora	wild four o'clock
Monarda didyma	bee balm
Myosotis sylvatica	forget me not
*Nemophila maculata	five spot
*Nemophila menziesii	baby blue eyes
*Oenothera biennis	evening primrose
*Oenothera caespitosa	gumbo lily
Oenothera lamarckiana	evening primrose
Oenothera missouriensis	sundrops
*Oenothera pallida	white evening primrose
Papaver nudicaule	Iceland poppy
Papaver rhoeas	corn poppy
Penstemon digitalis	beard tongue
Penstemon grandiflorus	beard tongue
Penstemon smallii	beard tongue
Penstemon strictus	beard tongue
*Petalostemon purpureum	prairie clover
*Phacelia campanularia	desert bell
*Phacelia tanacetifolia	tansy phacelia

Phlox drummondii	annual phlox
*Ratibida columnaris	prairie coneflower
Rudbeckia fulgida	coneflower
Rudbeckia hirta	black-eyed Susan
*Rudbeckia laciniata	coneflower
Salvia coccinea	scarlet sage
Silene armeria	catchfly
*Sisyrinchium angustifolium	blue-eyed grass
*Solidago canadensis	meadow goldenrod
*Solidago spathulata	narrow goldenrod
Stokesia laevis	Stoke's aster
Stylomecon heterophylla	wind poppy
Thymus serpyllum	creeping thyme
Tradescantia virginiana	spiderwort
Trifolium incarnatum	crimson clover
Venidium fastuosum	African daisy
Verbena goodingii	verbena
*Verbena stricta	hoary vervain
Viola cornuta	Johnny-jump-up
*Zinnia grandiflora	little golden zinnia

THE TOP TEN

The following list is not designed as a balanced mixture of wildflowers and should not be used as such. The flowers included on this list are noted for their adaptability and reliability. They are all generally hardy and easy to grow from seed in the Southwest.

*Collinsia heterophylla	Chinese houses
*Coreopsis lanceolata	lance-leaved coreopsis
*Coreopsis tinctoria	annual coreopsis
*Eschscholzia californica	California poppy
*Gaillardia aristata	Indian blanket
*Gaillardia pulchella	annual Indian blanket
*Machaeranthera tanacetifolia	prairie aster
*Oenothera caespitosa	gumbo lily
*Ratibida columnaris	prairie coneflower
*Rudbeckia laciniata	coneflower

GRASSES

When you plant a naturalized area, be sure to plant some native grasses to fill in niches that cannot be filled with the wildflowers. These grasses will help open up the meadow and serve as a foil for the colorful wildflowers. Naturally occurring meadows are characterized by a mixture of grasses and wildflowers. For instance, prairie areas contain up to seventy percent grasses. Do not use lawn or turf grasses — they will quickly overrun the wildflowers. The following species are good to use in the Southwest, and they compete well with the wildflowers.

Bouteloua gracilis	blue grama
Buchloe dactyloides	buffalo grass
Oryzopsis hymenoides	Indian ricegrass

PLANTS THAT TOLERATE DRY CONDITIONS

Because so much of this region receives little rainfall, you should plant species that can withstand dry conditions. As always, use as many species native to your region as possible. In the lists that follow, these species are marked with an *. Although they can all get by with little water, these species have other growth requirements that may be very different from one to another. Be sure to check soil and temperature requirements for each before planting. Even though these plants are drought tolerant, the seeds need moisture to germinate and the young plants need moisture to establish themselves.

Achillea millefolium X	yarrow
Ammi majus	bishop's flower
Centaura cyanus X	bachelor's button
Clarkia amoena	farewell to spring
Clarkia unguiculata	elegant clarkia
Collinsia heterophylla	Chinese houses
Coreopsis tinctoria	annual coreopsis
Cosmos bipinnatus	cosmos
Cosmos sulphureus	orange cosmos
Echinacea purpurea	purple coneflower
Eschscholzia californica	California poppy
Gaillardia pulchella	annual Indian blanket
Gazania rigens	treasure flower
Geum triflorum	prairie smoke
Gilia capitata	blue thimble flower
Helianthus annuus	sunflower
Ipomopsis rubra	standing cypress
Layia platyglossa	tidy tips
Liatris spicata	blazing star
Linanthus grandiflorus	mountain phlox
Linaria vulgaris	butter and eggs
Linum grandiflorum rubrum	red flax
Lobularia maritima	sweet alyssum
Lupinus texensis	bluebonnet
Mentzelia lindleyi	blazing star
Phacelia campanularia	desert bell
Phacelia tanacetifolia	tansy phacelia
Rudbeckia hirta	black-eyed Susan
Verbena goodingii	verbena

PLANTS FOR CUTTING

To some people, the best aspect of having a meadow area is the number of cut flowers that it makes readily available. Even a small area can yield an abundant supply of cut flowers throughout the growing season.

Achillea millefolium X	yarrow
Ammi majus	bishop's flower
Asclepias tuberosa	butterfly weed
Centaurea cyanus X	bachelor's button
Chrysanthemum leucanthemum X	ox-eye daisy
Clarkia species	farewell to spring
Collinsia heterophylla	Chinese houses
Coreopsis lanceolata	coreopsis
Coreopsis tinctoria	annual coreopsis
Cosmos bipinnatus	cosmos
Daucus carota	Queen Anne's lace
Erigeron speciosus	Oregon fleabane
Gaillardia aristata	Indian blanket
Gaillardia pulchella	annual Indian blanket
Gypsophila paniculata	baby's breath
Helianthus annuus	sunflower
Layia platyglossa	tidy tips
Rudbeckia hirta	black-eyed Susan
Venidium fastuosum	cape daisy

PLANTS FOR HIGH ALTITUDES

The following species are adaptable to high altitudes and are good to use in the mountains.

Achillea millefolium	yarrow
Aquilegia caerulea	blue columbine
Aquilegia formosa	scarlet columbine
Campanula rotundifolia	bluebell
Castilleja miniata	giant red paintbrush
Centaurea cyanus	bachelor's button
Chrysanthemum leucanthemum	ox-eye daisy
Cichorium intybus	chicory
Daucus carota	Queen Anne's lace
Echinacea purpurea	purple coneflower
Epiblobium angustifolium	fireweed
Erigonum umbellatum	sulphur flower
Geum triflorum	prairie smoke
Iris missouriensis	blue flag iris
Liatris punctata	dotted gayfeather
Linanthus grandiflorus	mountain phlox
Linum perenne lewisii	blue flax
Machaeranthera tanacetifolia	prairie aster

*Oenothera caespitosa	gumbo lily
*Penstemon barbatus	scarlet beard tongue
Penstemon strictus	beard tongue
Phlox drummondii	annual phlox
*Sisyrinchium angustifolium	blue-eyed grass
Thymus serpyllum	creeping thyme
*Verbena goodingii	verbena

SEASONAL BLOOM

You can have good color in your meadow during all parts of the growing season if you pay some attention to the blooming times of the different species. The following lists should help you find some favorites for each season. There will be great variation as to actual time of bloom depending on growing conditions, local weather, and when the seeds were sown or the plants set out. These are general guidelines. As always, use as many native species as possible (marked with an *).

SPRING:

*Aquilegia caerulea	blue columbine
Arabis alpina	rock cress
Baptisia australis	false indigo
Centaurea cyanus	bachelor's button
Cerastium bierbersteinii	snow in summer
*Collinsia heterophylla	Chinese houses
Dianthus barbatus	sweet William
Erysimum hieraciifolium	Siberian wallflower
*Eschscholzia californica	California poppy
*Fritillaria pudica	yellow bell
*Iris missouriensis	blue flag iris
*Layia platyglossa	tidy tips
*Linanthus grandiflorus	mountain phlox
Linaria maroccana	spurred snapdragon
Linum grandiflorum rubrum	red flax
*Mentzelia lindleyi	blazing star
*Nemophila menziesii	baby blue eyes
Papaver rhoeas	corn poppy
Penstemon digitalis	beard tongue
Penstemon smallii	beard tongue
*Phacelia campanularia	desert bell
*Sisyrinchium angustifolium	blue-eyed grass
Stokesia laevis	Stoke's aster
*Stylomecon heterophylla	wind poppy
Viola cornuta	Johnny-jump-up

SUMMER:

Achillea millefolium	yarrow
Ammi majus	bishop's flower
Anagallis arvensis	pimpernel
Asclepias tuberosa	butterfly weed
Baptisia australis	false indigo
Belamcanda chinensis	blackberry lily
Bidens aristosa	tickseed sunflower
Campanula rotundifolia	bluebell
Castilleja miniata	giant red paintbrush
Centaurea cyanus	bachelor's button
Chrysanthemum coronarium	garland chrysanthemum
Chrysanthemum leucanthemum	ox-eye daisy
Cichorium intybus	chicory
Clarkia amoena	farewell to spring
Clarkia concinna	red ribbons
Clarkia pulchella	deerhorn clarkia
Clarkia unguiculata	elegant clarkia
Collinsia heterophylla	Chinese houses
Consolida orientalis (same as *Delphinium ajacis*)	rocket larkspur
Coreopsis lanceolata	lance-leaved coreopsis
Coreopsis tinctoria	annual coreopsis
Cosmos bipinnatus	cosmos
Daucus carota	Queen Anne's lace
Dimorphotheca sinuata	African daisy
Echinacea purpurea	purple coneflower
Epilobium angustifolium	fireweed
Erigeron speciosus	Oregon fleabane
Eriogonum umbellatum	sulphur flower
Eschscholzia californica	California poppy
Gaillardia aristata	Indian blanket
Gaillardia pulchella	annual Indian blanket
Gazania rigens	treasure flower
Gypsophila elegans	annual baby's breath
Gypsophila paniculata	baby's breath
Helenium autumnale	sneezeweed
Helianthus annuus	sunflower
Ipomopsis rubra	standing cypress
Lathyrus latifolius	sweet pea
Lavatera trimestris	tree mallow
Liatris pycnostachya	blazing star
Linanthus grandiflorus	mountain phlox
Linum grandiflorum rubrum	red flax
Lupinus perennis	lupine

*Lupinus succulentus	succulent lupine
*Machaeranthera tanacetifolia	prairie aster
Monarda didyma	bee balm
*Oenothera biennis	evening primrose
Phlox drummondii	annual phlox
*Ratibida columnaris	prairie coneflower
Rudbeckia hirta	black-eyed Susan
Silene armeria	catchfly
Venidium fastuosum	African daisy

FALL:

Achillea millefolium	yarrow
Bidens aristosa	tickseed sunflower
Echinacea purpurea	purple coneflower
Gypsophila paniculata	baby's breath
*Helianthus annuus	sunflower
*Machaeranthera tanacetifolia	prairie aster
*Oenothera biennis	evening primrose
Solidago juncea	goldenrod

DATA FROM MEADOW PROJECTS

(1) Location: New Mexico

Description: slightly more than two acres of dry, flat, sandy soil with pH of 8 to 9.

Soil preparation: The area was cleared and selected spaces tilled, leaving most of the vegetation intact to reduce wind erosion. The area was fertilized with Osmocote 18-6-12.

Planting: Seeds collected locally from the wild were broadcast in the fall. Over the past two years up to thirty pounds of seeds have been used in this area.

Maintenance: The most time-consuming months are May and October due to the need for hand weeding and reseeding (averaging one hour per week). Maintenance time during the months of June through September averaged two to three hours per month.

Dominant flowers: scorpion flower, evening primrose, purple mat, blackfoot daisy, bush penstemon, coneflower, purple aster, gayfeather, desert zinnia.

Comments: If watered more frequently the area would have been more lush and had more variety. This individual chose not to water frequently because (1) the idea behind establishing the area was low maintenance and (2) because she "likes the serendipity of new arrivals after rains."

(2) Location: Arizona

Description: a 13,000-square-foot pond reclamation project

Soil preparation: The area was very disturbed from building a pond and putting in water lines. There was no vegetation. They rototilled what they could and put jute mesh on the banks. Ammonium nitrate was applied to the soil at a rate of one pound per 1000 square feet.

Planting: A commercial "dry blend" mixture of seeds was supplemented with other seeds collected from the wild to total about twenty-five pounds. Seeds were raked into the topsoil and then mulched with bark.

Maintenance: Approximately eight hours per month during July, August, and September were needed to weed out invasive species. A weed-eater was used on the very invasive yellow clover.

Dominant flowers: California poppy, blue flax, sunflowers, coreopsis, purple aster, purple coneflower, butterfly weed, evening primrose, penstemons.

Comments: Perhaps better results would have been obtained by planting in July and watering well.

(3) Location: California

Description: approximately one acre of dry land with alkaline soils.

Soil preparation: Mushroom compost, horse manure, and sewage sludge were added to the soil.

Planting: Most of the planting was done by plugging in plants grown in 2- to 3-inch pots. These were mulched with newspapers and wood chips. Direct seeding was done in small patches. The seed was obtained from the wild and from botanical gardens and commercial sources.

Maintenance: The area is controlled by hand weeding; a bit of herbicidal spraying; baiting for snails, slugs and pillbugs; and trapping for gophers. It is watered as needed.

Dominant species: California poppies, sunflowers, penstemon species, goldenrod.

Comments: The area was initially planted with a mixture of many different species. More weeds than wildflowers appeared, so the procedures described above were tried with much greater success.

(4) Location: California

Description: 100 square feet of dry flat land with neutral soil.

Soil preparation: The soil was not disturbed so as not to encourage weeds.

Planting: Seeds were collected from the wild and sown in pots. Seedlings were planted directly into the meadow area.

Maintenance: There is much hand weeding of weeds during June. The area is watered once a month during the summer.

Dominant flowers: During the spring members of the lily and mustard families are dominant. During the summer, the area is dominated by members of the sunflower family.

RESOURCES

INSTITUTIONS AND ORGANIZATIONS

The following organizations and institutions might be able to supply more information about growing native plants in the Southwest. In addition, check with your county extension agencies, state government offices, local garden clubs, and local chapters of the Soil Conservation Society.

Arizona

Arizona Native Plant Society
Box 18519
Tucson, Arizona 85731

Arizona Sonoran Desert Museum
Tucson, Arizona 85731

Boyce Thompson Southwest Arboretum
Superior, Arizona 85273

Desert Botanical Garden
1201 North Galvin Parkway
Phoenix, Arizona 85008

Transition Zone Horticultural Institute
P. O. Box 670
Flagstaff, Arizona 86002

Tucson Botanical Garden
2150 Avernon Way
Tucson, Arizona 85712

California

California Native Plant Society
2380 Ellsworth St., Suite D
Berkeley, California 94794

Fullerton Arboretum
California State University
Fullerton, California 92634

Rancho Santa Ana Botanic Garden
1500 North College Ave.
Claremont, California 91711

Santa Barbara Botanical Garden
1212 Mission Canyon Rd.
Santa Barbara, California 93101

Nevada

Northern Nevada Native Plant Society
Box 8965
Reno, Nevada 89431

New Mexico

Native Plant Society of New Mexico
Box 5917
Santa Fe, New Mexico 87502

NURSERIES AND SEED COMPANIES

The nurseries and seed companies listed below are not recommended, but are listed merely as possible sources. No attempt has been made to determine the quality of the seeds or plants available from these sources.

Agua Fria Nursery
1409 Agua Fria St.
Santa Fe, New Mexico 87501

Albright and Towne, Inc.
5143 Port Chicago Highway
Concord, California 94520

Appleton Forestry
1369 Tilton Rd.
Sebastopol, California 95472

Bay View Gardens
1201 Bay St.
Santa Cruz, California 95060

Berkeley Horticultural Nursery
1310 McGee Ave.
Berkeley, California 94703

Bernando Beach Native Plant Farm
Box 145, Star Route 7
Veguita, New Mexico 87062

Blue Oak Nursery
2731 Mountain Oak Lane
Rescue, California 95672

California Flora Nursery
Box 3, Somers and D. Street
Fulton, California 95439

Richard R. Clinebell
1874 Church St.
San Francisco, California 94131

Curtis and Curtis Seed Co.
Star Route, Box 8A
Clovis, New Mexico 88101

Desert Enterprises
P. O. Box 23
Morristown, Arizona 85342

Dry Country Plants
3904 Highway 70 East
Las Cruces, New Mexico 88001

Environmental Seed Producers
P. O. Box 5904
El Monte, California 91734

Greenhouse Garden Center
2450 South Curry St.
Carson City, Nevada 89701

H-H Forest Tree Nursery
P. O. Box 479
Sebastopol, California 95472

Hubbs Brothers Seed Co.
1015 North 35th St.
Phoenix, Arizona 85008

J.L. Hudson Seedsman
P. O. Box 1058
Redwood City, California 94064

Las Pilitas Nursery
Star Route, Box 23X
Santa Margarita, California 93453

Los Patios, Inc.
P. O. Box 1346
Corrales, New Mexico 87408

Miller Farms Nursery
1828 Central Ave.
McKinleyville, California 95521

Native Sons Wholesale Nursery
379 W. El Campo Rd.
Arroyo Grande, California 93420

New Mexico Native Plants Nursery
309 West College
Silver City, New Mexico 88061

Plants of the Southwest
1570 Pacheco St.
Sante Fe, New Mexico 87501

Redwood City Seed Co.
P. O. Box 361
Redwood City, California 94064

Redwood Nursery
2800 El Rancho Dr.
Santa Cruz, California 95060

Southwest Native Seeds
Box 50503
Tucson, Arizona 85703

Weber Nursery
237 Seeman Dr.
Encinitas, California 92024

Wildland and Native Seeds
Foundation
2402 Hoffman Dr., N.E.
Albuquerque, New Mexico 87110

Wild Seed
P. O. Box 27751
Tempe, Arizona 85282

SELECTED READING

Brown, Lauren. *The Audubon Society Nature Guide to Grasslands.* Alfred A. Knopf, New York; 1985.

Kearney, Thomas H., and Robert H. Peebles. *Arizona Flora.* University of California Press; 1960.

Lenz, Lee W., and John Dourley. *California Native Trees and Shrubs for Garden and Environmental Use in Southern California and Adjacent Areas.* Rancho Santa Ana; 1981.

Munz, Phillip A., and David D. Keck. *A California Flora.* University of California Press; 1973.

Natural Vegetation Committee-SCSA, Arizona Chapter. *Landscaping with Native Arizona Plants.* University of Arizona Press, Tucson, Arizona; 1985.

Ricketts, William. *Wildflowers of the United States* (Volume 4, Southwest). McGraw Hill, New York; 1966.

Schmidt, Marjorie G. *Growing California Natives.* University of California Press; 1980.

Ryan, Julie E., and Sally Wasowski. *Landscaping with Native Texas Plants.* Texas Monthly Press, Austin, Texas; 1985.

Tierney, G., and P. Hughes. *Roadside Plants of Northern New Mexico.* The Lightening Tree Press, Santa Fe, New Mexico; 1983.

CHAPTER FOURTEEN

Texas
And
Oklahoma

The eastern edge of Texas and the southeastern corner of Oklahoma are composed of Southeastern mixed forests and are included in the Southeastern region of this book. This chapter covers the remainder of these two states, an area which is made up of mixed prairie, short-grass prairie, and warm desert.

CONDITIONS TO CONSIDER IN TEXAS AND OKLAHOMA

NATURALLY OCCURRING PLANT COMMUNITIES

The natural plant communities of central Texas and Oklahoma and northward towards Canada are mixed prairies. The boundaries of these grasslands shift with changing weather patterns: one type of grassland slowly blends into another, depending on the amount of available moisture. Even within each grassland community, ecosystems will change. Gullies that might collect and hold extra rainfall will be able to support a different type of vegetation than, for example, a nearby rocky knoll that can hold little moisture. Rainfall generally decreases from east to west, varying from 23 inches annually on the eastern edge to 14 inches on the western border of the mixed prairie. The rains are not evenly distributed and come primarily during the late summer and fall months. The lack of moisture has resulted in less organic matter in the soil and a greater accumulation of salts. High winds and subsequent rapid evaportation rate must also be taken into consideration by gardeners in this area.

The panhandle of Oklahoma and northern Texas are made up of short-grass prairie. This type of grassland extends northward to Canada; its western boundary is the Rocky Mountains and the eastern border varies depending on available moisture and topography. The elevation of this area rises from 2,500 feet on the eastern edge to 5,000 feet where it meets the Rocky Mountains. The terrain is marked periodically by canyons and rough buttes. The precipitation is very low, in some areas as low as 10 inches annually, and it generally occurs during May, June, and July. Plants quickly use up the available moisture and go dormant by late summer. High winds and frequent hailstorms contribute to the difficult growing conditions of this area.

The desert areas of western Texas lie in the Chihuahuan Desert. This area is characterized by fine-textured heavy soils, very hot summers, and very dry conditions that are occasionally alleviated by a late summer storm. Growing conditions are poor and vegetation is sparse, dominated by the low creosote bush, yucca, mesquite, and cacti.

NOXIOUS WEEDS

The type of weed you will get in your meadow garden will in large part depend on the amount of extra watering you give the area. The better conditions you give your desired plants, the better conditions you will be giving the undesirables. You can expect problems from hedge parsley, sonchus species, rye grass, Johnson grass, and broom weed.

WHEN TO PLANT

The best time to plant most wildflowers in this region is in the fall, particularly for those species that bloom in the spring. Seeds of summer- and fall-blooming plants can be sown up until mid-March. By planting in the fall, you eliminate the need for pre-treating many of the seeds, for the natural freezing and thawing cycles of winter will break the dormancy of many species. For those species that you want to start indoors and transplant for early bloom, place the seeds in the refrigerator for one month before you sow them. Allow them to grow another month indoors before you transplant them.

MAINTENANCE

During the first few years of a meadow project, you will need to remove large and aggressive weeds by hand or by spot spraying with a general herbicide. The area should be mowed annually, usually in late July after most of the seeds have ripened. If autumn rains create tall growth from weeds, an additional mowing should be done in late winter.

PROBLEM WILDFLOWERS

Some wildflowers incouded in seed mixtures might become invasive and aggressive in Texas and Oklahoma. Be aware of their potentially invasive characteristics and use them wisely and only in a situation where you can control them.

Achillea millefolium   yarrow
Bidens aristosa   tickseed sunflower

Centaurea cyanus	bachelor's button
Daucus carota	Queen Anne's lace
Erigeron species	fleabanes
Helianthus annuus	sunflower

MEADOW PLANTS THAT GROW IN TEXAS AND OKLAHOMA

Creating a combination of wildflowers and native grasses that will thrive and compete together compatibly involves knowing the conditions of your own meadow area. The first step, of course, is to choose plants that do grow in your region. Even this is not easy, however, for the wonderful diversity and variety of growing conditions presented within this region make it impossible to know exactly what will grow where. Your own backyard might contain just the right conditions to grow a plant that does not normally do well in your area. For this reason, use the following lists as guidelines, but don't hesitate to experiment and try to grow some favorites that might not be on these lists. The following lists were based on recommendations from botanists and horticulturists from universities, botanical gardens, arboretums, and native plant societies, as well as the sage advice of many "dirt gardeners" who live in these states.

Although cultural requirements for the following species will vary tremendously, it is possible to grow each of these species somewhere within this region. Many of these species are not native to these states, and some are even cultivated flowers rather than wildflowers, but they were included in this list due to their presence within many commercial premixed wildflower blends. Species that are endangered or threatened or difficult to obtain are not included. On the list below and those that follow, species native to these states are marked with an *; species that have a tendency to become invasive are marked with an X; and unmarked species are non-native, but usually non-invasive.

Achillea millefolium X	yarrow
Achillea millefolium rubra	red yarrow
Ammi majus	bishop's flower
Anagallis arvensis	pimpernel
Aquilegia canadensis	columbine
Arabis alpina	rock cress
Argemone aurantica	white prickly poppy
Argemone hispida	white prickly poppy
Argemone mexicana	yellow prickly poppy
Asclepias curassavica	sunset flower
Asclepias incarnata	swamp milkweed
Asclepias tuberosa	butterfly weed
Aster ericoides	aster
Aster lineariifolius	aster
Aster novae-angliae	New England aster

Aurinia saxatilis	basket of gold
Baptisia australis	false indigo
Baptisia leucantha	wild white indigo
Belamcanda chinensis	blackberry lily
Bidens aristosa X	tickseed sunflower
Campanula rotundifolia	bluebell
Castilleja indivisa	Texas paintbrush
Castilleja integra	grassland paintbrush
Castilleja sessiflora	downy paintbrush
Centaurea cyanus X	bachelor's button
Cerastium bierbersteinii	snow in summer
Chrysanthemum leucanthemum	ox-eye daisy
Cichorium intybus X	chicory
Claytonia virginica	spring beauty
Consolida orientalis	
(same as *Delphinium ajacis*)	rocket larkspur
Coreopsis lanceolata	lance-leaved coreopsis
Coreopsis tinctoria	annual coreopsis
Cosmos bipinnatus	cosmos
Cosmos sulphureus	orange cosmos
Daucus carota X	Queen Anne's lace
Delphinium virescens	prairie larkspur
Dianthus barbatus	sweet William
Digitalis purpurea	foxglove
Dodecatheon meadia	shooting star
Dodecatheon pulchellum	western shooting star
Dracopis amplexicaulis	
(same as *Rudbeckia amplexicaulis*)	coneflower
Echinacea purpurea	purple coneflower
Epilobium angustifolium	fireweed
Erigeron speciosus	Oregon fleabane
Eschscholzia californica	California poppy
Eupatorium perfoliatum	boneset
Gaillardia aristata	Indian blanket
Gaillardia pulchella	annual Indian blanket
Gazania rigens	treasure flower
Geranium maculatum	wild geranium
Gypsophila elegans	annual baby's breath
Gypsophila pariculata	baby's breath
Helenium autumnale	sneezeweed
Helianthus annuus X	sunflower
Helianthus maximiliani	Maximilian sunflower
Iberis umbellata	candytuft
Ipomopsis rubra	standing cypress
Iris cristata	dwarf crested iris

Lathyrus latifolius X	sweet pea
*Liatris aspera	rough blazing star
*Liatris mucronata	blazing star
*Liatris punctata	dotted gayfeather
*Liatris pycnostachya	blazing star
Linaria maroccana	spurred snapdragon
*Linum perenne lewisii	blue flax
Lupinus perennis	perennial lupine
*Lupinus subcarnosus	Texas bluebonnet
*Lupinus texensis	bluebonnet
Lychnis chalcedonica	Maltese cross
*Machaeranthera tanacetifolia	prairie aster
*Mentzelia decapetala	blazing star
*Mirabilis multiflora	wild four o'clock
*Monarda citriodora	lemon mint
*Monarda fistulosa	bergamot
Nemophila menziesii	baby blue eyes
Nemophila maculata	five spot
*Oenothera biennis	evening primrose
*Oenothera missouriensis	sundrops
*Oenothera speciosa	evening primrose
Papaver rhoeas	corn poppy
*Penstemon barbatus	scarlet beard tongue
*Penstemon grandiflorus	beard tongue
*Petalostemon purpureum	prairie clover
Phacelia campanularia	desert bell
*Phlox drummondii	annual phlox
*Phlox pilosa	western phlox
*Ratibida columnaris	prairie coneflower
*Rudbeckia hirta	black-eyed Susan
*Salvia coccinea	scarlet sage
Silene armeria	catchfly
Sisyrinchium angustifolium	blue-eyed grass
*Solidago altissima	tall goldenrod
*Solidago odora	scented goldenrod
*Solidago sempervirens	seaside goldenrod
Thymus serpyllum	creeping thyme
*Tradescantia ohiensis	spiderwort
Trifolium incarnatum	crimson clover
Venidium fastuosum	African daisy
*Verbena bipinnatifida	verbena
*Verbena stricta	hoary vervain
Vernonia altissima	ironweed
Viola cornuta	Johnny-jump-up

THE TOP TEN

The following list is not designed as a balanced mixture of wildflowers and should not be used as such. The flowers included on this list are noted for their adaptability and reliability. They are all generally hardy and easy to grow in this region.

*Coreopsis tinctoria	annual coreopsis
*Gaillardia pulchella	annual Indian blanket
*Helianthus maximiliani	Maximilian sunflower
*Ipomopsis rubra	standing cypress
*Monarda citriodora	lemon mint
*Oenothera speciosa	evening primrose
Papaver rhoeas	corn poppy
*Phlox drummondii	annual phlox
*Ratibida columnaris	prairie coneflower
*Rudbeckia hirta	black-eyed Susan

(Number eleven has to be *Lupinus subcarnosus,* the Texas bluebonnet. It did not make it to the top ten because it is not considered "easy" from seed. It will germinate, but it takes time and patience.)

GRASSES

When planting sunny, naturalized areas, it is important to include some non-spreading grasses to fill in niches that the wildflowers cannot fill. Grasses are a foil for the wildflowers and create an openness which is basic to the charm of a meadow or grassland area. In Texas and Oklahoma there are several grasses that will help to bind the soil but will spread with moderation, traits that make them desirable as meadow grasses. Beware of turf grasses and many tall, cool-season annual grasses that will crowd out the wildflowers. Some of the best native grasses to grow in the meadow are:

Bothriochloa sacchariodes	silver bluestem
Bouteloua gacilis	blue grama
Buchloe dactyloides	buffalo grass
Panicum virgatum	switchgrass
Sorghastrum nutans	Indian grass
Schizachyrium scoparium	
(same as *Andropogon scoparius*)	little bluestem

SEASONAL BLOOM

You can have good color in your meadow during all parts of the growing season, if you pay some attention to the blooming times of the different species. The following lists should help you find some favorites for each season. There will be great variation as to actual time of bloom depending on growing conditions, local weather, and when the seeds were sown or when the plants were set out. These are general guidelines. As always, use as many native species as possible (marked with an *).

SPRING:

*Aquilegia canadensis	columbine
Arabis alpina	rock cress
Aurinia saxatilis	basket of gold
*Castilleja indivisa	Texas paintbrush
*Castilleja integra	grassland paintbrush
*Castilleja sessiflora	downy paintbrush
Centaurea cyanus X	bachelor's buttons
Cerastium bierbersteinii	snow in summer
Claytonia virginica	spring beauty
Consolida orientalis (same as Delphinium ajacis)	rocket larkspur
Dianthus barbatus	sweet William
Eschscholzia californica	California poppy
Geranium maculatum	wild geranium
*Iris cristata	dwarf crested iris
Linaria maroccana	spurred snapdragon
*Linum perenne lewisii	blue flax
*Lupinus subcarnosus	bluebonnet
*Lupinus texensis	bluebonnet
Nemophila menziesii	baby blue eyes
Papaver rhoeas	corn poppy
*Penstemon digitalis	beard tongue
Phacelia campanularia	desert bell
*Phlox drummondii	annual phlox
*Sisyrinchium angustifolium	blue-eyed grass
Viola cornuta	Johnny-jump-up

SUMMER:

Achillea millefolium	yarrow
Achillea millefolium rubra	red yarrow
Ammi majus	bishop's flower
Anagallis arvensis	pimpernel
Arabis alpina	rock cress
*Asclepias incarnata	swamp milkweed
*Asclepias tuberosa	butterfly weed
*Baptisia australis	false indigo
Belamcanda chinensis	blackberry lily
*Campanula rotundifolia	bluebell
Centaurea cyanus	bachelor's button
Cerastium bierbersteinii	snow in summer
Chrysanthemum leucanthemum	ox-eye daisy
Cichorium intybus	chicory
Coreopsis lanceolata	lance-leaved coreopsis
*Coreopsis tinctoria	annual coreopsis

Cosmos bipinnatus	cosmos
Cosmos sulphureus	orange cosmos
Daucus carota	Queen Anne's lace
*Delphinium virescens	prairie larkspur
Dianthus barbatus	sweet William
*Dodecatheon pulchellum	western shooting star
Echinacea purpurea	purple coneflower
*Epilobium angustifolium	fireweed
Erigeron speciosus	Oregon fleabane
Eschscholzia californica	California poppy
Gaillardia aristata	Indian blanket
*Gaillardia pulchella	annual Indian blanket
Gazania rigens	treasure flower
Gypsophila elegans	annual baby's breath
Gypsophila paniculata	baby's breath
*Helenium autumnale	sneezeweed
*Helianthus annuus	sunflower
Iberis umbellata	candytuft
*Ipomopsis rubra	standing cypress
Lathyrus latifolius	sweet pea
*Liatris pycnostachya	blazing star
Linaria maroccana	spurred snapdragon
Lupinus perennis	lupine
Lychnis chalcedonica	Maltese cross
*Machaeranthera tanacetifolia	prairie aster
*Mirabilis multiflora	wild four o'clock
*Monarda citriodora	lemon mint
*Monarda fistulosa	bergamot
*Oenothera biennis	evening primrose
*Oenothera missouriensis	sundrops
Papaver rhoeas	corn poppy
*Phlox drummondii	annual phlox
*Ratibida columnaris	prairie coneflower
*Rudbeckia hirta	black-eyed Susan
*Salvia coccinea	scarlet sage
Silene armeria	catchfly
*Solidago odora	scented goldenrod
Thymus serpyllum	creeping thyme
*Tradescantia ohiensis	spiderwort
Trifolium incarnatum	crimson clover
Venidium fastuosum	African daisy
*Verbena bipinnatifida	verbena
Viola cornuta	Johnny-jump-up

FALL:

Achillea millefolium	yarrow
Asclepias incarnata	swamp milkweed
Aster ericoides	aster
Aster lineariifolius	aster
Belamcanda chinensis	blackberry lily
Bidens aristosa	tickseed sunflower
Echinacea purpurea	purple coneflower
Gypsophila paniculata	baby's breath
Helianthus annuus	sunflower
Helianthus maximiliani	Maximilian sunflower
Liatris punctata	dotted gayfeather
Machaeranthera tanacetifolia	prairie aster
Oenothera biennis	evening primrose
Solidago altissima	tall goldenrod
Solidago sempervirens	seaside goldenrod

ALL-ANNUAL MIXTURE

For those who love color and want to replant yearly, a mixture of all annuals will present a meadow with a riot of color from spring until fall. Although many species will reseed, to be assured of a good display, you should collect or purchase seeds and replant every year. This is the least natural kind of meadow, but in some circumstances, it is a goody way to have a naturalized look. By sowing seeds annually, you can be assured of good color and diversity in the meadow every year without having to wait for the slower perennial plants to get established.

Ammi majus	bishop's flower
Anagallis arvensis	pimpernel
Bidens aristosa	tickseed flower
Centaurea cyanus X	bachelor's button
Coreopsis tinctoria	annual coreopsis
Cosmos bipinnatus	cosmos
Cosmos sulphureus	orange cosmos
Dracopis amplexicaulis (same as *Rudbeckia amplexicaulis*)	coneflower
Eschscholzia californica	California poppy
Gypsophila elegans	annual baby's breath
Helianthus annuus	sunflower
Linaria maroccana	spurred snapdragon
Lupinus texensis	bluebonnet
Machaeranthera tanacetifolia	prairie aster
Mentzelia decapetala	blazing star
Nemophila menziesii	baby blue eyes
Papaver rhoeas	corn poppy
Phacelia campanularia	desert bell

*Phlox drummondii   annual phlox
Silene armeria   catchfly
Trifolium incarnatum   crimson clover
Vendium fastuosum   African daisy

SHORT MEADOW PLANTS

When you live in an area that has strict lawn laws based on height, you might consider using dwarf or naturally low-growing plants. Small and low-growing plants are also useful for very small meadow areas or those that are closely confined. Heights will vary depending on growth conditions, but on the whole these species grow no taller than 24 inches.

Achillea millefolium rubra	12-24 in. red yarrow
Anagallis arvensis	6-12 in. pimpernel
*Aster lineariifolius	24 in. aster
Aurinia saxatilis	6-12 in. basket of gold
*Campanula rotundifolia	10-15 in. bluebell
*Castilleja integra	6-18 in. grassland paintbrush
*Castilleja sessiflora	6-18 in. downy paintbrush
Cerastium bierbersteinii	8 in. snow in summer
Chrysanthemum leucanthemum	12-24 in. ox-eye daisy
*Claytonia virginica	4-6 in. spring beauty
Coreopsis lanceolata	24 in. lance-leaved coreopsis
Dianthus barbatus	24 in. sweet William
*Dracopis amplexicaulis (same as Rudbeckia amplexicaulis)	20 in. coneflower
Erigeron speciosus	24 in. Oregon fleabane
Eschscholzia californica	12 in. California poppy
Gaillardia aristata	18-24 in. Indian blanket
*Gaillardia pulchella	12-24 in. annual Indian blanket
Gazania rigens	12 in. treasure flower
Geranium maculatum	12-24 in. wild geranium
Gypsophila elegans	12-20 in. annual baby's breath
Lathyrus latifolius	trailing vine, sweet pea
*Linum perenne lewisii	24 in. blue flax
*Lupinus texensis	12 in. bluebonnet
Lychnis chalcedonica	24 in. Maltese cross
*Machaeranthera tanacetifolia	18 in. prairie aster
Nemophila maculata	6 in. five spot
Nemophila menziesii	10 in. baby blue eyes
*Oenothera missouriensis	20 in. sundrops
*Phlox drummondii	20 in. annual phlox
*Phlox pilosa	24 in. western phlox
*Salvia coccinea	24 in. scarlet sage
Silene armeria	24 in. catchfly

*Sisyrinchium angustifolium	6-10 in. blue-eyed grass
Thymus serpyllum	3 in. creeping thyme
Trifolium incarnatum	8-14 in. crimson clover
Venidium fastuosum	24 in. African daisy
Viola cornuta	4-6 in. Johnny-jump-up

PLANTS THAT TOLERATE VERY DRY CONDITIONS

Because so much of this region receives little rainfall, it is best to use species that can withstand dry conditions. Although all the plants on the list below can do without much water, these species have other growth requirements that may be very different from one another. Be sure to check soil and temperature requirements for each before planting. Even if a species is listed as drought tolerant, the seeds need moisture to germinate, and young plants need moisture to establish themselves. Once established, they should be able to do with very little water. As always, use as many native species as possible.

Ammi majus	bishop's flower
*Argemone aurantica	prickly poppy
Argemone hispida	white prickly poppy
*Argemone mexicana	yellow prickly poppy
Centaurea cyanus X	bachelor's button
Cerastium bierbersteinii	snow in summer
Cichorium intybus X	chicory
Eschscholzia californica	California poppy
Gaillardia aristata	Indian blanket
*Gaillardia pulchella	annual Indian blanket
Gazania rigens	treasure flower
*Helianthus annuus	sunflower
*Helianthus maximiliani	Maximilian sunflower
Mentzelia decapetala	blazing star
Phacelia campanularia	desert bell
*Ratibida columnaris	prairie coneflower
*Rudbeckia hirta	black-eyed Susan

PLANTS FOR CUTTING

To some people, the best aspect of having a meadow area is the number of cut flowers that it makes readily available. Even a small area can yield an abundant supply of cut flowers throughout the growing season. For tips on treating cut flowers see Chapter 6.

*Aquilegia canadensis	columbine
*Asclepias tuberosa	butterfly weed
*Aster ericoides	aster
*Aster lineariifolius	aster

Aster novae-angliae	New England aster
Centaurea cyanus X	bachelor's button
Chrysanthemum leucanthemum	ox-eye daisy
Coreopsis lanceolata	lance-leaved coreopsis
*Coreopsis tinctoria	annual coreopsis
Cosmos bipinnatus	cosmos
Cosmos sulphureus	orange cosmos
Daucus carota X	Queen Anne's lace
Erigeron speciosus	Oregon fleabane
Gaillardia aristata	Indian blanket
*Gaillardia pulchella	annual Indian blanket
Gypsophila elegans	annual baby's breath
Gypsophila paniculata	baby's breath
*Helenium autumnale	sneezeweed
*Helianthus annuus	sunflower
*Liatris aspera	rough blazing star
*Liatris punctata	dotted gayfeather
*Liatris pycnostachya	prairie blazing star
*Lupinus texensis	bluebonnet
*Phlox pilosa	western phlox
*Ratibida columnaris	prairie coneflower
*Rudbeckia hirta	black-eyed Susan
Venidium fastuosum	African daisy

PLANTS TO ATTRACT BIRDS AND BUTTERFLIES

Birds and butterflies will find your meadow, just as they do any area with a profusion of flowers. However, if you would like to plant a few extra species that birds (particularly hummingbirds) and butterflies are especially attracted to, choose some of the following.

Achillea millefolium	yarrow
Ammi majus	bishop's flower
*Aquilegia canadensis	columbine
*Asclepias tuberosa	butterfly weed
Aurinia saxatilis	basket of gold
Centaurea cyanus	bachelor's button
Chrysanthemum leucanthemum	ox-eye daisy
Coreopsis lanceolata	lance-leaved coreopsis
Cosmos bipinnatus	cosmos
Daucus carota X	Queen Anne's lace
Dianthus barbatus	sweet William
*Helianthus annuus	sunflower
*Helianthus maximiliani	Maximilian sunflower
*Ipomopsis rubra	standing cypress
*Liatris species	blazing stars
*Monarda fistulosa	bergamot

Salvia coccinea   scarlet sage
Trifolium incarnatum   crimson clover

DATA FROM MEADOW PROJECTS

(1) Location: Texas

Description: ¼ acre of flat, dry area with alkaline soil.

Soil preparation: To reduce the problem with weeds, the soil was disturbed as little as possible. The soil was loosened by raking.

Planting: Seeds obtained from a commercial seed company were broadcast at the rate of ten pounds per acre. The area was then raked lightly to obtain better soil/seed contact. In those areas where the seeds were still visible, bagged compost was used as a mulch to cover lightly. The surface was then firmed with a hand-pushed, water-filled sod roller.

Maintenance: The plants were watered until they became established and then only when they showed water stress. Selective spraying and weeding controls aggressive weed species, and the area is mowed annually during mid-summer after the seeds have ripened.

Dominant wildflowers: bluebonnet, phlox, pink primrose, coreopsis, annual gaillardia, lemon mint, black-eyed Susan, Mexican hat, Maximilian sunflower.

(2) Location: Texas

Description: flat area of approximately 4,800 square feet; alkaline soil.

Soil preparation: Flail mowing was done to scarify the soil.

Planting: A commercial mixture of seeds was spread by a cyclone spreader and by hand broadcasting. The amount of seed used was based on the recommendations of the seed company. After seeding the area was raked and then tamped with a lawn roller.

Maintenance: After the plants were established, the area was not watered. Annual mowing was done in October.

Dominant wildflowers: black-eyed Susan, standing cypress, annual phlox, annual gaillardia, Maximilian sunflower, blazing star, evening primrose, goldenrod species.

RESOURCES

INSTITUTIONS AND ORGANIZATIONS

The following list includes institutions and organizations within Texas and Oklahoma that might be able to give you additional advice on estblishing meadow areas or growing native plants. In addition, check with your county extension agencies, state governments, local Soil Conservation Society chapters, and local garden clubs.

Oklahoma

> The Oklahoma Native Plant Society
> Route 1, Box 157
> Durant, Oklahoma 74701

Texas

Austin Nature Center
401 Deep Eddy
Austin, Texas 78703

Beautify Texas Council
P. O. Box 2251
Austin, Texas 78768

Brazos County Arboretum
College Station, Texas 77840

Chihuahuan Desert Research Institute
P. O. Box 1334
Alpine, Texas 79803

Greenhills Environmental Center
7575 Wheatland Re.
Dallas, Texas 77024

The Houston Arboretum and Nature Center
4501 Woodway Dr.
Houston, Texas 77024

Mercer Arboretum
22306 Aldine-Westfield Rd.
Humble, Texas 77338

The National Wildflower Research Center
2600 FM 973 North
Austin, Texas 78725

The Native Plant Society of Texas
P. O. Box 23836
Texas Women's University Station
Denton, Texas 76204

San Antonio Botanical Center
555 Funston Place
San Antonio, Texas 78209

South Texas Plant Materials Center
Caesar Kleberg Wildlife Research Institute
Texas A and I Unviersity
P. O. Box 218
Kingville, Texas 78363

Texas A and M University
Department of Horticulture
College Station, Texas 77840

Texas Department of Highways
Landscape Division
11th and Brazos
Austin, Texas 78701

Texas Wildflower Preservation Society
Department of Biology
East Texas State University
Commerce, Texas 75428

Wild Basin Wilderness Preserve
P. O. Box 13455
Austin, Texas 78711

NURSERIES AND SEED COMPANIES

The nurseries and seed companies listed below sell wildflower seeds. These are not recommendations, but merely possible sources. No research has determined the quality of materials offered.

Aldridge Nursery, Inc.
Route 1, Box 8
Von Ormy, Texas 78073

Alexanders Bluebonnet Seed Co.
8917 Sam Carter Dr.
Austin, Texas 78736

Containerzied Plants, Inc.
Route 5, Box 143
Brenham, Texas 77833

Greenhills Center
Geoffrey Stanford
7575 Wheatland Rd.
Dallas, Texas 75249

Green Horizons
500 Thompson Dr.
Kerrville, Texas 78028

Hilltop Herb Farm
Box 866
Cleveland, Texas 75215

Douglass W. King Co., Inc.
P. O. Box 20320
San Antonio, Texas 78286

J'Don Seeds International
P. O. Box 10998-533
Austin, Texas 78766

Lone Star Growers (wholesale only)
Route 9, Box 220
San Antonio, Texas 78227

Magnolia Seed, Hardware,
and Implement Co.
8401 Sovereign Row
Box 5650
Dallas, Texas 75222

Meanwhile Farm
Box 240
Wimberley, Texas 78676

Melot's, Inc.
P. O. Box 154
Bethany, Oklahoma 73008

Mosteller Seeds
2205 Bitter Creek
Austin, Texas 78744

Native Design Nursery
16318 Bandera Highway
Helotes, Texas 78023

Native Plant Nursery Oakhill
Burford L. Westlund
792 Oakdale Dr.
Austin, Texas 78745

Native Son Nursery
Sheryl McLaughlin
507 Lockhart Dr.
Austin, Texas 78704

Nicholson Seed
2700 Logan
Box 154-87
Dallas, Texas 75215

Sharp Brothers Seed Co.
4378 Canyon Dr.
Amarillo, Texas 79109

Swamp Fox Herbs
P. O. Box 33105
Austin, Texas 78764

Valley View Nursery
Box 400, Route 1
Park Hill, Oklahoma 74451

George Warner Seed Co., Inc.
P. O. Box 1448
Hereford, Texas 79045

Wildseed, Inc.
John R. Thomas
16526 Park Row Blvd.
Houston, Texas 77084

SELECTED READING

Abbott, Carol. *How to Know and Grow Texas Wildflowers*. Green Horizons Press.

Ajilvsgi, Geyata. *Wildflowers of Texas*. Shearer Pub.; 1984.

Correll, Donovan, and Marshall C. Johnson. *Manual of the Vascular Plants of Texas*.

Gould, Dr. Frank. *Common Texas Grasses*. Texas A & M University Press; 1978.

Gould, Dr. Frank. *The Grasses of Texas*. Texas A & M University Press; 1975.

Irwin, Howard S., and Mary M. Wills. *Roadside Flowers of Texas*. University of Texas Press; 1961.

Jones, Fred B. *Flora of the Texas Coastal Bend*. Rob and Bessie Welder Wildlife Foundation, Sinton, TX; 1975.

Loughmiller, Lynn and Campbell. *Texas Wildflowers: A Field Guide*. University of Texas Press. Austin, TX; 1984.

Ryan, Julie E., and Sally Wasowski. *Landscaping with Native Texas Plants*. Texas Monthly Press, Austin, Texas; 1985.

Warnock, Dr. Barton H. *Wildflowers of the Big Bend*. Sul Ross State University, Alpine, TX 79830.

Warnock, Dr. Barton H. *Wildflowers of the Guadalupe Mountains and the Sand Dune Country, Texas*. Sul Ross State University; 1974.

CHAPTER FIFTEEN

The
West

Colorado, Idaho, western Kansas, Montana, western Nebraska,
northern Nevada, North Dakota, eastern Oregon, South Dakota, Utah,
eastern Washington, Wyoming

CONDITIONS TO CONSIDER IN THE WEST

NATURALLY OCCURRING PLANT COMMUNITIES

The eastern edge of this region is tall-grass prairie, though much of this
area is now used for agriculture, supporting crops such as corn and wheat.
The original flora was dominated by a few species of grasses: big
bluestem, little bluestem, prairie cordgrass, needlegrass, June grass, and
prairie dropseed. Spring brings a quantity of wildflowers, lending exciting
color and diversity to the grassland. Rainfall averages between 15 and 20
inches per year.

Just to the west of the tall-grass prairie is an area called short-grass
plains or mixed prairie. This is a tremendous slope, rising in elevation
from 2,500 feet on the eastern edge to 5,000 feet in the west where it
meets the Rocky Mountains. The soils are heavier and less fertile, and
precipitation is very low, usually occurring in the summer. The timing of
the rains makes for a long season of wildflowers. The vegetation is much
more open than in the tall-grass prairie and is dominated by buffalo grass,
grama grass, and little bluestem.

West of this dry plain, the vegetation changes as dramatically as the
elevation. Precipitation is very low at the base of the mountains, averaging
10 to 20 inches annually, but it can reach an average of 40 inches or more
in high mountain valleys, usually falling in the form of snow.

West of the Rocky Mountains precipitation again is drastically reduced. The region between the mountains and the west Pacific Northwest
is considered a cold desert; precipitation averages between 5 and 20 inches
annually, and it usually comes in winter and not during the growing
season. In addition to the low precipitation, hot summer temperatures,
and cold winters, the possibility of frost in any month makes growing a
meadow garden a challenge in this area. Because of the adverse conditions

of the summer and winter months, most of the wildflowers bloom during the spring. The soils are generally alkaline and contain high concentrations of salt. This area consists of steep, dry mountains and deep basins. The constant changes in elevation create quite a variety of growing conditions, and it is possible to grow a number of plants with very diverse needs within a small area. The dominant vegetation, sagebrush covers millions of acres. Because of its location — between the Rocky Mountains on the eastern edge and the Sierra Nevadas and Cascade Mountains to the west — this region is sometimes called an intermountain grassland.

NOXIOUS WEEDS

Watering to give life to a meadow will also give life to a variety of unwanted guests, some of which might even become serious pests. Generally, the biggest problems with weeds will be from the perennial grasses such as Kentucky bluegrass, cheat grass, meadow fescue, and quackgrass. Other weeds that might give you problems are cheeseweed, bindweed, thistles, pigweed, lamb's quarters, mulleins, white and yellow sweet clover, and alfalfa.

WHEN TO PLANT

With the variety of weather conditions present in this area and the possibility of frost during so much of the year, temperature is not as important a factor in deciding when to plant as is available precipitation. If you have water available, you can plant during spring, early summer, or fall. If you plant in spring, mid-April to mid-May are usually the best times to plant, depending on your altitude and the length of your growing season. A fall planting should be done as late as the soil can be worked. Again, depending on the altitude and subsequent growing season, November seems to be the best month. In the arid intermountain grassland, a fall sowing is recommended to take advantage of the autumn and winter rains. Sowing in the fall and exposing the seeds to winter conditions will help to break dormancy of many seeds that might otherwise need pretreatment.

MAINTENANCE

Hand weeding of undesirable species will be necessary for the first year or two. Supplying enough water to get seedlings and plants established is very important. The amount of water needed thereafter will depend on local weather conditions and on the type of plants used. A good rule of thumb is to water when the plants begin to show stress. An annual mowing of the area is necessary to help control weeds and to prevent dense vegetation from shading out smaller, sun-loving plants.

PROBLEM WILDFLOWERS

The following wildflowers are sometimes included within a seed mixture, but they might become invasive and overly aggressive and thus outgrow their welcome in this region. This is not to say that they cannot be used, but be aware of the possibility of their becoming a pest and use them wisely. Check your local noxious weed list, and avoid planting any species listed.

Achillea millefolium	yarrow
Centaurea species	knapweed, bachelor's button
Chrysanthemum leucanthemum	ox-eye daisy
Daucus carota	Queen Anne's lace
Gypsophila paniculata	baby's breath
Lathyrus latifolius	sweet pea
Linaria genistifolia dalmatica	Dalmation toadflax
Linaria vulgaris	butter and eggs
Rudbeckia hirta	black-eyed Susan
Verbascum thapsus	mullein

MEADOW PLANTS THAT GROW IN THE WEST

Choosing a combination of wildflowers and grasses that will thrive in the harsh conditions presented in so many parts of the west is quite a challenge. Choose plants that are adaptable to drought conditions, to cut down on watering costs; that are suitable, so they will grow together compatibly and not choke one another out; and that are beautiful, so their presence will be a constant source of delight for you. The first step, of course, is to choose plants that will grow in your region. However, even this is difficult because the wonderful diversity and variety of growing conditions presented within this region make it impossible to know exactly what will and will not grow here. Your own backyard might contain just the right conditions to grow a plant that does not normally do well in your area. For this reason, don't hesitate to experiment and try some favorites, even if they are not on these lists. The following lists were based on recommendations from botanists and horticulturists from universities, botanical gardens, arboretums, and native plant societies, as well as the sage advice of many "dirt gardeners" who live in the West.

Although cultural requirements for the following species will vary tremendously, it is possible to grow each of these species somewhere within this region. Many of these species are not native to the western region; some are actually cultivated flowers rather than wildflowers. They were included on this list due to their presence within many commercial premixed wildflower blends. Species that are endangered, threatened, or difficult to obtain are not included on this list. On this list and those that follow, species native to the west are marked with an *; species that can become invasive are marked with an X; and unmarked species are non-native but generally non-invasive.

Achillea millefolium X	yarrow
Ammi majus	bishop's flower
Anagallis arvensis	pimpernel
Anemone occidentalis	chalice cup
Anemone patens	pasqueflower
Aquilegia caerulea	blue columbine
Aquilegia canadensis	columbine
Aquilegia chrysantha	golden columbine
Aquilegia flavescens	yellow columbine
Aquilegia formosa	scarlet columbine
Arabis alpina	rock cress
Argemone hispida	white prickly poppy
Asclepias tuberosa	butterfly weed
Aster novae-angliae	England aster
Aurinia saxatilis	basket of gold
Baptisia australis	false indigo
Camassia leichtlinii	coastal camas
Camassia quamash	camas
Campanula carpatica	bluebell
Campanula rotundifolia	bluebell
Castilleja coccinea	Indian paintbrush
Centaurea cyanus X	bachelor's button
Cerastium bierbersteinii	snow in summer
Cerastium tomentosum	snow in summer
Cheiranthus cheiri	wallflower
Chrysanthemum carinatum	painted daisy
Chrysanthemum coronarium	garland chrysanthemum
Chrysanthemum leucanthemum X	ox-eye daisy
Cichorium intybus	chicory
Clarkia amoena	farewell to spring
Clarkia pulchella	deerhorn clarkia
Claytonia lanceolata	spring beauty
Clematis columbiana	Columbia clematis
Consolida orientalis (same as *Delphinium ajacis*)	rocket larkspur
Coreopsis lanceolata	lance-leaved coreopsis
Coreopsis tinctoria	annual coreopsis
Cosmos bipinnatus	cosmos
Daucus carota X	Queen Anne's lace
Delphinium bicolor	delphinium
Delphinium cardinale	scarlet larkspur
Delphinium nelsonii	Nelson's larkspur
Dianthus barbatus	sweet William
Dianthus deltoides	maiden pink

Digitalis purpurea	foxglove
*Dodecatheon pulchellum	western shooting star
Echinacea angustifolia	pale purple coneflower
Echinacea purpurea	purple coneflower
*Epilobium angustifolium	fireweed
*Erigeron compositus	cutleaf fleabane
*Erigeron peregrinus	showy fleabane
*Erigeron speciosus	Oregon fleabane
*Eriogonum umbellatum	sulphur flower
*Eriophyllum lanatum	Oregon sunshine
Erysimum capitatum	wild wallflower
Erysimum hieraciifolium	Siberian wallflower
*Erythronium grandiflorum	fawn lily
*Erythronium hendersonii	Henderson's fawn lily
*Eschscholzia californica	California poppy
Eupatorium maculatum	Joe-pye weed
*Fritillaria lanceolata	mission bells
*Fritillaria pudica	yellow bell
*Gaillardia aristata	perennial gaillardia
Gaillardia pulchella	annual Indian blanket
Gazania rigens	treasure flower
Geranium maculatum	wild geranium
*Geranium viscosissimum	red wild geranium
*Geum triflorum	prairie smoke
Gilia aggregata	sky rocket
Gilia capitata	blue thimble flower
Gypsophila elegans	annual baby's breath
Gypsophila paniculata X	baby's breath
*Helenium autumnale	sneezeweed
*Helianthus angustifolius	sunflower
*Helianthus annuus	sunflower
Hesperis matronalis	dame's rocket
*Heuchera cylindrica	alum root
Iberis umbellata	candytuft
*Iris douglasiana	Douglas iris
*Iris missouriensis	blue flag iris
*Iris tenax	tough leaf iris
Lathyrus latifolius X	sweet pea
Lavatera trimestris	tree mallow
Layia platyglossa	tidy tips
*Liatris punctata	dotted gayfeather
Liatris pycnostachya	blazing star
Liatris scariosa	blazing star
Liatris spicata	blazing star
Linanthus grandiflorus	mountain phlox

Linaria maroccana	spurred snapdragon
Linum grandiflorum rubrum	red flax
Linum perenne lewisii	blue flax
Lobularia maritima	sweet alyssum
Lupinus perennis	lupine
Lupinus texensis	bluebonnet
Lychnis chalcedonica	Maltese cross
Machaeranthera tanacetifolia	prairie aster
Mentzelia decapetala	blazing star
Mimulus lewisii	monkey flower
Mirabilis jalapa	four o'clock
Monarda citriodora	lemon mint
Monarda didyma	bee balm
Monarda fistulosa	bergamot
Myosotis sylvatica	forget me not
Nemophila menziesii	baby blue eyes
Oenothera biennis	evening primrose
Oenothera caespitosa	gumbo lily
Oenothera cheiranthifolia	beach sundrops
Oenothera hookeri	evening primrose
Oenothera pallida	white evening primrose
Papaver nudicaule	Iceland poppy
Papaver rhoeas	corn poppy
Penstemon barbatus	scarlet beard tongue
Penstemon digitalis	beard tongue
Penstemon deustus	hot rock beard tongue
Penstemon fruticosus	shrubby beard tongue
Penstemon grandiflorus	beard tongue
Penstemon heterophyllus	violet beard tongue
Penstemon palmeri	Palmer beard tongue
Penstemon rupicola	red beard tongue
Penstemon rydbergii	Rydberg beard tongue
Penstemon serrulatus	Cascade beard tongue
Penstemon smallii	beard tongue
Petalostemon purpureum	prairie clover
Phacelia companularia	desert bell
Phacelia sericea	silky phacelia
Phlox divaricata	blue phlox
Phlox drummondii	annual phlox
Ratibida columnaris	prairie coneflower
Rudbeckia hirta X	black-eyed Susan
Salvia coccinea	scarlet sage
Silene armeria	catchfly
Sisyrinchium bellum	blue-eyed grass
Solidago canadensis	meadow goldenrod

Solidago nemoralis	gray goldenrod
Solidago odora	scented goldenrod
Stokesia laevis	Stoke's aster
Thymus serpyllum	creeping thyme
Tradescantia virginiana	spiderwort
Trifolium incarnatum	crimson clover
Verbena goodingii	verbena
*Verbena stricta	hoary vervain
Vernonia altissima	ironweed
Viola cornuta	Johnny-jump-up

THE TOP TEN

The following list is not designed as a balanced mixture of wildflowers and should not be used as such. The flowers included on this list are noted for their adaptability and reliability. They are all generally hardy and easy to grow from seed in this region.

Chrysanthemum leucanthemum	ox-eye daisy
Coreopsis tinctoria	annual coreopsis
*Gaillardia aristata	Indian blanket
Gaillardia pulchella	annual Indian blanket
*Helianthus annuus	sunflower
Layia platyglossa	tidy tips
*Linanthus grandiflorus	mountain phlox
Monarda citriodora	lemon mint
*Ratibida columnaris	prairie coneflower
Rudbeckia hirta	black-eyed Susan

GRASSES

When you plant sunny, naturalized areas, it is important to include some non-spreading grasses to fill niches that the wildflowers cannot fill. The grasses create an open feeling that adds to the charm of a meadow garden. In the West the fescues (sheep and tall fescue) help to bind the soil and provide food for many species of birds, yet they reproduce in moderation, making them a desirable meadow grass. The native grasses are almost all bunch grasses and are both attractive and non-spreading, though they are slow growing and take a while to get established. Some of the native grasses that you might try are listed below.

Andropogon gerardii	big bluestem
Boutelona curtipendula	side oats grama
Buchloe dactyloides	buffalo grass
Scizachyrium scoparium	
(same as *Andropogon scoparius*)	little bluestem
Sorghastrum nutans	Indian grass

SEASONAL BLOOM

You can have good color in your meadow during all parts of the growing season if you pay attention to the blooming times of the different species. The following lists should help you find some favorites for each season. There will be great variation as to actual time of bloom, however, depending on growing conditions, local weather, and when the seeds were sown or when the plants were set out. These are general guidelines. As always, use as many native species as possible (marked with an *).

SPRING:

*Anemone patens	pasqueflower
*Aquilegia caerulea	blue columbine
Aquilegia canadensis	columbine
*Aquilegia chrysantha	golden columbine
*Aquilegia formosa	Sitka columbine
Aurinia saxatilis	basket of gold
*Baptisia australis	false indigo
*Camassia leichtlinii	coastal camas
*Camassia quamash	camas
Centaurea cyanus X	bachelor's button
Cerastium bierbersteinii	snow in summer
Cheiranthus cheiri	wallflower
*Claytonia lanceolata	spring beauty
*Clematis columbiana	Columbia columbine
Collinsia heterophylla	Chinese houses
Consolida orientalis	
(same as *Delphinium ajacis*)	rocket larkspur
*Delphinium cardinale	scarlet larkspur
*Delphinium nelsonii	Nelson's larkspur
Dianthus barbatus	sweet William
*Erigeron compositus	cutleaf fleabane
Erysimum hieraciifolium	Siberian wallflower
*Erythronium grandiflorum	fawn lily
*Eschscholzia californica	California poppy
*Fritillaria lanceolata	mission bells
*Fritillaria pudica	yellow bell
Geranium maculatum	wild geranium
*Iris missouriensis	blue flag iris
*Iris tenax	tough leaf iris
Linaria maroccana	spurred snapdragon
*Linum perenne lewisii	blue flax
Lobularia maritima	sweet alyssum
Lupinus texensis	bluebonnet
Mentzelia decapetala	blazing star
Papaver rhoeas	corn poppy
*Penstemon digitalis	beard tongue

Penstemon smallii	beard tongue
*Phacelia sericea	silky phacelia
Phlox divaricata	blue phlox
*Sisyrinchium bellum	blue-eyed grass
Stokesia laevis	Stoke's aster
Viola cornuta	Johnny-jump-up

SUMMER:

Achillea millefolium X	yarrow
Ammi majus	bishop's flower
Anagallis arvensis	pimpernel
Arabis alpina	rock cress
*Asclepias tuberosa	butterfly weed
Baptisia australis	false indigo
*Campanula rotundifolia	bluebell
*Castilleja miniata	giant red paintbrush
Centaurea cyanus X	bachelor's button
Cerastium bierbersteinii	snow in summer
Chrysanthemum carinatum	painted daisy
Chrysanthemum coronarium	garland chrysanthemum
Chrysanthemum leucanthemum X	ox-eye daisy
Cichorium intybus	chicory
Clarkia amoena	farewell to spring
*Clarkia pulchella	deerhorn clarkia
Consolida orientalis (same as *Delphinium ajacis*)	rocket larkspur
Coreopsis lanceolata	lance-leaved coreopsis
Coreopsis tinctoria	annual coreopsis
Cosmos bipinnatus	cosmos
Daucus carota X	Queen Anne's lace
Dianthus barbatus	sweet William
Echinacea purpurea	purple coneflower
*Epilobium angustifolium	fireweed
*Erigeron peregrinus	showy fleabane
*Erigeron speciosus	Oregon fleabane
*Eriogonum umbellatum	sulphur flower
*Eriophyllum lanatum	Oregon sunshine
*Eschscholzia californica	California poppy
Eupatorium maculatum	Joe-pye weed
*Gaillardia aristata	Indian blanket
Gaillardia pulchella	annual Indian blanket
Gazania rigens	treasure flower
*Geranium viscosissimum	red wild geranium
*Geum triflorum	prairie smoke
*Helenium autumnale	sneezeweed

Helianthus annuus	sunflower
Iberis umbellata	candytuft
Lathyrus latifolius X	sweet pea
Lavatera trimestris	tree mallow
*Liatris punctata	dotted gayfeather
Liatris pycnostachya	blazing star
Liatris scariosa	blazing star
Liatris spicata	blazing star
Linaria maroccana	spurred snapdragon
Lobularia maritima	sweet alyssum
Lychnis chalcedonia	Maltese cross
*Machaeranthera tanacetifolia	prairie aster
*Mimulus lewisii	red monkey flower
Mirabilis jalapa	four o'clock
Monarda didyma	bee balm
Myosotis sylvatica	forget me not
Oenothera biennis	evening primrose
Oenothera pallida	white evening primrose
Papaver rhoeas	corn poppy
*Penstemon barbatus	scarlet beard tongue
*Penstemon deustus	hot rock beard tongue
*Penstemon fruticosus	shrubby beard tongue
*Penstemon palmeri	Palmer beard tongue
*Penstemon rydbergii	Rydberg beard tongue
*Penstemon serrulatus	Cascade beard tongue
Phlox drummondii	annual phlox
*Ratibida columnaris	prairie coneflower
Rudbeckia hirta X	black-eyed Susan
Salvia coccinea	scarlet sage
Silene armeria	catchfly
Solidago odora	scented goldenrod
Thymus serpyllum	creeping thyme
Tradescantia virginiana	spiderwort
Trifolium incarnatum	crimson clover
*Verbena stricta	hoary vervain
Vernonia altissima	ironweed
Viola cornuta	Johnny-jump-up

FALL:

Achillea millefolium X	yarrow
Aster novae-angliae	New England aster
Echinacea purpurea	purple coneflower
*Erigeron peregrinus	showy fleabane
*Eriogonum umbellatum	sulphur flower
*Helianthus annuus	sunflower

*Machaeranthera tanacetifolia	prairie aster
Oenothera biennis	evening primrose
*Solidago canadensis	meadow goldenrod
Solidago odora	scented goldenrod

PLANTS FOR HIGH ALTITUDES

The species listed below are especially adaptable to the high altitudes found in many parts of this region.

Achillea millefolium X	yarrow
*Aquilegia caerulea	Colorado columbine
*Camassia quamash	common quamash
*Campanula rotundifolia	bluebell
*Clematus columbiana	Columbia clematis
*Erigeron peregrinus	showy fleabane
*Eriophyllum lanatum	Oregon sunshine
*Erysimum capitatum	wild wallflower
*Erythronium grandiflorum	fawn lily
*Gaillarda aristata	Indian blanket
*Heuchera cylindrica	alum root
*Iris missouriensis	blue flag iris
*Linum perenne lewisii	blue flax
*Mimulus lewisii	red monkey flower
*Nemophila menziesii	baby blue eyes
*Oenothera caespitosa	gumbo lily
*Oenothera pallida	white evening primrose
*Penstemon fruticosus	shrubby beard tongue
*Penstemon heterophyllus	violet beard tongue
*Penstemon rupicola	red beard tongue
*Penstemon serrulatus	Cascade beard tongue
*Penstemon strictus	beard tongue
*Phacelia sericea	silky phacelia
*Ratibida columnaris	prairie coneflower
Rudbeckia hirta X	black-eyed Susan

PLANTS FOR CUTTING

To some people the best aspect of having a meadow area is the number of cut flowers it makes readily available. Even a small area can yield an abundant supply of cut flowers throughout the growing season.

Ammi majus	bishop's flower
Achillea millefolium X	yarrow
*Aquilegia caerulea	blue columbine
Aquilegia chrysantha	golden columbine
*Asclepias tuberosa	butterfly weed
Aster novae-angliae	New England aster

Centaurea cyanus X	bachelor's button
Chrysanthemum carinatum	painted daisy
Chrysanthemum leucanthemum X	ox-eye daisy
Coreopsis lanceolata	lance-leaved coreopsis
Coreopsis tinctoria	annual coreopsis
Cosmos bipinnatus	cosmos
Daucus carota X	Queen Anne's lace
Delphinium species	larkspurs
Echinacea purpurea	purple coneflower
Erigeron peregrinus	showy fleabane
Eriophyllum lanatum	Oregon sunshine
Erythronium hendersonii	Henderson's fawn lily
Gaillardia aristata	Indian blanket
Gaillardia pulchella	annual Indian blanket
Gilia capitata	blue thimble flower
Gypsophila elegans X	annual baby's breath
Gypsophila paniculata X	baby's breath
Helenium autumnale	sneezeweed
Helianthus annuus	sunflower
Heuchera cylindrica	alum root
Iris douglasiana	Douglas iris
Layia platyglossa	tidy tips
Lupinus species	lupines
Monarda citriodora	lemon mint
Phlox divaricata	blue phlox
Ratibida columnaris	prairie coneflower
Solidago nemoralis	goldenrod
Solidago odora	scented goldenrod

PLANTS THAT TOLERATE VERY DRY CONDITIONS

Because so much of this region receives little rainfall, you will be wise to plant species that are drought tolerant. Although all the species listed below can do with little water, these species have widely varying growth requirements. Be sure to check soil and temperature requirements for each species before planting. Even though the species is drought tolerant, the seeds need moisture to germinate and young plants need moisture to get established. As always, use as many species native to your region as possible.

Achillea millefolium X	yarrow
Ammi majus	bishop's flower
Argemone hispida	white prickly poppy
Centaurea cyanus X	bachelor's button
Cichorium intybus	chicory
Clarkia amoena	farewell to spring
Coreopsis tinctoria	annual coreopsis

Cosmos bipinnatus	cosmos
Echinacea purpurea	purple coneflower
*Erigeron compositus	cutleaf fleabane
*Eriogonum umbellatum	sulphur flower
*Eriophyllum lanatum	Oregon sunshine
*Eschscholzia californica	California poppy
*Gaillardia aristata	Indian blanket
Gaillardia pulchella	annual Indian blanket
Gazania rigens	treasure flower
*Geum triflorum	prairie smoke
Gilia capitata	blue thimble flower
*Helianthus annuus	sunflower
Layia platyglossa	tidy tips
Liatris spicata	blazing star
Linaria maroccana	spurred snapdragon
Linum grandiflorum rubrum	red flax
Lobularia maritima	sweet alyssum
Lupinus texensis	bluebonnet
Nemophila menziesii	baby blue eyes
*Ratibida columnaris	prairie coneflower
Rudbeckia hirta X	black-eyed Susan
Verbena goodingii	verbena

SHORT MEADOW PLANTS

For areas where lawn laws are a problem, one solution is to use only short-growing plants in your meadow. These species are also good to use in areas that are very small or closely confined. Environmental conditions for growing these plants will vary a great deal, so be sure to check on each species' requirements before choosing it for your meadow. Although the heights of plants vary enormously from one area to another due to differences in growing conditions, the following plants generally grow no taller than 24 inches.

Achillea millefolium rubra	12-24 in. red yarrow
Anagallis arvensis	6-21 in. pimpernel
Arabis alpina	16 in. rock cress
Aurinia saxatilis	6-12 in. basket of gold
*Camassia quamash	12-18 in. camas
*Campanula rotundifolia	10-15 in. bluebell
Campanula carpatica	12-24 in. bluebell
Castilleja coccinea	12-24 in. Indian paintbrush
Cheiranthus cheiri	24 in. wallflower
Chrysanthemum leucanthemum X	12-24 in. ox-eye daisy
Coreopsis lanceolata	24 in. lance-leaved coreopsis
Dianthus barbatus	24 in. sweet William
Dianthus deltoides	6-18 in. maiden pink

*Erigeron speciosus	24 in.	Oregon fleabane
*Eriogonum umbellatum	6 in.	sulphur flower
*Erythronium grandiflorum	4-12 in.	fawn lily
*Eschscholzia californica	12 in.	California poppy
*Fritillaria pudica	6 in.	yellow bell
*Gaillardia aristata	18-24 in.	Indian blanket
Gaillardia pulchella	12-24 in.	annual Indian blanket
Gazania rigens	12 in.	treasure flower
Geranium maculatum	12-24 in.	wild geranium
*Geum triflorum	12-18 in.	prairie smoke
Gilia capitata	24 in.	blue thimble flower
Gypsophila elegans	12-20 in.	annual baby's breath
*Iris missouriensis	12-18 in.	blue flag iris
*Iris tenax	18-24 in.	Oregon iris
Lathyrus latifolius X		trailing vine, sweet pea
Linum grandiflorum rubrum	14 in.	red flax
*Linum perenne lewisii	24 in.	blue flax
Lobularia maritima	12 in.	sweet alyssum
Lupinus perennis	24 in.	lupine
Lupinus texensis	12 in.	bluebonnet
Lychnis chalcedonica	24 in.	Maltese cross
*Machaeranthera tanacetifolia	18 in.	prairie aster
Myosotis sylvatica	6-15 in.	forget me not
Nemophila menziesii	10 in.	baby blue eyes
*Oenothera pallida	14 in.	white evening primrose
Papaver nudicaule	24 in.	Iceland poppy
Phlox drummondii	20 in.	annual phlox
Phlox divaricata	8-12 in.	blue phlox
Salvia coccinea	24 in.	scarlet sage
Silene armeria	24 in.	catchfly
Sisyrinchium bellum	24 in.	blue-eyed grass
Solidago nemoralis	24 in.	gray goldenrod
Stokesia laevis	24 in.	Stoke's aster
Thymus serpyllum	6 in.	creeping thyme
Tradescantia virginiana	24 in.	spiderwort
Trifolium incarnatum	8-14 in.	crimson clover
Viola cornuta	5-8 in.	Johnny-jump-up

PLANTS TO ATTRACT BIRDS AND BUTTERFLIES

Birds and butterflies will find your meadow, just as they do any area with a profusion of flowers. However, if you would like to plant a few extra species that birds (particularly hummingbirds) and butterflies are especially attracted to, choose some of the following.

*Aquilegia formosa	Sitka columbine
*Asclepias tuberosa	butterfly weed
Aster species	asters
Aurinia saxatilis	basket of gold
Chrysanthemum species	chrysanthemum
Cosmos bipinnatus	cosmos
Daucus carota X	Queen Anne's lace
Dianthus barbatus	sweet William
Gaillardia species	Indian blankets
Gilia aggregata	sky rocket
Gilia capitata	blue thimble flower
*Helianthus annuus	sunflower
Lobularia maritima	sweet alyssum
Penstemon species	penstemons
Phlox species	phlox
Salvia coccinea	scarlet sage

ALL-ANNUAL MIXTURE

For those who love color and want to replant yearly, a mixture of all annuals will present a meadow with a riot of color from spring until fall. Although many species will reseed, to be assured of a good display, you should collect or purchase seeds and replant every year. This is the least natural kind of meadow, but in some circumstances, it is a good way to have a naturalized look. By sowing seeds annually, you can be assured of good color and diversity in the meadow every year without having to wait for the slower perennial plants to become established. This type of meadow is particularly useful for short-term landscaping, as in an empty lot that you have access to for only a year or two.

Ammi majus	bishop's flower
Anagallis arvensis	pimpernel
Centaurea cyanus X	bachelor's button
Clarkia amoena	farewell to spring
*Clarkia pulchella	deerhorn clarkia
Consolida orientalis	
(same as Delphinium ajacis)	rocket larkspur
Coreopsis tinctoria	annual coreopsis
Cosmos bipinnatus	cosmos
*Dracopis amplexicaulis	
(same as Rudbeckia amplexicaulis)	coneflower
*Eschscholzia californica	California poppy
Gaillardia pulchella	annual Indian blanket
Gilia capitata	blue thimble flower
Gypsophila elegans X	annual baby's breath
*Helianthus annuus	sunflower
Lavatera trimestris	tree mallow

Layia platyglossa	tidy tips
Linaria maroccana	spurred snapdragon
Linum grandiflorum rubrum	red flax
Myosotis sylvatica	forget me not
Machaeranthera tanacetifolia	prairie aster
Nemophila menziesii	baby blue eyes
Papaver rhoeas	corn poppy
Phlox drummondii	annual phlox
Silene armeria	catchfly
Trifolium incarnatum	crimson clover

DATA FROM MEADOW PROJECTS

(1) Location: Utah

Description: three acres of irrigated rolling hillside with alkaline soil.

Soil preparation: The area was cleaned, scarified, and pulverized to a depth of at least 4 inches. Four inches of clean topsoil with a pH between 5.5 to 7.7 was brought in.

Planting: The area was seeded in October with a mechanical spreader at a rate of six pounds per 1,000 square feet. It was raked and hydromulched (combination of water and "silva mulch") at a rate of 1,400 pounds per acre. Fertilizer was applied with the hydromulching.

Maintenance: The area is watered at a rate of 2 inches per week during the summer months.

Dominant flowers: purple coneflower, lance-leaved coreopsis, California poppy, annual baby's breath, blue flax, white evening primrose, narrow leaf penstemon, Palmer penstemon.

Comments: Heavier hydromulching during planting would be helpful.

(2) Location: Colorado

Description: 315 square feet on a dry, flat surface.

Soil preparation: The area was rototilled.

Planting: A commercial mixture was used, with the emphasis on plants able to withstand dry conditions. Planting was done in mid-May.

Maintenance: The area was thoroughly watered until plants were established, and then was watered intermittent (approximately once a month) for the remainder of the summer. The area was mowed in mid-June, which slowed down the blooming times and had an unknown effect on the weeds.

Dominant flowers: alyssum, baby's breath, catchfly, corn poppy, California poppy, spurred snapdragon, corn flower, plains coreopsis, clarkias, tidy tips, annual gaillardia.

Comments: The area lost a great deal of diversity after two years, as dominant species took over.

(3) Location: Colorado

Description: dry, flat area.

Soil preparation: The soil was "ripped" in late February to uproot weeds and break up the soil.

Planting: A commercial mixture using seeds from plants 24 inches tall or less was applied at a rate of six pounds per acre with a mechanical spreader in mid-April. Overseeding was done in mid-May, and the area was mowed to a height of 3 inches in early October.

Maintenance: Several hours per week were spent controlling weeds during the summer. The area was kept watered through June.

First year flowering schedule: baby's breath dominant in June; corn poppy dominant in July; scarlet flax, prairie aster, candytuft, wallflower, rocket larkspur, coreopsis, blue flax, spurred snapdragon, African daisy, annual gaillardia, corn poppy, catchfly and black-eyed Susan present in August; *Rudbeckia* dominant in September.

Comments: The second year most of the perennials did well, including blue flax, wallflower, Maltese cross, black-eyed Susan, and corn poppy. Field clover presented a serious weed problem. Controlling the weeds in June is important.

RESOURCES

INSTITUTIONS AND ORGANIZATIONS

The following list includes institutions and organizations within the West that might be able to give you additional advice on growing native plants. In addition, check with your county extension agencies, state governments, local Soil Conservation Society chapters, and local garden clubs.

Colorado

The Denver Botanical Gardens
909 York St.
Denver, Colorado 80206

Idaho

Idaho Native Plant Society
Pahove Chapter
Box 9451
Boise, Idaho

Kansas

Kansas Landscape Arboretum
Route 5
Abilene, Kansas 67410

Nebraska

> Nebraska Statewide Arboretum
> 112 Forestry Sciences Laboratory
> University of Nebraska-East Campus
> Lincoln, Nebraska 68583-0823

Nevada

> Northern Nevada Native Plant Society-Pahove Chapter
> Box 8965
> Reno, Nevada 89507

Oregon

> Native Plant Society of Oregon
> 393 Fulvue Dr.
> Eugene, Oregon 97405

Utah

> Utah Botanical Garden
> 1817 North Main
> Farmington, Utah 84025

Washington

> Washington Native Plant Society
> Department of Botany
> University of Washington
> Seattle, Washington 98195

Wyoming

> Wyoming Native Plant Society
> 1603 Capitol Avenue
> Cheyenne, Wyoming 82001

NURSERIES AND SEED COMPANIES

The nurseries and seed companies listed below sell wildflowers. The quality of their materials, however, is unknown. These are not recommendations, but merely possible resources.

Applewood Seed Co.
P. O. Box 10761, Edgemont Station
Golden, Colorado 80401

Arrow Seed Co., Inc.
Box 722
Broken Bow, North Dakota 68822

Clifty View Nursery
Route 1, Box 509
Bonner Ferry, Idaho 83805

Dandelion Enterprises
3416 Tanarack Dr.
Boise, Idaho 83703

E.C. Moran
Box 327
Stanford, Montana 59479

Forestfarm
990 Tetherow Rd.
Williams, Oregon 97544

Globe Seed and Feed Co., Inc.
Box 445
Twin Falls, Idaho 83301

Grassland West Co.
P. O. Box A
Culdesac, Idaho 83524

Greer Gardens
1280 Goodpasture Island Rd.
Eugene, Oregon 97401

Jacklin Seed Company
W. 5300 Jacklin Ave.
Post Falls, Idaho 83854

McLaughlin's Seeds
Buttercup's Acre
Mead, Washington 99021-0550

Moses Lake Conservation District
Box 415, Route 3
Moses Lake, Washington 99837

Native Plants, Inc.
9180 South Wasatch Blvd.
Sandy, Utah 84092

Northplan Seed Producers
N.A.P.G. Inc.
P. O. Box 9107
Moscow, Idaho 83843

Northwest Biological Enterprises
23351 Boskey Dell Lane
West Linn, Oregon 97068

Plants of the Wild
P. O. Box 866
Tekoa, Washington 99033

Paul Schlitz
1098 Road 19, Star Route
Powell, Wyoming 82435

Winterfield Ranch Seed Co.
Box 97
Swan Valley, Idaho 83449

Carhart Feed and Seed
P. O. Box 55, Third and Guyman
Dove Creek, Colorado 81324

Treehouse Nursery
7450 Valmont Rd.
Boulder, Colorado 80301

SELECTED READING

Craighead, John J., Frank C. Craighead, Jr., and Ray J. Davis. *A Field Guide to Rocky Mountain Wildflowers.* Houghton Mifflin, Boston; 1963.

Kruckeberg, Arthur. *Gardening with Native Plants of the Pacific Northwest, an Illustrated Guide.* University of Washington Press, Seattle, Washington, and London, England; 1982.

Niehaus, Theodore F., and Charles L. Ripper. *A Field Guide to Pacific States Wildflowers.* Houghton Mifflin Co., Boston; 1976.

Ricketts, William. *Wildflowers of the United States* (Volume 6, Central, Mountain, and Plains States). McGraw Hill, New York; 1966.

Spellenberg, Richard. *The Audubon Society Field Guide to North American Wildflowers* (Western). Alfred A. Knopf, New York; 1979.

Sunset Magazine and Book Editors. *New Western Garden Book.* Sunset-Lane Publishing Co., 1979.

Part Three

Introduction

Some of our most beautiful native plants are the meadow wildflowers. Many of these wildflowers, such as black-eyed Susans and ox-eye daisies are quite common. However, when we plant them from seed and nurture them as they grow, they tend to take on a new charm for us. When you plant a meadow garden, you may find that your attitude about many of these common wildflowers changes, as you discover the beauty inherent in all flowers, no matter how common. Discovering beauty in a hardy flower is much easier than trying to find it in a beautiful and unusual, but temperamental, species that does not want to grow.

All the wildflowers are adapted to environmental conditions within their natural range, but only if they are growing in an area similar to their natural habitat. For example, butterfly weed grows easily in Georgia, but only where it gets good drainage and plenty of sun. In a moist, woody area, it simply will not thrive. When you cultivate wildflowers, the best rule of thumb is to mimic the plant's natural habitat as closely as possible.

Knowing about the individual wildflowers, their cultural requirements, when they bloom, what color they are, how tall they get, and other physical characteristics, is important in creating a well-balanced meadow garden. When you are cooking, you don't throw together different kinds of ingredients just because you like each of them. You have to pay attention to how they go together and how they complement one another. The same is true of planting a meadow garden. Plant the wildflowers that you like best, but only if their growing requirements are similar and if they blend together well. Try some different species to spice up your meadow, but stick to a good basic recipe of native wildflowers that grow easily and are compatible with one another.

Horticultural knowledge about our native plants is increasing at a wonderful rate — but never fast enough. As we begin to understand more about our wildflowers we will know more about how to grow them, where they will grow best, and the most effective means of propagation. The following information was compiled from research by experts in every region of the country. However, it is from you, the wildflower gardener, that the best information will come. As you learn more about growing the wildflowers that can be found in your region, share this knowledge with others. The native plants represent a treasure house of potential wealth in agriculture, medicine, and horticulture. Take part in the fun of discovering this treasure.

Yarrow

BOTANICAL NAME: *Achillea millefolium* (a-KILL-ee-ah mil-eh-FO-lee-um)

COMMON NAME: yarrow

FAMILY: Compositae

GROWING RANGE: all regions of the United States (it can become invasive and difficult to control in several areas)

NATURAL RANGE: Europe and western Asia

BLOOMS: May — September

HEIGHT: 36 inches

COLOR: white

TYPE: perennial

DESCRIPTION: The attractive dark green leaves are finely dissected and almost fernlike. They are quite aromatic, especially when crushed. The blossoms are white or cream colored and occur in clusters at the top of the stems.

ENVIRONMENTAL PREFERENCE: This plant needs full sun but can easily adapt to either dry or moist conditions. When it has become established, it is quite drought tolerant. Although able to grow in many different type of soils, it seems to prefer a light soil. A soil that is too rich produces abundant foliage but smaller flowers. The plant is hardy to -30° F.

PROPAGATION: The easiest and fastest method of propagation is plant division. The parent plants produce an abundance of strong white rhizomes which form colonies that can be easily divided. It is best to plant these divisions in early spring or during the fall months. Space them 6 to 12 inches apart, and set the rhizomes ½ inch deep. To plant seeds in a flat, sow sparingly on the surface of the soil because light is necessary for germination. Keep the soil evenly moist until germination occurs. The plant rarely self-sows, but it spreads readily by underground runners. Planting rate for a pure stand is one pound per acre.

The yarrows are native to Europe but have naturalized quite well throughout the United States. This plant is exceptionally hardy, and established colonies can take more abuse than grass. It is an excellent plant to use on hillsides and areas that need erosion control, because the rhizomes form mats that help to hold the soil in place. The plant does have a real tendency to become invasive in certain areas. Regions in which it seems to be a potential problem include the Midwest, mountain regions, the Northeast, the Southeast, and the West. Be aware of this potential and use the plant sparingly. Picking the faded blossoms will help keep the plant from looking too weedy and will help prolong the blooming period.

The aromatic leaves have been used for centuries for medicinal purposes. They were most frequently used to stanch the flow of blood from a wound, a use reflected in its many names such as woundwort, nosebleed, bloodwort, staunchgrass, and staunchweed. Modern research has proven that the leaves contain chemicals that are effective in helping blood to clot more quickly. The leaves were also made into salves and solutions used to soothe bruises and burns and to cure earaches.

The name *Achillea* is from the Greek hero Achilles who was said to carry the plant with him always to treat wounded soldiers.

OTHER SPECIES: *A. millefolium rubra.* The red yarrow grows to a height of only 18 to 24 inches and does not seem to be quite as aggressive as the wild white form. Propagation methods are similar to the white form. Planting rate is one pound per acre.

A. filipendulina. Gold yarrow or fernleaf yarrow differs from the *millefolium* in that the leaves are gray green, slightly hairy, and finely dissected. It grows taller than the other varieties, often reaching a height of 60 inches. The flowers occur in heads that are 4 to 6 inches across and are a lovely gold yellow color. When planted, they should be spaced 18 inches apart and should be divided after four years to maintain vigor. Propagation techniques are similar to that of *A. millefolium.* Suggested planting rate is ½ pound per acre.

BOTANICAL NAME: *Ammi majus* (AM-mee MAY-jus)
COMMON NAME: Bishop's flowers
FAMILY: Umbelliferae
GROWING RANGE: all regions of the United States
NATURAL RANGE: northeastern Africa and Eurasia
BLOOMS: June — August
HEIGHT: 36 inches
COLOR: white
TYPE: annual
DESCRIPTION: The leaves are finely dissected with sharply toothed margins. The blossoms occur in terminal umbels that are up to 6 inches across. The petals are shorter than the stamen.
ENVIRONMENTAL PREFERENCE: Other than requiring full sun, this plant is not particular about its growing conditions. It can withstand soil that is light or heavy and even sterile. Once established, its water requirements are minimal.
PROPAGATION: Bishop's flowers starts from seed very easily and also reseeds successfully. Although it looks very much like Queen Anne's lace (*Dancus carota*), the two plants are in different genera and should not be confused. *Ammi majus* rarely becomes as aggressive or weedy looking as *Daucus carota*. Even so, within a mixture it should be used sparingly. The plant has naturalized throughout North America and is used extensively in the cut-flower trade. Planting rate is two pounds per acre.

Bishop's flowers

This European native has flowers that are good to use in bouquets and flower arrangements. The airy blossoms add nice texture to the meadow.

Scarlet pimpernel

BOTANICAL NAME: *Anagallis arvensis* (an-ah-GAL-iss ar-VEN-sis)
COMMON NAME: scarlet pimpernel
FAMILY: Primulaceae
GROWING RANGE: all regions of the United States (may be difficult to control in some areas)
NATURAL RANGE: Europe
BLOOMS: June — August
HEIGHT: 4 — 12 inches
COLOR: orange to scarlet
TYPE: annual
DESCRIPTION: This plant is rather sprawling and has low branches. Although the starlike flowers are tiny (only ¼ inch across), they are profuse.
ENVIRONMENTAL PREFERENCE: Pimpernel will grow in light or heavy soil but seems to prefer sand. It will grow either in full sun or partial shade and needs little water.
PROPAGATION: It grows easily from seed, germinating best at a temperature of 65 to 75° F. The seeds will germinate in ten to twenty days. Suggested planting rate is four pounds per acre.

This highly adaptable little plant has been called poor man's weatherglass or shepherd's clock because the small flowers close up during cloudy weather and in the late afternoon. The plant was used frequently in home remedies and was reputed to be a cure for melancholy. The genus name refers to this, for *Anagallis* is from the Greek word meaning "to delight" or "to make laughter." Scarlet pimpernel was sometimes used as a symbol for assignation and change. The name pimpernel is from the Latin word *piperinella*, which means "little peppers" for the seeds of the plant look like pepper seeds. Touching the leaves often causes a rash on the skin.

White and blue forms of this plant are also available.

BOTANICAL NAME: *Aquilegia canadensis* (ak-qui-LEE-jee-ah can-ah-DEN-sis)
COMMON NAME: columbine
FAMILY: Ranunculaceae
GROWING RANGE: all regions of the United States
NATURAL RANGE: Nova Scotia to Florida; west to Minnesota and Tennessee

BLOOMS: April — June
HEIGHT: 36 inches
COLOR: red and yellow
TYPE: perennial
DESCRIPTION: The flowers are drooping and bell-like with five long spurs pointing upwards, and they are often as long as 2 inches. The leaves are divided many times.
ENVIRONMENTAL PREFERENCE: This plant is often found in the wild on steep slopes and in dry, open areas. Under cultivation, similar conditions are beneficial, though it will not tolerate overly dry or soggy soils. It prefers slightly acidic to neutral soil that is rich in humus with good drainage. It will take full sun or light shade. Do not plant columbine in too rich a soil: in rich soil it will yield lush foliage and inferior flowers.
PROPAGATION: Because the plant does not divide or transplant well, it is best to grow columbine from seed. The seeds should be sown as soon as they are ripe or in the fall, because they need a period of damp cold. If you want to wait until spring to sow, place seeds in the refrigerator in damp vermiculite or sand for three to four weeks. When you sow, place the seeds on top of the growing medium or soil, for the seeds need light to germinate. This plant self-sows readily, and seedlings will bloom during the second year. Collect seeds from the end of May to early June.

Columbine

Although they are usually considered woodland plants, the columbines are wonderful species to use at the edge of a meadow where they will get a bit of shade. Mixing several species in mass plantings makes quite a show. Many cultivars have been developed from the wild columbines, but these will revert back if planted from seed. The columbines do suffer damage from leaf miners — those little insects that eat tunnels through the leaves, leaving trails or patterns. This makes the foliage look a bit peculiar, but it does not affect the blossoms. There is a possibility, however, that the leaf miners will spread to other plants in the meadow.

The configuration of the flower has given it many unusual common names, such as meeting house — the spurs made some people think of ''heads in a circle.'' The genus name is from the latin word for eagle, for some people thought that these spurs looked like an eagle's claw. The name columbine is from the Latin word for dove, for the spurs reminded still others of doves' heads in a circle.

Columbine has been used for centuries to cure various ailments. Concoctions made from the plant were used as a cure for measles, smallpox, jaundice, abdominal pains, and liver ailments. Perhaps the most unusual use of the columbine was as a lion tonic: it was fed to them in the spring to revive their strength.

The columbines make fine cut flowers. After picking the blossoms, plunge them immediately into warm, salty water and then into clean, warm water to the base of the flowers, Columbines are symbols of cuckoldry and a deserted lover, so be careful when you bestow this as a gift!

OTHER SPECIES: *A. caerulea.* Native to the Rocky Mountains, the Colorado or blue columbine is a lovely species to use in full sun or partial shade where good moisture is available. It blooms from April through June. Planting rate is suggested at 112 ounces per acre.

A. vulgaris. This species is from Europe and was introduced to our country because of its lovely little violet, pink, or white blossoms. It produces generous numbers of flowers if it is grown in temperate, cool climates in light, sandy soil with moderate amounts of moisture. It grows no taller than 12 inches, and it blooms in May and June.

A. formosa. Scarlet columbine is found most often in the Pacific Northwest. It prefers open, rocky areas and alpine meadows. Common names are scarlet columbine and Sitka columbine.

A. chrysantha. The golden columbine is generally 2 to 4 feet tall and ranges from the Rocky Mountains to Texas. The flowers are a clear yellow color and have long, downward-pointing spurs.

A. flavescens. The yellow columbine is native from Alberta to British Columbia and in Colorado, Utah, and Oregon. It grows up to 24 inches tall. It is an alpine species that adapts to cultivation quite well.

Rock cress

BOTANICAL NAME:　*Arabis alpina* (AIR-ah-biss al-PINE-ah)
COMMON NAME:　rock cress
FAMILY:　Cruciferae
GROWING RANGE:　all regions except the Southeast
NATURAL RANGE:　mountains of Europe
BLOOMS:　May — July
HEIGHT:　16 inches
COLOR:　white
TYPE:　perennial
DESCRIPTION:　This low, tufted plant has an abundance of soft, gray green leaves. The small (½ inch) flowers nearly cover the plant in spring and early summer. The basal leaves are found in clusters, and the fragrant flowers occur in racemes, or short stalks. Under good conditions this plant can spread to 24 inches.
ENVIRONMENTAL PREFERENCE:　Rock cress needs full sun and well-drained soil. It should be cut back after flowering.
PROPAGATION:　It grows from seed very well and will reseed readily. The seeds need light to germinate and should be sown on the surface. Seeds germinate in about fifteen days. Germination occurs

most rapidly at temperatures of 65 to 70° F. Rock cress can also be grown from root cuttings taken in mid to late summer.

Often plants that are sold as *Arabis alpina* are actually a closely related species, *Arabis caucasica*, or wall cress. This species is hardier, is more dependable, and can withstand hotter and drier conditions. It looks very much like the rock cress, having gray green leaves and white flowers. It is well suited for hot, dry areas, particularly in rock gardens or among rocks in the meadow.

The genus name is from Arabia, the original home of many species.

BOTANICAL NAME: *Argemone hispida* (ar-GEM-oh-nee HISS-pid-ah)
COMMON NAME: white prickly poppy
FAMILY: Papaveraceae
GROWING RANGE: Midwest, Southeast, Southwest, Texas-Oklahoma, West
NATURAL RANGE: Wyoming south to Mexico, west to California
BLOOMS: June — August
HEIGHT: 20 — 32 inches
COLOR: white
TYPE: perennial
DESCRIPTION: The white flowers are 2 ½ to 4 inches across, and the foliage is a lovely silver gray color. The plant does have harsh prickles, however.
ENVIRONMENTAL PREFERENCE: This plant needs full sun and dry, sandy, well-drained soil.
PROPAGATION: Sow seeds where they are to grow and keep them moist until they germinate.

White prickly poppy

The bright white flowers of white prickly poppy will last through even the hottest summers, and once established, the plant is drought tolerant. The genus name is from the Greek word *argemon,* meaning "cataract of the eye"; some plant of this genus was once thought to cure cataracts or eye disorders.

OTHER SPECIES: *A. alba.* This plant is native to the South-eastern United States and is found naturally in dry, open areas.

A. mexicana. The yellow prickly poppy is native to tropical America. It grows easily from seed. The blossoms have an unusual scent, and the seedpods are quite prickly.

A. platyceras. This native of North America, Central America, and South America is considered one of the most beautiful species of this genus. It grows from 1 to 4 feet tall and has white blossoms.

Common milkweed

BOTANICAL NAME: *Asclepias incarnata* (ass-KLEE-pee-us in-car-NAY-tah)

COMMON NAME: swamp milkweed

FAMILY: Asclepiadaceae

GROWING RANGE: Midwest, Northeast, Southeast, Texas-Oklahoma, and West (may be difficult to control in some areas)

NATURAL RANGE: Nova Scotia south to Florida and west to Utah

BLOOMS: August — October

HEIGHT: to 48 inches

COLOR: pink

TYPE: perennial

DESCRIPTION: The stem of this plant is quite stout and smooth, the leaves smooth and lance shaped. The flowers are deep pink to mauve, and the seedpods are quite attractive.

ENVIRONMENTAL PREFERENCE: Although the common name alludes to the fact that the plant can take very wet and soggy conditions, these are not requirements. The plant seems to do equally well in drier conditions. This makes it an ideal plant to use in poorly drained areas of a meadow. It does need full sun.

PROPAGATION: Swamp milkweed is easily grown from both cuttings and root divisions taken in early spring or fall. The seeds need a period of cold stratification and should be sown in the fall or placed in the refrigerator for several weeks. The seeds can best be gathered in October. Plants grown from seed will not bloom until the third growing season.

The milkweeds can be a disturbing pest — they have a tendency to become invasive and outgrow their welcome, particularly in the Midwest and the Northeast. They can be controlled by pulling up the stalks as they appear. If you want just one colony of plants, you could try this suggestion: plant them in barrels and then bury the barrels below the surface of the soil. In theory, at least, the barrels will keep the plant from spreading to become a nuisance. Another control measure is to be sure to pick the seedpods before the seeds have a chance to disperse.

Both the family and genus names come from the Greek god of medicine. Aesculapius. Unfortunately, modern testing has found no real medicinal use for the plant, although it was used for centuries to cure various ills, including dysentery and asthma. The Quebec Indians used the root as a contraceptive, and the Shawnee Indians used the sap to take away warts. The Delaware Indian name for milkweed boiled with dumplings is *pee-too-can-oh-uk*.

There are 1,900 species of milkweeds, all of which depend on insects for pollinization. The monarch butterfly is often called the milkweed butterfly, because its larvae feed on the plant so often. Goldfinches are also particularly attracted to the milkweeds, because they use the soft down from the seeds to line their nests. Deer can often be seen feeding on the young shoots and flowers.

OTHER SPECIES: *A. syriaca.* The common milkweed, native from New Brunswick south to Georgia and Oklahoma, will grow in nearly any soil in full fun. It needs to be used toward the back of an area, because it grows to a height of 3 to 5 feet.

A. curassavica. Sunset flower is native to California, the Southeast, the Southwest, and Texas, and it will grow in most other regions. The plant grows to a height of 3 feet and has an attractive cluster of red flowers. It needs much more moisture than the other species listed but is good for attracting butterflies and hummingbirds. Suggested planting rate is 208 ounces per acre.

A. amplexicaulis. The blunt-leaved or sand milkweed is a prairie milkweed with greenish flowers tinged with purple. It grows 2 to 2 ½ feet tall and has wavy leaves that clasp the stem. Native from New England to Nebraska, south to Florida and Texas, it blooms in June and July.

Butterfly weed

BOTANICAL NAME: *Asclepias tuberosa* (ass-KLEE-pee-us too-bur-OH-sah)
COMMON NAME: butterfly weed
FAMILY: Asclepiadaceae
GROWING RANGE: all regions of the United States
NATURAL RANGE: Midwest, Northeast, Southeast, Southwest, Texas, West
BLOOMS: June — September
HEIGHT: 12 — 36 inches
COLOR: orange
TYPE: perennial
DESCRIPTION: The bright orange umbels of flowers are borne on multiple flowering stems, which are rough and hairy but do not exude the milky sap that is generally characteristic of this family. The blossoms are followed by milkweed-type pods which break open, releasing hundreds of seeds carried by silky parachutes.
ENVIRONMENTAL PREFERENCE: The most important requirement of this plant is well-drained soil. If it is planted in soil that is too rich or heavy and damp the roots will rot. Soil that is sandy or gritty and neutral or slightly acidic is perfect for this plant. Although it prefers full sun, it can withstand partial shade. It seems to be quite adaptable and has been recorded as being hardy to -30° F.
PROPAGATION: Because of its deep taproot, this plant is very difficult to move when it is mature. Best propagation methods include planting seeds and taking root cuttings.

For ease of collecting and cleaning, seeds should be collected before the down is formed, just before the pods begin to split open. The seeds seem to benefit from cold stratification, so place them in damp sand in the refrigerator for several weeks before planting. Unless you live in a very mild region, an alternative to this method is to sow the fresh seeds in the fall and allow them to overwinter. Seedlings grown in a flat should be moved to 4-inch pots when the second pair of leaves appears. If allowed to become root bound, the seedlings will quickly wilt and die. When transplanting, disturb the roots as little as possible. Cuttings from the roots of mature plants can be taken in the fall. Two-inch sections of the root should be placed in a mixture of sand and peat moss. To keep the sections upright, cut an angle at the bottom of each section. Keep the cuttings evenly moist until a good root system is established.

Young plants can be transplanted with a fair degree of success. If the root is cut to a 4-inch length, new feeder roots will be produced, creating a more compact plant. The eye of the root should be placed at a depth of 2 inches.

The butterfly weed is one of the few wildflowers that will grow in nearly every region of the country without becoming weedy or invasive. The bright blossoms range in color from a yellow orange to a nearly red orange. Once the plant is established it can grow to bushel-barrel size if it is in a suitable location. It sends down a tap root that becomes impervious to burrowing animals, fire, or over-zealous wildflower pickers. It does very well as a cut flower and cutting the blossoms will prolong the blooming period. It is also useful as a dried flower and will retain much of its color. The dried pods are also used in dried flower arrangements.

This plant was once called pleurisy root because early pioneers believed that it would cure pleurisy, which it unfortunately does not. Another common name is chigger weed: people erroneously believed that the plant harbored great numbers of chiggers. The down formed with the seeds was used as stuffing in pillows.

New England aster

BOTANICAL NAME: *Aster novae-angliae* (ASS-ter NOV-ee — AN-glee-eye)
COMMON NAME: New England aster
FAMILY: Compositae
GROWING RANGE: all regions of the United States (may be difficult to control in some areas)
NATURAL RANGE: Vermont to Alabama; west to North Dakota and to New Mexico
BLOOMS: August — October
HEIGHT: 3 — 5 feet

COLOR: lavender to pink

TYPE: perennial

DESCRIPTION: This bushy plant has bright lavender ray flowers with gold disk flowers found at the end of branches. The flower heads are small, the stem rather sticky.

ENVIRONMENTAL PREFERENCE: New England aster prefers slightly acidic, well-drained soil. It does best in full sun but will tolerate light shade. It likes cool, moist roots, so if the summers get quite hot in your area, mulch around these plants if possible. Too rich soil or not enough sunlight will result in sprawling plants.

PROPAGATION: This plant rarely appears in seed mixtures because germination of the seed is variable and because the seeds are difficult to collect in great quantities. The seeds form two to three weeks after the plant blooms. The seeds will benefit from a period of moist stratification and should be planted in the fall or placed in damp sand in the refrigerator for a few weeks. The seedlings often do not stay true to the color of the parent plant. The plants can be divided easily, and the best time to do this is during late fall. The plants need to be divided every two to three years to retain their vigor. When planting, place the clumps 1 to 2 feet apart, and place the roots down one inch and the rhizomes at soil level.

More than seventy-five species of asters grow in the United States. The name aster is from the Greek word meaning star, which is the way the blossoms are shaped. The asters were sacred to the Greek gods and goddesses, and people believed that these delicate little plants were made from star dust. Asters had a variety of uses, including curing snake bites, driving away snakes, and curing the bite of a mad dog. There were used as a symbol of elegance and love.

OTHER SPECIES: Each region of the country boasts a different set of Aster species. The following species are recomended because they are particularly lovely or do especially well in cultivation. These are only guidelines, however; find out what your local asters are and, if appropriate, introduce them into your own meadow.

A. azureus. The deep blue of this species makes it especially appealing to the gardener. Its natural range is from western New York and Minnesota, south to Georgia and Alabama. It blooms from early September through October, reaching a height of about 4 feet. Unchallenged, this plant can get rather coarse and rangy looking, but competition from other plants seems to hold it in check. It will self-sow readily or can be transplanted from divisions taken in fall or early spring.

A. cordifolius. This native of the Eastern woodlands is a good speciman to use in light shade, as is *A. conspicuus* from the West Coast. This blue-violet flower can grow up to 6 feet high.

A. ericoides. The heath aster is native from Maine to Pennsylvania, west to Missouri and Texas. It is found in dry, open spaces and the flowers are usually white, sometimes tinged with blue or pink.

A. laevis var. Geyeri. The smooth aster is native to much of North America, its range extending from the Yukon south to New Mexico and eastward to Maine and Georgia. This is one aster that does not need seed stratification and will often bloom late the first season. Blossoms are pale blue to purple, and the plant can grow to 3½ feet. Its natural habitat is moist prairie and wood borders.

A. lateriflorus. Native from Quebec to Minnesota, south to Florida and Texas, the calico aster is often found in dry, open areas and on beaches. The blossoms are pale purple or white and the plant can grow up to 4 feet tall.

A. lineariifolius. Native to Quebec and Maine, south to Florida and west to Wisconsin, Missouri, and Texas, the sandpaper aster, or pine starwort, is easy to cultivate. It readily self-sows and can be divided in late fall. It needs full sun and well-drained soil. A bushier plant can be obtained by pinching out the early buds until about the first of July. Violet-colored blossoms appear from August till frost and because it grows to a height of only 2 feet, it is a useful plant for the rock garden.

Basket of gold

BOTANICAL NAME: *Aurinia saxatilis* (ah-REE-na sacks-ah-TILL-iss) (same as *Alyssum saxatile)*

COMMON NAME: basket of gold

FAMILY: Cruciferae

GROWING RANGE: all regions of the United States

NATURAL RANGE: Europe and Turkey

BLOOMS: April — June

HEIGHT: 8 — 12 inches

COLOR: yellow

TYPE: perennial

DESCRIPTION: A multitude of small, bright, four-petaled flowers (1 to 3 inches across) occur on branching stems. The foliage is silver gray and will stay on the plant all year. If the soil is not too rich, this plant forms a nice spreading mat.

ENVIRONMENTAL PREFERENCE: Basket of gold likes well-drained soils, although it has been recorded as growing quite well in soil with a high clay content. It will grow in full sun or partial shade and is generally hardy and easy to grow.

PROPAGATION: To grow this plant from seed, it is best to sow the seed in the spring in flats or in a sheltered spot in the meadow or garden. Suggested planting rate per acre is four pounds. If you use established plants, set them out in early spring and space them 12 inches apart. After the plant blooms, cut back the stems to half their length to stimulate new growth. Some pests that might be a problem include caterpillars, slugs, and snails.

Alyssum saxatile is actually an old name for the plant that is now called *Aurina saxatilis*. Many catalogs still call the plant by its old name. By any name it is a bright addition to a meadow area. It is particularly useful for the border or for a low-growing meadow. If used in a general mixture it often gets lost among the taller plants. In more formal situations, it is particularly useful in the rock garden.

Basket of gold was introduced to the United States from Crete in the early 1700s. It boasts many common names, including gold tuft because of the color, and madwort based on the plant's one-time reputation as a cure for hydrophobia and other mental disorders. The genus name *Alyssum* comes from the greek word *alysson,* meaning without rage or without madness.

False indigo

BOTANICAL NAME: *Baptisia australis* (bap-TEE-see-ah os-TRAIL-iss)

COMMON NAME: false indigo

FAMILY: Leguminosae

GROWING RANGE: Midwest, Northeast, Southeast, Southwest, Texas-Oklahoma, West

NATURAL RANGE: Pennsylvania, south to North Carolina and Tennessee

BLOOMS: late May — July

HEIGHT: 3 — 4 feet

COLOR: Indigo blue

TYPE: perennial

DESCRIPTION: This bushy plant has leaves that look somewhat like those of clover and are blue green. The blue flowers occur on upright racemes. The sap, when exposed to air, turns a purplish color, and the leaves turn black when dried. The foliage, quite graceful and arching, is especially attractive.

ENVIRONMENTAL PREFERENCE: Although it seems to do best in sandy soils, it will tolerate heavier soils with good drainage. It likes full sun or light shade and a slightly sweet soil with a pH of seven or a bit more.

PROPAGATION: Plant false indigo in the spring or fall while the plant is dormant. Set the plants 2 feet apart, and place the upper eye of the root 2 inches below soil level. If using divisions from older plants, trim the old root back to 3 inches. The seeds are formed in pods and will rattle when ripe. If bugs or pests are present in the seedpod, place a "no-pest strip" into a storage bag for a few days along with the seeds. Before you sew seeds, soak them overnight in hot water to soften the seed coat. Germination will be variable, but for best results the seeds should be planted outdoors in the spring when the soil temperature is about 70° F. The first seedlings should appear within a few weeks and will continue to appear for several weeks afterward. Avoid overwatering, as the seedlings are subject to mildew. Some of the seedlings will bloom the third year and some not until the fifth year. Transplanting seems to be a more reliable method of propagation, and certainly it will bring blossoms sooner.

Baptisias are attractive, easy-to-grow wildflowers that do well under cultivation. They are generally long-lived and trouble free. They work well planted in masses or as individual specimen plants. Because they have such attractive foliage and develop such nice spread, some species can even be used as a deciduous hedge. They are especially good on banks or steep hillsides because they develop extensive root systems which are useful for erosion control.

The interesting seedpods are wonderful for dried flower arrangements. Pick the entire seeding stalk in early fall just as the pods are beginning to show a little black and hang them upside-down in an airy place to ripen.

The genus name is from the Greek word *baptizein,* which means "to dye" and refers to this plant's pigment, which was used as a substitute for indigo. The species name means "southern" and refers to the plant's origin — the southern part of the United States.

Although the leaves resemble clover, this plant is not edible and even may be considered poisonous.

OTHER SPECIES: *B. leucantha.* This species grows 3 to 6 feet tall and is native to moist areas from Michigan and Ohio to Nebraska and Texas. The pea-like flowers are white, sometimes tinged with purple.

B. leucophaea. Native from Michigan and Minnesota south to Arkansas and Texas, the blossoms of this plant are cream colored or yellow. It can withstand a bit drier conditions than *B. australis* and is considered one of the best species of this genus to use in the garden. It blooms in April and May and grows 12 to 18 inches tall.

B. pendula. The wild white indigo, native to the southern United States, has attractive foliage and is a lovely white in bud and in full bloom. The leaves and buds are on gray stalks, and the flowers open to a startlingly beautiful white. The young plants seem to prefer a rich, loose soil and will develop a good root system the first year. They flower sparsely the second year and produce an abundance of bloom the third season and for many seasons thereafter.

B. tinctoria. The yellow wild indigo or yellow rattleweed is native to the region from Massachusetts, south to Florida, and west to Minnesota. It blooms in June and July and grows 2 to 3 feet tall. It seems to thrive in any poor, dry soil and is truly drought tolerant. When established, the plants will self-sow readily, or they can be divided in early spring and transplanted then. The blue green leaves will remain attractive until frost. This plant was once placed in the harnesses on horses to help keep away flies. For this reason, it was also known as horseweed.

BOTANICAL NAME: *Belamcanda chinensis* (bell-am-CAN-da chi-NEN-sis)
COMMON NAME: blackberry lily
FAMILY: Iridaceae
GROWING RANGE: all regions except the Pacific Northwest
NATURAL RANGE: China and Japan
BLOOMS: July — September
HEIGHT: 24 — 36 inches
COLOR: orange
TYPE: perennial

Blackberry lily

DESCRIPTION: The flat, sword-shaped leaves are similar to those of the cultivated iris, and the bright orange blossom is speckled with red and is lilylike. The blossom opens up to be 1½ to 2 inches wide.
ENVIRONMENTAL PREFERENCE: This plant needs an airy, open spot in the meadow and rather rich garden soil to do well.
PROPAGATION: The blackberry lily is one of the easiest of all perennials to grow from seed. The seeds are gathered in the fall, stored over the winter in the refrigerator and then planted in spring, producing blossoms in two years. If you plant rhizomes rather than seeds, place them 1 inch deep and 1 foot apart, since this plant forms large clumps.

This plant from the Orient has escaped from cultivation and naturalized in many areas of the country. Recaptured and put into a meadow, it adds wonderful texture, color and variety to the area. Since many lilies and irises grow in naturally occurring meadow areas, the blackberrry lily looks right at home in a manmade meadow.

The name blackberry lily comes from the seed pod which, when open, shows a seed mass that looks very much like a blackberry. The spotted flower is the basis for another name, leopard flower.

BOTANICAL NAME: *Bidens aristosa* (BY-denz ar-iss-TOE-sah)
COMMON NAME: tickseed sunflower
FAMILY: Compositae
GROWING RANGE: Midwest, Northeast, Southeast, Texas-Oklahoma
NATURAL RANGE: New England, south to Virginia, west to Texas, and north to Missouri and Minnesota

BLOOMS: August — October
HEIGHT: 1 — 5 feet
COLOR: yellow
TYPE: annual
DESCRIPTION: An abundance of small yellow daisylike flowers are borne on several branches. The flower heads are 1 to 2 inches wide, and the leaves are 6 inches long and opposite.
ENVIRONMENTAL PREFERENCE: Quite an adaptable plant, this sunflower will perform best with full sun and good moisture. It will tolerate a good bit of shade, but reduced flowering will be the cost. It should be grown in a naturally moist area.

This plant is a very poor competitor and cannot be used close to other plants. This limits its use in the meadow, but if enough open space can be made for it, it is a lovely addition to the September landscape.

PROPAGATION: The seeds need at least thirty days of moist cold before they will germinate. the easiest way to accomplish this is by sowing the seeds in the fall. Wait until after the first or second frost to collect the seeds. Sow them immediately, for the seeds lose viability very quickly and cannot be stored effectively.

This plant germinates so easily and reliably from seed that it is a shame that it will not tolerate neighbors. It can be planted in masses, but it will not compete well with grasses and other perennials. The seeds of this plant are probably better known than the blossoms for they will stay with you after a walk through the woods in the fall. The seeds are known by a variety of names including stick tights, beggar's ticks, and tickseed. They can be easily removed with the flat edge of a knife blade. The name *Bidens* is from the Greek words meaning "two teeth" and refers to the two hooks on the seed capsule.

OTHER SPECIES: *B. polylepis.* This species is very similar to *B. aristosa,* and cultural and propagation techniques are the same.

Tickseed sunflower

Camas

BOTANICAL NAME: *Camassia quamash* (kam-ASS-ee-ah QUAM-ash)
COMMON NAME: camas
FAMILY: Liliaceae
GROWING RANGE: West and Pacific Northwest
NATURAL RANGE: southeastern British Columbia, west to Montana and northern Oregon and Idaho
BLOOMS: April — May
HEIGHT: 12 — 18 inches
COLOR: blue, blue violet
TYPE: perennial

DESCRIPTION: The stems bear several loose clusters of deep blue flowers. The grasslike leaves dry quickly after the plant blooms.

ENVIRONMENTAL PREFERENCE: Camas need full sun or light shade and average to moist soil with plenty of water while it is growing.

PROPAGATION: Plant the bulbs in the fall after the weather has cooled, and place them 3 to 4 inches apart. It does very well from seed, although germination is very slow, taking sometimes as long as six months or more. Sow the seeds in flats ⅛ inch deep.

A wonderful plant to naturalize in a meadow, camas adds delicate blue color to the spring landscape. It is also very good for rock gardens, or to plant around rocks found in the meadow. The camas was an important source of food for many Northwestern Indian tribes, and fields where the bulbs were abundant were fiercely defended. The white man also used the bulbs for food; *Camassia* was eaten by many explorers and settlers. Where it was found in abundance, it was even used sometimes for hog food. Due to this exploitation, camas is no longer found in great abundance. It is easy to confuse this plant with *Zigadenus venenosus*, the death camas, which is extremely poisonous.

OTHER SPECIES: *C. leichtlinii*. This plant, which is native from British Columbia to California, can be found most often in moist soils.

BOTANICAL NAME: *Campanula rotundifolia* (kam-PAN-yew-lah row-tun-di-FOE-lee-ah)

COMMON NAME: bluebell

FAMILY: Campanulaceae

GROWING RANGE: all regions of the United States (some species may become quite invasive and difficult to control)

NATURAL RANGE: California north to Alaska and east to the Atlantic

BLOOMS: June — September

HEIGHT: 6 — 20 inches

COLOR: blue

TYPE: perennial

DESCRIPTION: A tuft of basal leaves is formed in the spring, from which comes thin wiry stems with an abundance of thimble-sized nodding blue flowers, either in clusters or singly.

ENVIRONMENTAL PREFERENCE: Good drainage and full sun is important, sandy loam or regular garden soil preferable. This plant needs regular watering.

PROPAGATION: Division of the clumps is the easiest and most reliable method of propagation. These can be divided and replanted in late spring after the basal foliage has appeared, or in late summer or fall. Position the plants with their basal foliage at soil level. If you use

Bluebell

offshoots from the clump, plant them 1 to 2 inches deep. Germination from seed is variable, but under good conditions using seeds is a viable means of propagation. Place the tiny seeds in a flat or in soil that will remain undisturbed. They need stratification, so either plant in the fall or place the seeds in the refrigerator for several weeks. The first seedlings will begin to appear after fifteen to twenty days. They will germinate most quickly at a temperature of 60 to 70° F.

Although bluebell requires more attention and richer soil than many of the other meadow plants, it would be a versatile and lovely addition to your area. It is particularly suited to a protected corner or among rocks.

The name *Campanula* is from the Latin word for bell and actually means "little bell." The species name refers to the basal leaves and means "round-leaved." The common name harebell may refer to the fact that this plant can often be found growing in open fields or meadows where hares might be found. Another possible origin of this name is that witches were said to have used this plant to turn themselves into hares. Other common names for this species include Scotch harebell, bluebell, bluebells of Scotland, and witches' thimbles.

There are many species of Campanulas, some of which adapt themselves well to cultivation. Others become noxious weeds. One of the worst offenders is *Campanula rapunculoides*. It is an offensively persistent plant and very hard to eradicate if allowed a foothold in the garden or meadow. Prevention is the best cure — just don't plant it.
OTHER SPECIES: *C. carpatica*. This species from the Carpathian Mountains in central Europe has had many cultivars developed from it. Grown most often in the Southwestern United States, it is reasonably frost free and has been said to be hardy to -30° F. It prefers well-drained soil and appreciates a little extra watering. The flowers can be either blue or white and occur on upright stems.

Indian paintbrush

BOTANICAL NAME: *Castilleja coccinea* (kas-til-EE-ah kock-SIN-ee-ah)
COMMON NAME: Indian paintbrush
FAMILY: *Scrophulariaceae*
GROWING RANGE: Midwest, Northeast, Southeast, Texas-Oklahoma, Southwest, West
NATURAL RANGE: Massachusetts to Ontario; south to South Carolina, Mississippi, and Oklahoma
BLOOMS: June — August
HEIGHT: 12 — 24 inches
COLOR: red
TYPE: annual or biennial

DESCRIPTION: It is the bracts of this plant that create its beauty. They are large, red, and fan shaped, and the small yellow green flowers can be found growing on a short, dense spike in the axils of the bracts.

ENVIRONMENTAL PREFERENCE: This plant is quite difficult to get established, but once it is, it will grow under a wide variety of conditions. It seems to do best among perennial plants.

PROPAGATION: It is difficult to transplant this plant or to get good growth from seeds. Planting the fresh seeds in a grassy area might meet with some success. Also, the seeds can be included with chopped turf in a soil mixture. Cold stratification of the seeds seems to speed germination.

This plant is rarely found in gardens because of the difficulty in propagation. However, once a stand is growing, it seems to tolerate many kinds of environmental conditions and will probably thrive. There is some controversy as to whether or not this genus is parasitic on the roots of sagebrush and other perennials. For many years all species were considered parasitic, but now only the annual species *(C. indivisa)* is thought to exhibit parasitic characteristics, and this only in the early stages of germination.

The legend of its origin says that an Indian brave was painting a picture and was having a difficult time capturing the vibrant colors of the sunset. Frustrated, he asked for help and the Great Spirit gave him paintbrushes dripping with bright colors. The Indian finished his picture and threw away the paintbrushes. Wherever the brushes landed, this flower began to grow.

The Indians used this plant to soothe burned skin or to cure the burning sting of the centipede.

OTHER SPECIES: *C. sessiflora.* The downy paintbrush is a short perennial that blooms from March to June or later. It can be found throughout the Great Plains.

C. indivisa. The Texas paintbrush is an annual that grows to a height of 16 inches and blooms from March to June. It is hemiparasitic on the roots of perennials, particularly during germination stages.

BOTANICAL NAME: *Centaurea cyanus* (sen-TAW-ree-ah sigh-AN-us)
COMMON NAME: bachelor's button
FAMILY: Compositae
GROWING RANGE: all regions of the United States (may be difficult to control in many regions)
NATURAL RANGE: Europe and the Near East
BLOOMS: April — August
HEIGHT: 30 inches

Bachelor's button

COLOR: blue

TYPE: annual

DESCRIPTION: The foliage is gray green and slightly fuzzy. The 1-to 2-inch blossoms, made up of both disk and ray flowers, are bright blue and are found at the ends of slender stems.

ENVIRONMENTAL PREFERENCE: This very hardy plant is both salt and drought tolerant. It grows in full sun or light shade and prefers neutral or basic soil. It can grow in dry, heavy, or light soil, but it does not like clay and poorly drained soil.

PROPAGATION: Bachelor's button grows very easily from seed. Sow it outdoors where you want it to grow, either in spring after the last frost or in the fall where winters are mild. It will sprout in ten days in the spring and will produce blossoms beginning in about three months. It does not like to be transplanted.

The very characteristics that make bachelor's button tolerant of so many different conditions also make it overly aggressive in many areas. Be conscious of its invasive potential, and use it wisely.

Several cultivars have been formed from this plant, and it is now possible to get bachelor's buttons that are pink or dwarf, growing only 18 inches tall.

The name bachelor's button comes from the flower bud, which is round and hard and looks somewhat like a button. In England young women would wear this flower as a sign that they were not married and were looking for an appropriate bachelor. An old superstition was that the girl who wore this flower in her apron pocket would get the bachelor of her choice. Other common names for this plant are bluebottle, for the color of the blossom, and cornflower, for it was often found growing in England in the corn fields (corn was a name given to all grain, not just the American maize).

Snow in summer

BOTANICAL NAME: *Cerastium bierbersteinii* (ser-ASS-tee-um by-er-ber-STINE-ee-eye)

COMMON NAME: snow in summer

FAMILY: Caryophyllaceae

GROWING RANGE: all regions of the United States (may be difficult to control in some areas)

NATURAL RANGE: Crimea

BLOOMS: April — August

HEIGHT: 8 inches

COLOR: white

TYPE: perennial

DESCRIPTION: This is a low-growing, mat-forming little plant, covered with small (½ to ¾ inch), white flowers. The foliage is silver gray, each leaf measuring about ¾ inch long. It will spread two to three feet in one growing season.

ENVIRONMENTAL PREFERENCE: Growing equally as well in mild and cold climates, coast or desert, this is a very adaptable plant, though optimum growing conditions for it would include good drainage and full sun with a bit of shade during the hottest part of the day. Standing water from poorly drained soil will cause root rot. It can take very dry conditions, but it will grow faster with a little water.

PROPAGATION: Seeds will germinate in approximately fifteen days, so sow seeds where you want them to grow in spring or divide the clumps in spring or fall.

Snow in summer is not a very long-lived plant. For best results replant it every few years. Useful in the rock garden, in border areas of the meadow, or in low-growing meadows, snow in summer does have a tendency to become overly aggressive.

OTHER SPECIES: *C. tomentosum.* This closely related species is found more often under cultivation. It is evergreen, and the flowers are slightly smaller. It is originally from the mountains of Italy and Sicily.

Wallflower

BOTANICAL NAME: *Cheiranthus cheiri* (care-AN-thus CARE-eye)
COMMON NAME: wallflower
FAMILY: Cruciferae
GROWING RANGE: Midwest, Northeast, Pacific Northwest, West
NATURAL RANGE: southern Europe
BLOOMS: April — May
HEIGHT: 24 inches
COLOR: orange
TYPE: perennial often grown as biennial
DESCRIPTION: This is a very compact flower with bright orange ¾ inch flowers on a spike occurring on short, stout stems. The lance-shaped leaves are dark green, and the whole appearance of the plant is that of a miniature shrub.

ENVIRONMENTAL PREFERENCE: Bright sun, good drainage, and moist, neutral soil are the basic requirements for growing this plant. For best blooms, the soil should not be overly rich. It performs best in cool coastal areas, and it really needs a cool growing season for best bloom. It grows well in England and is prized there as a garden favorite. Under the correct conditions it is hardy and easy to grow. If grown as a perennial, it might need winter protection in very cold areas.

PROPAGATION: Wallflower grows quite well from seeds which can be started indoors eight to ten weeks before the last frost. There are many cultivars, but these seem to resent meddling and very often revert back to species color when allowed to reseed.

Wallflower is rarely considered a wildflower in this country, but it is included in many meadow mixtures because it adds a bright spot of color and does well in many meadow environments.

The flowers are quite fragrant and were often carried in festival and celebrations. The name *Cheiranthus* is from two Greek words meaning "hand" and "flower" because they were used so often for bouquets, or flowers carried by hand. The language of wallflower is fidelity in misfortune or faithfulness in adversity. The darker colored varieties were known as bloody warrior and were planted at cottage windows to protect against invaders.

The flowers, stems, and seeds were used in medicines to cure ailments ranging from liver disorders to sore muscles.

Note: The plant often listed as *Cheiranthus allionii* is actually in a different genus and is correctly named *Erysimum hieraciifolium*. For information about this plant, see the section under that name.

Ox-eye daisy

BOTANICAL NAME: *Chrysanthemum leucanthemum* (kris-AN-tha-mum loo-KAN-thee-mum)
COMMON NAME: ox-eye daisy
FAMILY: Compositae
GROWING RANGE: all regions of the United States (may be difficult to control in some areas)
NATURAL RANGE: Europe and Asia
HEIGHT: 12 — 24 inches
BLOOMS: June — July
COLOR: white
TYPE: perennial
DESCRIPTION: White ray flowers surround yellow disk flowers. The stem is straight or slightly branched, and the basal leaves are deeply toothed.
ENVIRONMENTAL PREFERENCE: Ox-eye daisy performs best in full sun in ordinary garden soil. Too rich a soil will produce tall, spindly stems that fall over. It needs a good amount of moisture and should be watered weekly when rains are not sufficient.
PROPAGATION: Ox-eye daisy self-sows readily and is easily grown from seed. The seeds do best when sown when they are fresh. For a meadow area, sow them in late summer or fall. In mild areas some of the seeds will germinate immediately and may bloom the following summer. To start seeds indoors, sow in flats that are well drained with a soil temperature of about 70° F. Germination will be low, as with most members of the Compositae family, so sow plenty of seeds. The recommended planting rate is five pounds per acre. Large clumps can be divided in the fall and the divisions replanted immediately, spaced 6 to 12 inches apart. Spread the roots out, and plant the crown at soil

level. To retain their beauty and vigor, the clumps should be divided every two to three years.

Although this immigrant from Europe is bright and lovely, it can become invasive and outgrow its welcome in some areas of the country, particularly in the Midwest and the Pacific Northwest. Given sufficient moisture, it could be a pest in other areas, so don't let it reseed itself if it shows this potential in your area.

This is a plant that has been known and used for centuries. It was thought to hold many magical powers, including the ability to ward off thunder and lightening and tell fortunes (loves me, loves me not.). Medicinal properties that it was believed to contain included cures for chapped hands, bruised skin, smallpox, tumors, jaundice, broken bones, and toothaches. To dream of the daisies in the fall would mean a winter filled with bad luck. To dream of them in the spring would mean months of good fortune.

OTHER SPECIES: There is a dwarf variety available which seems to need less moisture. Other Chrysanthemums which closely resemble the daisy and would be suitable for planting in the meadow include:

C. Carinatum. Painted daisy, tricolor chrysanthemum, or summer chrysanthemum — all common names for this plant — is native to Morocco. It can be white, yellow, red or purple with a band of color at the base. It has deeply cut foliage with single daisylike flowers that make good cut flowers. It can be sown either in spring or fall in heavy or light soil in full sun. It blooms from June through September and grows to a height of only 18 to 36 inches. This plant may become a pest in the Western mountains and Pacific Northwest. Suggested planting rate is eight pounds per acre.

C. coronarium. Garland chrysanthemum, or crown daisy, is originally from the Mediterranean region. It has a stout, branched stem and yellow ray flowers. It grows to a height of 5 feet and blooms from April through September. It is grown frequently in the Orient as a vegetable, for the young leaves are quite tasty. This plant may become invasive in parts of the West. Suggested planting rate is five pounds per acre.

Chicory

BOTANICAL NAME: *Cichorium intybus* (si-CORE-ee-um in-TIE-bus)

COMMON NAME: chicory

FAMILY: Compositae

GROWING RANGE: all regions of the United States (may be difficult to control in many areas)

NATURAL RANGE: North Africa, Europe, Western Asia

BLOOMS: July — September

HEIGHT: 12 — 48 inches

COLOR: blue

TYPE: perennial

DESCRIPTION: The basal leaves which look somewhat like dandelion leaves, are deeply toothed and taper toward the ends. The upper leaves are much smaller. The flowers are bright, sky blue and are 1 to 2 inches across. Each ray flower is notched or jagged on the end.

ENVIRONMENTAL PREFERENCE: These plants need full sun and good drainage, though they are adaptable to a wide range of soil types. They will grow in clay and are drought tolerant. The acidity of the soil seems to affect the intensity of the blossom color.

PROPAGATION: Easily grown from seed, chicory germinates in approximately ten to fifteen days when the temperature range is between 65 and 75° F. If transplanting, dig deeply to get the entire taproot and plant 1 to 2 feet apart with the crown at soil level. It propagates best by sowing the seed and transplanting young plants.

Chicory is considered a weed by many and will outgrow its welcome if care is not taken. It is considered invasive in nearly every region of the country. Being a perennial, it will come back year after year, as well as reseed readily. It is a rather ragged-looking weed and is not really suitable for a garden, but the bright blue blossoms look very good in an open, naturalized area such as a meadow.

The roots are ground and used as a coffee substitute. Chicory coffee was said to be good for liver and gall bladder problems, and it has been considered a useful herb since Roman times.

Chicory blossoms last only a few hours, opening in the morning and then closing up by noon. They can be used as a cut flower if hardened overnight in warm water.

Other common names for this plant include ragged soldiers, blue sailors, wild succory, and bunk.

Farewell to spring

BOTANICAL NAME: *Clarkia amoena* (CLARK-ee-ah a-ME-nah)

COMMON NAME: farewell to spring

FAMILY: Onagraceae

GROWING RANGE: Pacific Northwest, Southwest, West

NATURAL RANGE: California

BLOOMS: June — August

HEIGHT: 12 — 36 inches

COLOR: pink, lavender, or white

TYPE: annual

DESCRIPTION: The flowers are made up of four fan-shaped petals and are 2 inches across. Several flowers can be found on a single flowering stalk.

ENVIRONMENTAL PREFERENCE: This plant does not do well in hot, humid weather and should not be planted anywhere that summer temperatures rise above 80° F. They need full sun and a light, sterile soil. Sandy soil with no fertilizer is just right. Though they need constant moisture for germination and during early growth, once established they need little water.

PROPAGATION: These grow well from seed planted either in fall or spring. As they are difficult to transplant, it is best to sow them where you want them to grow.

The common name farewell to spring comes from the fact that they bloom in late spring or early summer, and they seem to usher out one season while greeting the next. These are a favorite Western wildflower and are quite showy growing in the wild or in the garden or meadow. Breeders have developed several cultivars which have double flowers in all different shades, but the cultivars have a hard time competing with the simple beauty of the wild *Clarkias*. They make wonderful, long-lasting cut flowers. The seeds of several species were gathered by the Indians for food.

Clarkia was named for William Clark, the famous explorer who, with Meriwether Lewis, first crossed the Rocky Mountains in 1806.

OTHER SPECIES: *C. concinna.* This species, also native to California, is called red ribbons. It prefers partial shade and is an excellent choice for the border area between woods and meadow. It has low-growing, attractive foliage and deeply cut, bright pink petals. It grows to a height of 18 inches.

C. pulchella. The petals of this species have three lobes — a broad central one and two narrow outer ones. Taken together they resemble a deer's antlers — thus the common name, deerhorn clarkia. The petals are deep pink to magenta, and the plant grows 8 to 18 inches high. Deerhorn clarkia prefers full sun to light shade and is good for naturalizing in a meadow. It is native from the Rocky Mountains to the Pacific coast.

C. unquiculata (un-qwick-you-LAY-ta). The elegant clarkia, as this is called, is a salmon to purplish color and blooms in May and June. It grows to a height of 36 inches. This plant is considered easy to grow and will tolerate a wide variety of environmental conditions. It is native to California and is commonly found on dry slopes with sunny exposures, but it will tolerate light shade. It will germinate in seven to fourteen days if the temperature is between 65° and 75° F. If it likes its environment, it will self-sow readily.

Spring beauty

BOTANICAL NAME: *Claytonia virginica* (clay-TONE-ee-ah ver-JIN-i-kah)
COMMON NAME: spring beauty
FAMILY: Portulacaceae
GROWING RANGE: Midwest, Northeast, Southeast, Texas-Oklahoma
NATURAL RANGE: Ontario to Quebec and southern New England, south to Georgia, and west to Louisiana and Texas, north to Minnesota.
BLOOMS: March — May
HEIGHT: 4 — 6 inches
COLOR: pink
TYPE: perennial
DESCRIPTION: The small blossoms are actually white with red stripes but look pink from a distance. The leaves are grasslike and are much taller than they are wide. There can be as many as fifteen flowers from the same tuber.
ENVIRONMENTAL PREFERENCE: This species prefers a moist, rich woodland but will also do well in drier woodland soil if it's given ample water during the blooming season. The soil should be neutral to slightly acid. It needs filtered sunlight or open shade.
PROPAGATION: The tubers of this plant are tiny — just about the size of a pea. These should be planted 3 inches deep. Although the plant seems to readily self-sow, it is difficult to collect the tiny seeds.
OTHER SPECIES: *Claytonia lanceolata.* The Western spring beauty is quite adaptable and can be found from the snow line in the mountains down to low desert areas. The flowering racemes may hold as many as fifteen white or light pink blossoms.

A good plant to use in a woodland area bordering the meadow, spring beauty can form very large colonies of delicate blossoms. They disappear soon after blooming, however, so they should be planted in among other plants. The blossoms should not be picked for a cut flower for they do not last. The tubers are edible and are described as tasting somewhat like a baked potato and a roasted chestnut. Spring beauty is of particular interest to geneticists for it has an unstable number of chromosomes: there are fifty possible chromosomal combinations. This is highly unusual for both the plant and animal families.

BOTANICAL NAME: *Collinsia heterophylla* (kol-LIN-see-ah het-er-oh-FILL-ah)
COMMON NAME: Chinese houses
FAMILY: Scrophulariaceae
GROWING RANGE: Northeast, Pacific Northwest, Southwest

NATURAL RANGE: California
BLOOMS: April — July
HEIGHT: 24 inches
COLOR: white and lavender
TYPE: annual
DESCRIPTION: Tiers of snapdragonlike flowers occur on stems up to 24 inches long. The lower lips of the blossoms are a rose purple color and the upper ones white. The leaves are narrow and triangularly shaped.
ENVIRONMENTAL PREFERENCE: An adaptable plant, this will grow in full sun or shade, and will tolerate both wet and dry conditions. It will perform best in a rich, moist soil.
PROPAGATION: Seeds of this plant will germinate in seven to ten days at 60° to 70° F. The germination rate is low — only 50 percent — so be sure to sow sufficient numbers of seeds. It will self-sow readily. Recommended planting rate for this species is six pounds per acre.

The common name, Chinese houses, comes from the arrangement of flowers, which really do look like miniature pagodas. Although it is rarely grown in the Southeast, it should grow well in the Northeast as well as the western part of the country. It makes nice cover for bulbs, has a long blooming period, and is excellent as a cut flower. The genus name is for a botanist, Zaccheus Collins, who lived in Philadelphia in the late 1700s.

Chinese houses

BOTANICAL NAME: *Coreopsis lanceolata* (kor-ee-OP-sis lan-see-oh-LAY-tah)
COMMON NAME: coreopsis
FAMILY: Compositae
GROWING RANGE: all regions of the United States
NATURAL RANGE: Michigan, south to Florida and New Mexico
BLOOMS: May — August
HEIGHT: 24 inches
COLOR: yellow
TYPE: perennial
DESCRIPTION: The bright yellow blossoms are 2 to 2½ inches across and are made up of (usually) eight petals with jagged edges. The basal leaves are lance shaped and 3 to 6 inches long.
ENVIRONMENTAL PREFERENCE: Found naturally in sandy, rocky areas, this species likes well-aerated soil that is not too rich. Too rich a soil will result in more leaves than flowers. It will do well in full sun or light shade with regular watering.
PROPAGATION: Clumps can be divided in spring or fall. Remove a few leaves to reduce water loss and replant them immediately. Germination rate from the seeds is high, and seeds will sprout after only a week. They need light to germinate, so sow seeds on the surface and be sure to keep them sufficiently moist.

Coreopsis

Coreopsis provides bright, sunny spots in the meadow. This plant is easily grown from seed and competes well with grasses. Although it is relatively short-lived, it reseeds readily and a healthy stand should perpetuate itself for a long time. It is generally hardy and easy to grow and will flower abundantly. Suggested planting rate is ten pounds per acre. A dwarf variety (18 inches tall) is available.

The name coreopsis is from two Greek words — *koris,* meaning "bedbug," and *opsis,* meaning "looks like" — and refers to the seeds which resemble small bugs or ticks. Another common name is tickseed. It was once believed that the seeds had the power to repel bugs of all kinds, so people would put them in their mattresses. Unfortunately, the seeds are only good for planting again to give us more blossoms.

OTHER SPECIES: *C. tinctoria.* This is an annual coreopsis called calliopsis. It is an airy plant with soft, fernlike foliage and a profusion of bright yellow or red flowers. Individual blossoms may be all yellow or all red or yellow with a band of red around the center. They need well-drained soil and frequent watering and do best if grown in only moderately rich soil. Sow the seeds outdoors in the meadow after the last frost and they should germinate within seven to ten days, producing flowers in about three months. The suggested planting rate is only two pounds per acre. This plant is native from Minnesota to Washington, south to Louisiana and California, and is both a prolific bloomer and a good cut flower. There is a dwarf variety available, growing only 8 inches tall.

Cosmos

BOTANICAL NAME: *Cosmos bipinnatus* (KOS-mose by-pin-AH-tus)

COMMON NAME: cosmos

FAMILY: Compositae

GROWING RANGE: all regions of the United States

NATURAL RANGE: Mexico

BLOOMS: June — September

HEIGHT: 36 — 60 inches

COLOR: pink, white, red

TYPE: annual

DESCRIPTION: This is a very open, airy plant with soft, fernlike leaves and simple daisylike flowers.

ENVIRONMENTAL PREFERENCE: Cosmos does well in light, moderately rich soil with full sun. It is drought tolerant.

PROPAGATION: Cosmos is very easy to grow from seed, and it also transplants well. You can get very early blooms by starting the seeds indoors in late winter and putting them in the meadow after the last frost. They germinate most quickly at a temperature of 65° to 75° F. and will sprout within five to seven days, producing blossoms in two to three months.

Planted in masses, the soft blossoms and foliage of the cosmos will add interesting texture and color to the meadow in late spring and summer. they make very nice cut flowers if the newly opened blossoms are placed immediately in cool water.

Spanish priests grew this plant in mission gardens and were impressed with the ordered simplicity of the plant. They gave it the Greek name *cosmos*, which means "ordered universe." Today the plant is considered a symbol of harmony.

The Plant Introduction Center in Washington, D.C., in 1897 was looking for plants and flowers that would adapt well in American climates. Cosmos was brought in from Mexico in 1898 and was found to be especially good in Southwestern climates.

OTHER SPECIES: *C. sulphureus*. This plant is a bright orange, gold, or sometimes almost red color. It often produces semi-double or double flowers. Planting rate is suggested at fifteen pounds per acre.

Queen Anne's lace

BOTANICAL NAME: *Daucus carota*
COMMON NAME: Queen Anne's lace
FAMILY: Umbelliferae
GROWING RANGE: all regions of the United States (may become invasive in some areas)
NATURAL RANGE: Afghanistan
BLOOMS: June — August
HEIGHT: 4 — 5 feet
COLOR: white
TYPE: biennial
DESCRIPTION: The fernlike leaves of this plant form an attractive rosette from which the multi-branched flowering stem arises. The blossoms are terminal umbels of many small white florets. The center floret is usually a dark purple. After the plant blooms the flower head curls upward and inward forming a "nest."
ENVIRONMENTAL PREFERENCE: Quite an adaptable plant, Queen Anne's lace does not seem particular about the type of soil that it grows in, although good drainage is beneficial. It does need full sun for at least half the day. This plant naturalizes very easily.
PROPAGATION: Queen Anne's lace is easily propagated from seed, for there is usually a high percentage of germination within a few days. Sow it in the fall or in the spring when the ground is warm. The sowing should be very shallow. Rake carefully over the soil to lightly cover the seeds. The plants form a deep taproot and an attractive rosette of leaves. It blooms the second season, or sometimes late in the first

season. Young plants can be moved successfully if you take care to move the entire taproot. Seeds can be collected three to four weeks after the plant blooms when the umbel is brown and dried. The seeds should be dried and stored in a sealed bag in the refrigerator until used. The seeds have been reported to remain viable for up to six years under ideal conditions.

A native of Afghanistan, Queen Anne's lace has become naturalized in every region of this country. You will see it often during the summer months growing along the roadsides and in fields. It reseeds very easily and may become invasive, particularly in the Midwest and Southeast. Take care to remove the plants after they flower and before the seeds are scattered. Because it is a biennial, you can remove the entire plant since it will not bloom again anyway. Collect and replant the seeds you want so that you will not have more seedlings than you desire.

The root of the Queen Anne's lace, which contains carotin, when grated and mixed with oil, was used by mountain folk to soothe burned skin. Eating the center floret was thought to cure epilepsy. The name Queen Anne's lace came from the frilly blossom which looks somewhat like lace, and legend tells us that the odd-colored center floret came when a queen was making this lace and pricked her finger, causing a single drop of blood to fall.

Rocket larkspur

BOTANICAL NAME: *Delphinium virescens* (del-FIN-ee-um)
COMMON NAME: prairie larkspur
FAMILY: Ranunculaceae
GROWING RANGE: West, Midwest, Texas-Oklahoma, Southwest
NATURAL RANGE: Wisconsin, south to Missouri, Oklahoma, and Texas
BLOOMS: May — July
HEIGHT: 60 inches
COLOR: white
TYPE: perennial
DESCRIPTION: The white blossoms are arranged densely along long, tapering flowering spikes. The stems are stiff and erect.
ENVIRONMENTAL PREFERENCE: This plant should be grown in full sun or partial shade and prefers well-drained soil of average fertility and plenty of moisture. It will grow in soils with a high clay content, but not in soils high in acidity. It flowers best in cool weather and may not do well in parts of the lower South.
PROPAGATION: Prairie larkspur is easily grown from seed. Sow the seeds in the fall so they can benefit from a period of cold. Sow only ⅛ inch deep, and thin the seedlings to prevent crowding. If seeds are not used immediately, store them in an airtight container in the refrigerator. Suggested planting rate is ten pounds per acre.

All of the *Delphiniums* contain alkaloids that are harmful both to man and cattle, though apparently not to sheep. The name *Delphinium* is from the Greek word for dolphin: the shape of the closed buds resembles a dolphin. Probably because of its poisonous properties, the delphiniums were thought to hold magical powers. To place a leaf of the plant in front of an insect or snake was thought to take away the creature's strength. It was often put on children's hair to get rid of ''varmin'' and was sometimes used cautiously as a medicine.

OTHER SPECIES: Several species of *Delphinium* are native to different regions of the United States. Find out which ones grow in your area and try them out. There are species which will grow in full sun to open shade. Some of the best are listed below.

D. cardinale. Scarlet larkspur is native to California and will grow well in the Pacific Northwest and the Southwest. The suggested planting rate is 112 ounces per acre. It will grow in full sun to partial shade and needs a moderate amount of watering though it should not be watered during the summer dormancy period. It grows to be about 4 feet tall and is wonderful for attracting hummingbirds.

D. bicolor. Native to the west, this species can be found in abundance in the Black Hills. It blooms during May and June but dies down quickly after the seeds ripen, going into early dormancy and leaving a bare spot in the meadow or garden. It can be grown in light shade or full sun and prefers soil rich in humus. The flowers are a rich, dark, purple blue color.

D. ajacis. The true name for this species is *Consolida orientalis* or rocket larkspur. It is a European species that will grow in every region of the United States. It has an attractive white or pink or blue blossom and grows to a height of 24 to 48 inches.

Sweet William

BOTANICAL NAME: *Dianthus barbatus* (die-AN-thus bar-BAY-tuss)

COMMON NAME: sweet William

FAMILY: Caryophyllaceae

GROWING RANGE: all regions of the United States

NATURAL RANGE: Pyrenee and Carpathian mountains

BLOOMS: April — August

HEIGHT: to 18 inches

COLOR: pink, red, purple, violet

TYPE: perennial (often grown as annual or biennial)

DESCRIPTION: Many small (¾ inch) flowers are borne at the end of the flowering stem. It grows in clumps and has grass-like leaves.

ENVIRONMENTAL PREFERENCE: This plant grows best in well-drained soil and full sun but cannot tolerate extremely acidic soils. It prefers cool to moderately cool summer temperatures. Where the summers are hot it will need light shade during the hottest part of the day. It needs regular watering.

PROPAGATION: Sow seeds in early spring as soon as the soil can be worked, or set out young plants in the fall and mulch them lightly with peat moss or straw (preferably free of weed seeds), or perhaps best of all, evergreen boughs. If the seeds are sown when temperatures are around 70° F., they will sprout in about five days and will bloom in two to three months. It is extremely easy to start from tip cuttings of new growth. These can be placed in a growing medium made of sand, peat moss, and garden soil, or placed directly into light garden soil if given sufficient moisture.

Sweet William is almost always considered a garden flower but is included in many seed mixtures because it grows easily from seed and can withstand meadowlike conditions. It is very sweet scented — somewhat like cloves — and makes a good cut flower.

The generic name is from the Greek word meaning "divine flower." Presumably it was given to this plant because of its beauty and fragrance. The species name *barbatus* means "bearded" and refers to the fringe found within the flowers. The common name is said to have been given to this plant to honor William the Conqueror.

OTHER SPECIES: *D. deltoides.* Maiden pink, as this species is called, forms loose mats making it good for mass plantings. There are tufts of evergreen leaves, and the flowers are pink or white. It grows to a height of 6 to 18 inches and requires less water than *D. barbatus.* It is quite adaptable to a variety of conditions, blooms abundantly, and is easy to grow.

Foxglove

BOTANICAL NAME: *Digitalis purpurea* (di-ji-TAL-iss pur-pur-EE-ah)

COMMON NAME: foxglove

FAMILY: Scrophulariaceae

GROWING RANGE: all regions of the United States

NATURAL RANGE: Europe

BLOOMS: June — August

HEIGHT: 24 — 48 inches

COLOR: purple, pink, red, yellow, white

TYPE: biennial

DESCRIPTION: Flowers are thimble shaped and occur toward the top of tall spikes. The downy leaves are in rosettes.

ENVIRONMENTAL PREFERENCE: Light to full shade with moist, well-drained garden soil are necessities for this plant.

PROPAGATION: This is easily grown from seed, but be sure to sow on the surface for the seeds need light to germinate. It takes about twenty days for them to sprout, and the plants will not bloom until the second year.

Because this is a biennial, annual seeding will be necessary to have continuous blooms. Luckily, under good conditions, the species reseeds itself readily. The plant is quite poisonous and is the source for a drug which is a heart stimulant. The origin of the name foxglove has several possibilities. One fairy tale says that the blossoms were made like gloves and given to foxes by fairies so that the foxes could raid the chicken coop without getting caught. Other people say that the blossoms resemble a bell or an ancient instrument called a ''glew'' and that the name eventually changed from fox's glew to fox's glove and then foxglove.

BOTANICAL NAME: *Dimorphotheca sinuata* (di-mor-fo-TEK-ah sin-you-AY-tah) (same as *Dimorphotheca aurantiaca*)
COMMON NAME: African daisy or cape marigold
FAMILY: Compositae
GROWING RANGE: Southeast, Southwest, Texas-Oklahoma
NATURAL RANGE: South Africa
BLOOMS: May — August
HEIGHT: 12 inches
COLOR: orange or yellow
TYPE: annual
DESCRIPTION: The daisylike blossoms come in many shades, including a white variety that has a black center, and are 2½ to 4 inches across. The leaves have a few teeth or indentations. The plant is capable of forming large mounds.
ENVIRONMENTAL PREFERENCE: The African daisy likes lots of sun and heat. It can withstand alkaline soil and has low water requirements, but it needs good drainage. In very humid areas there are more leaves than flowers. This plant does not like a cool, moist coastal climate. It performs best in late winter or early spring in a warm, dry climate.
PROPAGATION: Easily grown from seed, the African daisy can be planted in late summer for fall color in mild regions. In cooler climates, you can sow it in spring and expect blooms in late summer. Suggested planting rate is fifteen pounds per acre.

African daisy

The generic name is from Latin words meaning ''two shapes of fruit'' and refers to the fact that the plant produces more than one form of seeds. The name *aurantiaca* means orange colored and refers to the color of the blossoms.
OTHER SPECIES: *D. pluvialis.* The white African daisy has a purple base. It grows to a height of only 6 inches and needs low to moderate water. The suggested planting rate is fifteen pounds per acre.

BOTANICAL NAME: *Dodecatheon meadia* (doe-dee-KATH-ee-on me-AD-ee-ah)

COMMON NAME: shooting star

FAMILY: Primulaceae

GROWING RANGE: all regions except the Southwest

NATURAL RANGE: Pennsylvania and southern Wisconsin, south to Alabama and eastern Texas

BLOOMS: May into June

HEIGHT: 10 — 15 inches

COLOR: pink

TYPE: perennial

DESCRIPTION: A rosette of leaves, sometimes reddish, appears in early spring. The flowering stalk is leafless and bears clusters of pink flowers, each with five reflexed petals. The foliage disappears in summer.

ENVIRONMENTAL PREFERENCE: This plant likes full sun to light shade with plenty of moisture while it is blooming. Once it is established, it is considered drought tolerant. The soil should be slightly acidic to neutral.

PROPAGATION: Although shooting star produces an abundance of seed, it is a plant slow to bloom from seed, usually taking three to four years. The seedlings are often fragile and difficult to transplant. Fresh seeds should be used and should be sown in the fall or given at least sixty days of cold stratification. Mature plants can be divided successfully after they bloom. To divide, break segments that contain eyes and at least 3 inches of root away from the original clump. Replant, and these divisions should bloom the second year. Root cuttings can be taken in early spring.

Shooting star

The shooting stars were particularly abundant in the prairies, and when settlers first came they called them "prairie pointers." The genus name is from the Greek words meaning "flower of the twelve gods." It is closely related to the garden cyclamen and is sometimes called the American cowslip.

Many other species of shooting stars are suitable for cultivation and will do well in full sun to moderate shade.

OTHER SPECIES: *D. pulchellum.* This species does particularly well in the West and Midwest and is native to southern Alaska and western Canada, south to Mexico. It flowers according to the weather — after a warm spring, it blooms in June; after a particularly cool spring, it will not bloom until later. If there is not sufficient moisture, it will not bloom at all.

BOTANICAL NAME: *Echinacea purpurea* (eck-in-AY-see-ah pur-pur-EE-ah)

COMMON NAME: purple coneflower

FAMILY: Compositae

GROWING RANGE: all regions

NATURAL RANGE: Ohio to Iowa, south to Louisiana and Georgia

BLOOMS: June — October

HEIGHT: 24 — 36 inches

COLOR: purple

TYPE: perennial

DESCRIPTION: Purple coneflower is rather a stiff and coarse plant, but the long-lasting, beautiful flowers make it a favorite wildflower to use in the meadow. The blossoms are a reddish purple and have an orange center, and the leaves are large and covered with bristles.

ENVIRONMENTAL PREFERENCE: Although it prefers a moist, rich soil, it will tolerate clay and seems adaptable to varying pH levels and will grow in either heavy or light soils. It does need well-drained soil, and often a shovel full of sand will help considerably. It needs full sun and once established, is considered drought tolerant.

PROPAGATION: This plant is easily grown from seed, which may be sown in either spring or fall. Germination may be somewhat unreliable; best results will come from sowing the seeds in flats and then transplanting the young plants to the meadow when they are large enough. Mature plants can be divided in fall or spring and can be separated down to a single stem. Seeds can be collected three to four weeks after the flowers fade. They can either be planted immediately or can be placed in the refrigerator in a sealed plastic bag for three to four weeks. The planting rate is recommended at twelve pounds per acre.

Purple coneflower

Although considered hardy and trouble free, purple coneflower is sometimes attacked by Japanese beetles. Where this is a problem with other plants, the purple coneflower should not be used. It competes well with the grasses and seems to be especially well suited to cooler climates. The generic name is from the Greek word *echinos*, meaning ''hedgehog'' and referring to the bristles on the plant.

OTHER SPECIES: *E. pallida.* Sometimes called pale purple coneflower, this species has very light pinkish purple blossoms. It is very easy to grow from seed, root cuttings, or divisions. It is native from the Midwest, southeast to Louisiana, Alabama, and Georgia.

BOTANICAL NAME: *Epilobium angustifolium* (ep-i-LOW-bee-um an-gus-ti-FOE-lee-um)

COMMON NAME: fireweed

FAMILY: Onagraceae

Fireweed

GROWING RANGE: all regions of the United States
NATURAL RANGE: North America and Eurasia
BLOOMS: July — August
HEIGHT: 2 — 6 feet
TYPE: perennial
DESCRIPTION: The bright pinkish red flowers are borne in spikelike clusters. The leaves are long, narrow, and willow-like.
ENVIRONMENTAL PREFERENCE: Needing full sun and moist soil, this species will not tolerate any shade.
PROPAGATION: This plant may be grown from seed or plant division. It spreads rapidly from reseeding and from a creeping root stalk.

As the common name suggests, fireweed can be found most often in recently burned areas. During World War II after London had been bombed, acres of fireweed could be seen carpeting the earth.

Many parts of the plant are considered edible and even tasty. The young shoots were boiled and eaten like asparagus, and the leaves were dried and made into tea or used fresh and raw in salads. Other parts of the plant were used to treat various ailments including asthma and whooping cough.

The generic name is from two Greek words meaning "upon the pod" and is descriptive of the blooming habits of the plant, as the flowers open in succession beginning at the bottom of the stem. Because of the willowlike leaves, another common name for this plant is willow herb or willowweed. Other common names include Oriental purple, blooming Sally, and wick-up.

Both taller growing and dwarf varieties are available.

Fleabane daisy

BOTANICAL NAME: *Erigeron speciosus* (air-RIDGE-er-on spee-see-OH-sus)
COMMON NAME: fleabane daisy
FAMILY: Compositae
GROWING REGION: all regions of the United States
NATURAL RANGE: southern British Columbia; south to Oregon, Arizona, and New Mexico; and east to Montana and South Dakota
BLOOMS: June — August
HEIGHT: 24 inches
COLOR: white to blue and lavender
TYPE: perennial
DESCRIPTION: The fleabanes are similar to asters, but the petals are threadlike and not flattened as they are in the asters. The leaves are narrow and pointed, and the blossoms are white with tinges of blue and lavender.
ENVIRONMENTAL PREFERENCE: This plant needs full sun to partial shade and will do well in any light, well-drained soil. It needs moderate watering but can take relatively dry, infertile soil. It is hardy to -20° F.

PROPAGATION: Although germination rate is low, the fleabane daisy is relatively easy to grow from seed sown thickly in the meadow or garden area. You can also propagate by dividing older plants in early spring.

If you happen to be pregnant while you are planting your meadow, the fleabane could be a very handy plant for you. An old superstition said that if a pregnant woman planted a seed of the fleabane, it would tell her the gender of her coming child. If it turned out to be tinged with pink, the child would be a girl; if tinged with blue, then a boy was on the way.

The generic name came from two Greek words meaning "spring" and "old man." This was appropriate for the fleabane for it blooms in the spring, and the thin white petals are suggestive of an old man's beard. The common name fleabane was given to this plant by early pioneers who believed that the blossoms had the power to repel fleas and other troublesome bugs and pests. They used it to stuff their mattresses, but, unfortunately, it proved to have no insect repelling properties.

OTHER SPECIES: Once you establish a meadow garden, chances are good that you will have at least one of the fleabanes growing there — even if you did not plant it. Although many species of fleabanes are rather weedy looking, they all seem to be more appreciated in Europe than they are here, and several kinds are cultivated in European gardens. Other species that might be considered for cultivation in your meadow include *E. pulchellus*, *E. annuus*, and *E. philadelphicus*.

E. canadensis contains glands that secrete a strong-smelling oil that acts as a plant inhibitor, preventing other plants from growing close by. Pull this species up if it appears in your meadow.

Sulphur flower

BOTANICAL NAME: *Eriogonum umbellatum* (air-ee-OG-oh-num um-bell-AY-tum)
COMMON NAME: sulphur flower
FAMILY: Polygonaceae
GROWING RANGE: Pacific Northwest, West, Texas-Oklahoma
NATURAL RANGE: from the east side of the Rocky Mountains to the mountains in the Northwest and Southwest
BLOOMS: June — September
HEIGHT: 4 — 12 inches
COLOR: orange or yellow
TYPE: perennial
DESCRIPTION: The *Eriogonum*s form lovely rosettes of rich, glossy leaves. The small blossoms occur at the end of long flowering stems in wide clusters, or umbels. As the flowers age, they turn to a reddish bronze, and by October the foliage is a bronze color also.

ENVIRONMENTAL PREFERENCE: This plant needs full sun to partial shade and is considered drought resistant. If given the correct growing conditions, it will adapt well to cultivation.

PROPAGATION: Sulphur flower is easily grown from seed and should be either sown directly where you want it or grown in a flat and then transplanted when small.

Eriogonums are particularly common in the Grand Canyon and Mesa Verde national parks. The individual blossoms are small, but the clusters are very nice in a dried flower arrangement.

OTHER SPECIES: There are at least 150 species of Eriogonums native to North America, particularly in the West, and different species seem to adapt to different environmental conditions. Another excellent species to introduce to the garden or meadow area is E. fasciculatum or arroyo buckwheat. It can grow to a height of 36 inches, can spread to 4 feet, and has white or pinkish blossoms. Because it spreads easily, it is often used for erosion control. It is native to California.

Wallflower

BOTANICAL NAME: *Erysimum hieraciifolium* (ee-RIS-i-mum hy-er-ACE-ee-eye-FOE-lee-um) (same as *Cheiranthus allionii*)

COMMON NAME: Siberian wallflower

FAMILY: Cruciferae

GROWING RANGE: Midwest, Pacific Northwest, Southeast, West, Southwest

NATURAL RANGE: north central and eastern Europe

BLOOMS: April — May

HEIGHT: 18 inches

COLOR: orange

TYPE: perennial

DESCRIPTION: A bushy plant with bright orange flowers, the wallflowers has long, narrow leaves that are 2 to 4 inches long.

ENVIRONMENTAL PREFERENCE: This plant needs full sun or partial shade and can withstand dry or moist conditions. It performs best where the summers are not too hot, preferring the climate of a cool, coastal area.

PROPAGATION: This grows easily from seeds sown in fall in mild climates and in early summer in cooler climates. Seedlings can be started indoors in early spring; they transplant well. Suggested planting rate is six pounds per acre.

Sometimes known as *Cheiranthus allionii*, this plant no longer belongs to this genus. Environmental conditions and propagation are similar to that of the English wallflower, *Cheiranthus cheirii*. Other common names for this plant include blister cress and treacle mustard.

BOTANICAL NAME: *Erythronium americanum* (ee-ree-THROW-nee-um ah-mer-i-kay-num)

COMMON NAME: fawn lily

FAMILY: Liliaceae

GROWING RANGE: Midwest, Northeast, Southeast, Texas-Oklahoma

NATURAL RANGE: Nova Scotia, south to Georgia, west to Tennessee, Arkansas, and Oklahoma, and north to Minnesota

BLOOMS: March — June

HEIGHT: 4 — 10 inches

COLOR: yellow

TYPE: perennial

DESCRIPTION: The foliage is very attractive, a mottled brown and green color. The flowers are found on the larger plants and only the plants which have two leaves will bear flowers. Many plants will have a single leaf and no flower. The blossoms are made up of sepals and petals (called tepals) that are reflexed back. The dark purple stamens are long and conspicuous.

Fawn lily

ENVIRONMENTAL PREFERENCE: The fawn lily is found naturally in moist areas under deciduous trees. It needs deep, fertile soil that's rich in organic matter and a constant supply of moisture. Mulch this plant heavily with rotted leaves to conserve moisture and keep the soil cool.

PROPAGATION: Propagation of this species is very slow. The seeds should be planted immediately and it will generally take from three to four years for the first blossoms to appear. Dividing clumps is another viable means of obtaining new plants. The offshoots from the mother plants should be divided when the plant goes dormant. The small bulbs should be planted with the narrow end up.

Generally considered a woodland plant, *E. americanum* is wonderful for naturalizing in a woodland border area where moisture is plentiful. It forms large colonies with interesting foliage and graceful yellow blossoms.

Because it takes such a long time to produce a flowering plant, when you buy plants from a nursery, be sure that they have been grown from proper propagation methods and not dug from the woods.

Other common names for the Western fawn lily are avalanche lily, glacier lily, and snow lily, all given because the plant has the habit of blooming just at snow line. The Eastern species also has a number of common names including dog tooth violet (though it is not a true violet), trout lily (because the mottled leaves resemble the skin of a trout and because it blooms during trout season), and adder's tongue (because of the long, protruding stamen). The genus name is from a

Greek word meaning red and was given because of the dark red mottled spots on the leaves. The leaves are edible and were eaten as a spring vegetable. The roots, also considered tasty, were stored in root cellars for winter fare. Tea made from the leaves was considered a cure for the hiccups.

OTHER SPECIES: *E. grandiflorum.* This plant is native from northern Oregon, east to western Colorado, Wyoming, and western Montana. It grows to a height of 6 to 8 inches and blooms in June and July. This species is best grown from seed, but be sure to transplant the seedlings when they are very young as they like to grow very deep, which helps them to become more drought resistant. Considered a good species for harsh climates, *E. grandiflorum* comes in yellow, white, and bicolor forms.

California poppy

BOTANICAL NAME: *Eschscholzia califonica* (es-KOLZ-ee-ah kal-i-FORN-i-kah)

COMMON NAME: California poppy

FAMILY: Papaveraceae

GROWING RANGE: all regions of the United States

NATURAL RANGE: California and Oregon

BLOOMS: April — August

HEIGHT: 18 inches

COLOR: orange

TYPE: annual or tender perennial

DESCRIPTION: The flowers are 2 to 3 inches wide and are made up of four large petals and many stamen. Numerous blossoms are found at the ends of slender stems.

ENVIRONMENTAL PREFERENCE: This plant is heat and drought tolerant but does not like soil that is continuously wet or overly rich. It needs full sun or light shade.

PROPAGATION: The tiny seeds should be scattered where you want them to grow, not transplanted. Water them thoroughly and keep them constantly moist until germination. In mild climates they can be sown in fall for earlier bloom, but the seeds are tender and may not overwinter in cooler climates. The recommended planting rate is five pounds per acre. In its native range, reseeding is quite common.

California's favorite wildflower, the California poppy is a sassy little sweetheart that has won the admiration and love of gardeners all over the country. Although breeders have developed strains that are double and range in color from golden cream and orange to pink and deep red, the simple orange blossoms of the natural wildflower still seem to be the favorite. In its native range in springtime, it covers the hillsides with its bright face during the day, only to close up at night.

The genus name is from Dr. J.F. Eschscholtz, a physician and botanist who came to the Pacific Northwest with the Russian exploration teams in 1816 and 1824.

OTHER SPECIES: *E. caespitosa.* This dwarf variety grows to a height of 9 inches. Environmental requirements and propagation techniques are similar to those of *E. californica.* Planting rate is five pounds per acre.

Joe-pye weed

BOTANICAL NAME: *Eupatorium maculatum* (yew-pa-TORE-ee-um mack-yew-LAY-tum)

COMMON NAME: Joe-pye weed

FAMILY: Compositae

GROWING RANGE: Midwest, Northeast, Southeast, Texas-Oklahoma

NATURAL RANGE: eastern North America

BLOOMS: August — September

HEIGHT: up to 72 inches

COLOR: wine, pinkish purple

TYPE: perennial

DESCRIPTION: This tall, stately species has terminal clusters of small purplish blossoms. The leaves occur in whorls of three or four and are toothed.

ENVIRONMENTAL PREFERENCE: Joe-pye weed prefers moist soil and full sun to partial shade. It is not particular as to the fertility of the soil that it grows in, but adding organic matter to poor soil will help the plants get established more quickly.

PROPAGATION: The seeds can be collected in September and early October. Sow them immediately where you want them to grow, or if that is not possible, place them in a sealed bag in the refrigerator for a spring planting. They will flower during their second season. The clumps should be divided every two or three years to keep them looking neat. Divide when the plants are dormant in late fall or in early spring as soon as the new growth appears. Separate the outer sections, and include at least one stem and several roots. Replant, and keep moist until established.

Joe-pye weed is a plant well worth our attention. For a moist spot, especially toward the back of the meadow garden, this plant is unsurpassed. Showing color in late summer and early fall, this blends well with the yellow goldenrods and purple asters that are also in bloom at this time. In the Appalachian Mountains this plant is called queen of the meadow. With a name like that, it should at least get a chance in your meadow — if you have the necessary conditions.

Joe-pye weed was thought to hold certain magical powers. For example, the Indians believed that if a man went courting a young woman, he would be assured of success if he had a piece of this plant in his mouth. Eating the roots and leaves of this plant was said to stimulate the appetite and improve the complexion. It was also considered strong medicine and was used to cure a variety of things including kidney disorders, fevers, problems with the nervous system, and typhoid fever. It was probably this last use that gave it its common name, for the Indian word for typhoid fever was *jopi.* The plant soon became known as *jopi* weed or eventually, Joe-pye weed. Another explanation for the origin of the name was that Joe Pye was an Indian medicine man who spend much of his life treating victims of typhoid fever using this plant.

OTHER SPECIES: *E. perfoliatum.* This plant is called boneset and is slightly shorter. It blooms in September and October.

E. fistulosum. While its requirements are similar to the other species, this plant can grow to a height of 10 feet.

Mission bells

BOTANICAL NAME: *Fritillaria pudica*
COMMON NAME: yellow bell
FAMILY: Liliaceae
GROWING RANGE: Pacific Northwest, Southwest, Texas-Oklahoma, West
NATURAL RANGE: British Columbia to California and New Mexico
BLOOMS: March — June
TYPE: perennial
COLOR: yellow
HEIGHT: 4 — 12 inches
DESCRIPTION: The single yellow flower is found nodding at the top of the flowering stem. The leaves are 2 to 8 inches long and grasslike. As the flowers age they turn rusty red or purplish.
ENVIRONMENTAL PREFERENCE: *Fritillarias* need dappled sun in well-drained soil. They are found naturally in grasslands among sagebrush and in open coniferous woods.
PROPAGATION: As with all the native lilies, propagation from seed is a slow process. It often takes four to six years to obtain flowering plants from seed. A faster means of propagation is by dividing the plants, and the best time to divide and transplant is in the fall when the tops begin to die down. Do not allow the bulbs to dry out.

The genus name is from the Latin word *fritillus,* which means "checkerboard" or "dice box" and refers to the markings on some species.
OTHER SPECIES: Western North America can boast of having more than twenty species of *Fritillaria.* They grow in a variety of soils and locations and altitudes. Some additional species that lend themselves well to cultivation are:

F. lanceolata. Mission bells or checker lily grows to a height of 12 to 48 inches and blooms from February to June.

F. pluriflora. This is the pink fritillary or adobe lily. It is native to California and the Pacific Northwest. It blooms in early spring.

BOTANICAL NAME: *Gaillardia aristata* (gah-LAR-dee-ah air-iss-TAY-ta)

COMMON NAME: perennial gaillardia or Indian blanket

FAMILY: Compositae

GROWING RANGE: all regions of the United States

NATURAL RANGE: North Dakota to Colorado, west to Oregon and Southwest Canada

BLOOMS: June — September

HEIGHT: 18 — 24 inches

COLOR: yellow and red

TYPE: perennial

DESCRIPTION: Large daisylike blossoms have a red domed center with yellow and red ray flowers. The leaves are lobed and linear shaped.

ENVIRONMENTAL PREFERENCE: Gaillardias need well-drained soil and full sunlight. They seem to resent too rich a soil, so do not add fertilizer. Once established, their water requirements are minimal, though occasional watering seems to extend the blooming period.

PROPAGATION: This plant is easily grown from seed sown outdoors in spring or started in flats in late winter. Seeds germinate in five to ten days at 65° to 75° F. Suggested planting rate is ten pounds per acre. You can also divide plants in early spring or take root cuttings in summer. This plant does not seem to consistently reseed itself, so you must reseed or put in new plants annually. Collect the seeds in October and store them, dry, in the refrigerator.

Indian blanket

The name Indian blanket was given to this plant because the jagged colored edges of the blossoms look like Indian blanket designs. The genus was named for a Frenchman famed for his enthusiastic support of the study of botany, Gaillard de Marentoneau.

OTHER SPECIES: *G. pulchella* (pull-SELL-ah). The cultural requirements for annual Indian blanket are similar to those of the perennial variety. It seems to thrive in heat, and is native from Virginia to Florida, west to New Mexico, and north to Colorado, Nebraska, and Missouri. Good drainage is essential. It will take approximately twenty days for the seeds to sprout, and the first blooms can be seen in three months. The blossoms are smaller than on *G. aristata,* but it makes an outstanding cut flower and blooms from mid-summer until frost.

Treasure flower

BOTANICAL NAME: *Gazania rigens* (gah-ZANE-ee-ah RING-genz) (same as *Gazania splendens*)
COMMON NAME: treasure flower
FAMILY: Compositae
GROWING RANGE: Midwest, Southeast, Southwest, Texas-Oklahoma, West
NATURAL RANGE: South Africa
BLOOMS: May — August
HEIGHT: 12 inches
COLOR: yellow, white, orange, red
TYPE: perennial
DESCRIPTION: This low-growing, clumping plant has flowers that are a variety of colors, about 3 inches across, and daisy-like. The foliage is an attractive silver gray, and the leaves are long and slender.
ENVIRONMENTAL PREFERENCE: This plant dislikes cold, damp winters and will not survive frigid temperatures. It likes well-drained, light, sterile soils and full sun. It is considered drought tolerant but appreciates occasional watering. It will benefit from a slow-acting fertilizer applied in spring.
PROPAGATION: Treasure flower will not overwinter in many areas, and cuttings should be taken in fall, as you would with cultivated geraniums. For the best cuttings, take the shoots closest to the crown and place in sand or other growing medium. Seeds should be sown in spring after the last frost and when the soil warms. Recommended planting rate is ten pounds per acre. Seeds should have complete darkness until they sprout (in about eight days), so cover with soil. It spreads by long, trailing stems.

The genus was named for Theodore of Gaza, a Greek scholar who translated Theophrastus and Aristotle from Greek to Latin in the fifteenth century.

This plant should be carefully placed in the meadow so that it will not get lost among the bigger plants. Choose the white or maroon varieties, which show up better among the multitude of yellow blossoms that seem to dominate the meadow during the summer months. Gazania is a low-growing plant, so a place toward the front of the meadow will show it to best advantage.

BOTANICAL NAME: *Geranium maculatum* (jer-AY-nee-um mack-yew-LAY-tum)
COMMON NAME: wild geranium
FAMILY: Geraniaceae
GROWING RANGE: Midwest, Northeast, Southeast, Texas-Oklahoma, West
NATURAL RANGE: Maine to Georgia, west to South Dakota and Arkansas

BLOOMS: April — June
HEIGHT: 12 — 24 inches
COLOR: magenta
TYPE: perennial
DESCRIPTION: The lavender to pink flowers are borne in loose clusters at the ends of slightly hairy stems. Each flower measures 1 to 1 ½ inches across and is composed of five petals, five pointed sepals, and ten stamens. The leaves are deeply lobed into five parts and get white spots on them as they age.

ENVIRONMENTAL PREFERENCE: The wild geranium will grow well in open woods as well as in a meadow. It likes neutral to slightly acid soil and prefers rich woodland or garden soil, so amend your soil with organic matter if necessary. It needs full sun or open shade. Plants with a bit of shade actually seem to produce more blossoms. Deep shade or crowded conditions will deter growth.

PROPAGATION: The seeds are rather difficult to collect because the seed capsules burst open with such surprising speed, shooting the seeds out great distances. The seeds need a period of cold stratification and should be planted outdoors in the fall. It sometimes takes two years, or two stratification periods, for the seeds to germinate. The seedlings should be left undisturbed for the first growing season and can be transplanted when they go dormant in the fall. It takes three years to get a bloom from plants started from seed. Plant division is a quicker method. After the small rhizomes are separated from the parent plant, they should be placed 1 inch deep with the eyes leading to the surface. Wild geraniums are best planted in groups of three or more.

Wild geranium

The fruit from members of the Geraniaceae family is long and pointed and has been the basis for many names for these plants. It is most often thought to resemble a crane's beak, and the family and generic name reflect this, as both are based on the Greek word for crane. A frequently used common name is crane's bill. The species name means spotted and refers to the leaves which get white spots on them as they age. Other common names include shameface (for the color of the flower), alum root, and rock weed, since it often grows on rocky slopes.

The plant has always been prized for its medicinal qualities and has been used for a variety of cures including treatment for sore throats, ulcers, dysentery, hemorrhages, and flesh wounds. In the language of flowers it is associated with constancy and availability.

OTHER SPECIES: *Geranium viscosissimum.* The red wild geranium is native from South Dakota to California. It is a perennial growing to 24 inches tall. The flowers are a purplish pink color and are ¾ inches long. It blooms from May to August and can be found in the wild in meadows and open woodland from lowlands to the mountains. Other common names for this species include sticky geranium and crane's bill.

Prairie smoke

BOTANICAL NAME: *Geum triflorum* (JEE-um try-FLOOR-um)
COMMON NAME: prairie smoke
FAMILY: Rosaceae
GROWING RANGE: Midwest, Northeast, Pacific Northwest, Southeast, Southwest, West
NATURAL RANGE: across northern North America
BLOOMS: April —June
HEIGHT: 12 — 18 inches
COLOR: purple
TYPE: perennial
DESCRIPTION: This plant is much more beautiful and conspicuous in seed form than while flowering. The flowers are small, are reddish brown or pink, and occur in groups of three. The leaves are deeply dissected and fernlike. The fruiting stalks have long, soft, feathery hairs that are quite attractive.
ENVIRONMENTAL PREFERENCE: Able to withstand poor, dry soils, established plants are considered drought resistant. This plant needs full to light sun, and there is a danger of damping off of the seedlings if there is too much moisture or shade. It does not compete well with grasses.
PROPAGATION: The seeds need no treatment and should be planted immediately. The plants may be divided in late summer and are easily transplanted.

Prairie smoke gives a wild and somewhat exotic look to the meadow garden and is an attractive plant for the entire growing season. The foliage is nice and neat and the pretty blossoms are followed by the outstanding and unusual fruiting stalks. On the prairies, where it is one of the first plants to appear, the wind catches the soft feathers creating an airy look as well as dispersing the seeds. The roots were once used to make a tea or a chocolatelike drink and in England were used to flavor wine. Medicinal value is minimum but it was at one time used to treat heart trouble. Other common names are purple avens and old man's whiskers or grandpa's whiskers. The dried fruiting stalks may be sprayed with hair spray to hold their shape for a dried bouquet.

BOTANICAL NAME: *Gilia capitata* (GIL-ee-ah cap-i-TAY-tah)
COMMON NAME: blue thimble flower
FAMILY: Polemoniaceae
GROWING RANGE: Pacific Northwest, Southwest, West
NATURAL RANGE: British Columbia, to central California, to western Idaho
BLOOMS: April — May
HEIGHT: 24 inches
COLOR: blue
TYPE: annual
DESCRIPTION: The bright blue, five-lobed flowers are often mistaken for phlox. This is an understandable mistake, for they do belong to the same family. It is a rather bushy plant, and the flowers occur in globe-shaped heads.
ENVIRONMENTAL PREFERENCE: Somewhat adaptable to a variety of conditions, gilia needs a relatively cool climate. Though it is drought tolerant, it will respond favorably to extra watering. It can take full sun or full shade. It is found naturally on grassy slopes in all of the pacific states.
PROPAGATION: This plant is easily grown from seeds by sowing in open ground in early spring. In addition, the plant puts out numerous rhizomes which are easily transplanted. Suggested planting rate is two pounds per acre.

Bird's eye gilia

The genus was named for an eighteenth-century Spanish botanist, Felipe Luis Gil.
OTHER SPECIES: *G. aggregata.* Called skyrocket or scarlet gilia, this plant can produce flowers from the middle of May until late summer. This bright red flower will grow to a height of 12 to 30 inches, and if grown in a suitable location, will reseed readily.

G. leptantha. With its neat growing habit and extended period of bloom, the showy blue gilia is a favorite wildflower for cultivation. It blooms during the summer months and can be grown in full sun or partial shade. Planting rate is five pounds per acre.

G. tricolor. This species, called bird's eyes, is one of the more adaptable gilias, preferring dry soil and full sun. It is hardy and easy to grow and will reseed readily. Suggested planting rate is two pounds per acre. The trumpet-shaped flowers are lavender and white with gold throats — hence the common name. The flowers are fragrant and hold their color when dried.

BOTANICAL NAME: *Gypsophila paniculata* (jip-SOF-i-lah pan-ick-yew-LAY-tah)
COMMON NAME: perennial baby's breath
FAMILY: Caryophyllaceae

Baby's breath

GROWING RANGE: all regions of the United States (it has a tendency to become invasive in some areas)

NATURAL RANGE: central and eastern Europe to central Asia

BLOOMS: July — October

HEIGHT: 36 inches

COLOR: white

DESCRIPTION: This is a much-branched, shrubby plant covered with tiny white blossoms during the summer months. The leaves are slender and pointed, 2 ½ to 4 inches long. The individual blossoms are only 1/16 inch wide, but there are hundreds to a spray.

ENVIRONMENTAL PREFERENCE: This plant cannot tolerate an acid soil and will not overwinter in poorly drained soggy soils. Though it does best in full sun, it can take partial shade. In very cold climates, it should be mulched during the winter. Once it is established, it should not be moved.

PROPAGATION: Seeds sown in the spring when temperatures range between 70° and 75° F. will germinate in ten days and will bloom during their second season of growth. Basal cuttings may be taken in the spring.

OTHER SPECIES: *G. elegans.* Annual baby's breath has cultural requirements similar to those of the perennial species. It grows to a height of 12 to 20 inches and blooms in July and August. The seeds will germinate in seven to ten days, and the first blooms generally appear in three months, It is originally from the Ukraine, eastern Turkey, and northern Iran. The flowers are somewhat larger than those of *G. paniculata,* but the plant flowers for only a short time. For continual bloom, seeds should be sown every few weeks during the spring.

Though baby's breath is generally considered a garden flower, its airy branches add nice texture to the meadow. Use it cautiously, however, for this plant does have the tendency to become invasive and hard to control, particularly in the Midwest and the West where it has escaped and adapted to life along the roadsides with amazing rapidity and has become a serious pest in some agricultural areas.

The genus name means "love chalk" and is descriptive of the growing requirements of the plant. If the soil is not suitably alkaline (pH of seven or higher), lime can be added at the time of planting. The common name baby's breath comes from the delicate, misty effect produced by the hundreds of tiny white flowers. This plant is often used both as a cut flower and dried. To dry, hang the flowering stalks upside down in a well-ventilated place. The species name *elegans* means "elegant" and refers to the general appearance of the flowers in bloom.

BOTANICAL NAME: *Helenium autumnale* (hell-EN-ee-um aw-tum-NAL-ee)

COMMON NAME: sneezeweed

FAMILY: Compositae

GROWING REGION: all regions of the United States

NATURAL REGION: Quebec to Florida and west to British Columbia and Arizona

BLOOMS: July — September

HEIGHT: 2 — 4 feet

COLOR: yellow/orange

TYPE: perennial

DESCRIPTION: This multi-branched plant has large yellow daisylike blossoms with a brown pompomlike center and many clasping leaves 2 to 4 inches long.

ENVIRONMENTAL PREFERENCE: This plant prefers full sun in soil rich in organic matter, and it seems to thrive in hot weather if it gets sufficient moisture. It does not perform well in dry soils but is quite tolerant of wet situations during the growing season. It is hardy to -35° F.

PROPAGATION: The easiest and fastest means of propagation is by division, and the clumps should be divided every two to three years to keep them healthy. Transplanting should be done in the spring when the soil warms.

Sneezeweed is such an unfortunate name for this plant, especially since it is totally unfounded. This pollen from the plant is too heavy to be airborne and really does not make people sneeze. Sneezeweed is a good plant to use for fall color and is particularly showy planted with the cardinal flower, which also likes a moist spot. The genus was named for Helen of Troy, and the species name indicates the blooming season.

Sneezeweed

BOTANICAL NAME: *Helianthus annuus* (he-lee-AN-thuss AN-new-us)

COMMON NAME: common sunflower

FAMILY: Compositae

GROWING RANGE: all regions of the United States (some species are considered invasive and difficult to control)

NATURAL RANGE: throughout the United States

BLOOMS: August — October

HEIGHT: 36 — 96 inches

COLOR: yellow

TYPE: annual

DESCRIPTION: The very large blossoms of this plant are between 3 and 6 inches wide. The ray flowers are yellow and the center disk flowers a reddish brown. The stems bear one or several flower heads.

ENVIRONMENTAL PREFERENCE: This is an adaptable plant, and the size of the blossoms is dictated by the amount of moisture it gets and

Common sunflower

the fertility of the soil. Although it will withstand poor, dry soil, it will perform better with richer soil and moderate watering. While it is considered hardy and easy to grow, it is subject to rusts in wet climates. The larger flowered varieties are more difficult to care for. This species exhibits allelopathy, the ability to inhibit the growth of other nearby plants. The inhibitor is released from decaying roots and rhizomes, so removing the roots after flowering will help this situation.

PROPAGATION:　Sunflowers are very easy to grow from seed sown in early spring.

Worshipped by the Inca Indians as a symbol of the sun, sunflowers were considered a prized plant by the early plant explorers. The seeds of this lofty American native were taken to Spain where they were cultivated and hybridized. The North American Indians planted the flowers and used the seeds for flour and oil. Early American settlers planted the sunflowers close to their homes, believing in the superstition that the bright yellow blossoms would ward off malaria. All parts of the plant are useful: the seeds for cooking and making soap, the leaves and stalks for fodder, fibers from the stalk for making cloth, and the young shoots for a spring vegetable. The genus name is from two Greek words: *helios*, meaning "sun," and *anthos*, meaning "flower."

OTHER SPECIES:　*H. angustifolius.* The narrow-leaved sunflower is found in swampy areas from New York to Florida, west to Missouri and Texas. It can tolerate drought as well as considerably wet conditions. If sown in spring after danger of frost has passed and when the soil is warm, the seeds should sprout in five days and bloom in two to three months.

H. grosseserratus. The saw tooth or big tooth sunflower is considered the best sunflower for cultivation, according to the *Prairie Propagation Handbook.* It blooms from September until October and seeds can be collected in November.

H. maximiliani. This tall perennial grows to a height of 8 feet and blooms in October. Native to Texas and New Mexico, this species is quite drought tolerant but can become somewhat aggressive.

Dame's rocket

BOTANNICAL NAME:　*Hesperis matronalis*
COMMON NAME:　dame's rocket
FAMILY:　Cruciferae
GROWING RANGE:　all regions of the United States
NATURAL RANGE:　Mediterranean Area
BLOOMS:　May — June
COLOR:　purple, white
HEIGHT:　24-36 inches
TYPE:　perennial
DESCRIPTION:　The flowers are phloxlike and are up to 2 inches across. They are borne in loose floral heads at the ends of the flowering stems.

ENVIRONMENTAL PREFERENCE: This plant will grow in full sun to partial shade and needs moist, well-drained soil.

PROPAGATION: Dame's rocket grows easily from seed but is rather short-lived and should be replanted annually. It will germinate in eight to twelve days at temperatures of 65° to 75° F. The planting rate for a pure stand is recommended at eight pounds per acre.

The large blossoms make a nice show in the late spring meadow. Their beauty is enhanced by a wonderfully sweet fragrance.

BOTANICAL NAME: *Iberis umbellata* (EYE-ber-iss um-bell-AY-tah)
COMMON NAME: candytuft
FAMILY: Cruciferae
GROWING RANGE: all regions of the United States
NATURAL RANGE: Mediterranean Area
BLOOMS: June — August
HEIGHT: to 16 inches
COLOR: white, pink, or lavender
TYPE: perennial (sometimes annual)
DESCRIPTION: This low, bushy plant has shiny green foliage in mounds of up to 2 feet across. There is an abundance of tiny white blossoms, each of which is only 1/8 to 1/2 inch across.
ENVIRONMENTAL PREFERENCE: Candytuft dislikes damp conditions and shade. It is a sunlover and prefers light, well-drained soil.
PROPAGATION: Grown from seed, it germinates in five to fourteen days and will bloom within two to three months. Sow in early spring after the last frost when the soil has warmed somewhat. After it flowers, cutting back the stalks will keep the plants from getting woody and open centered. Plant candytuft in groups of three or more toward the front of the meadow or border.

Candytuft

The common name candytuft comes from the word *Candia,* which is the ancient name for Crete. This member of the mustard family has been known and used for centuries for seasoning and is sometimes known as candy mustard. The genus is named for *Iberia,* the Roman name for ancient Spain and the original home for many species of this genus.

Considered a wonderful cure for rheumatism in American colonial days, it was always included in a herb garden.

BOTANICAL NAME: *Ipomopsis rubra* (ip-oh-MOP-sis REW-brah)
COMMON NAME: standing cypress
FAMILY: Polemoniaceae
GROWING RANGE: Midwest, Pacific Northwest, Southeast, Southwest, Texas-Oklahoma
NATURAL RANGE: South Carolina to Florida and west to Texas
BLOOMS: June — August
HEIGHT: 24 — 72 inches

Standing cypress

COLOR: red

TYPE: perennial or biennial

DESCRIPTION: This is a rather tall, erect plant with bright red tubular flowers. The leaves are deeply divided and cover the flowering stalk.

ENVIRONMENTAL PREFERENCE: Light, dry soil and full sun to partial shade are the best conditions for this plant. It needs good drainage but is drought resistant when established.

PROPAGATION: Grown as an annual, a biennial, and as a short-lived perennial, this plant grows well from seed and will usually produce blossoms the first growing season, particularly if it is started inside in early spring. When seeds are sown outdoors, suggested planting rate is six pounds per acre.

Texas plume, or standing cypress, as it is sometimes called, is an excellent plant to use along stream banks or in the back of the meadow. It gets rather large (up to 6 feet), so it should be placed in the correct location. It is closely related to the *Gilias* and is sometimes erroneously called a *gilia*. The color and configuration of the flowers makes Texas plume particularly good for attracting hummingbirds. Another common name is Spanish larkspur.

BOTANICAL NAME: *Iris cristata* (EYE-ris kris-TAY-tah)

COMMON NAME: dwarf crested iris

FAMILY: Iridaceae

GROWING RANGE: Northeast, Pacific Northwest, Southeast, Texas-Oklahoma

NATURAL RANGE: Maryland to Georgia and Oklahoma

BLOOMS: April

HEIGHT: 4 — 9 inches

COLOR: blue, purple

TYPE: perennial

DESCRIPTION: As the name suggests, these look like miniature iris. The single flowers have six parts, three downward curving petallike sepals and three upward curving petals. The leaves are sword shaped and can be up to 14 inches tall.

ENVIRONMENTAL PREFERENCE: Best planted on a hillside or slight incline, this iris must have good soil drainage. It seems to do fine in soil that is of average fertility and where it gets moderate amounts of moisture. It needs direct sun and performs best with a bit of dappled shade.

PROPAGATION: Propagation by seed is often difficult for only a few seeds are usually set. Division is easy and reliable. Divide the plants in late fall when they begin to go dormant, signaled by the tips of the foliage turning yellow. When dividing, include two or three fans with each division and replant immediately.

Because of the many colors found on a single iris, this family of plants was named for the goddess of the rainbow, Iris. It was the duty of this goddess to take the souls of women to the Elysian Fields, and for this reason, irises were often planted on the graves of women during the days of the Roman Empire.

Although it was used by the American Indians for various medical treatments, dwarf crested iris is somewhat poisonous, causing intestinal inflammation and shortness of breath if consumed in great quantities.

The iris is the basis for the *fleur de lis,* or flower of Louis, that was included on the French banner.

OTHER SPECIES: *I. tenax.* The Oregon blue flag or tough leaf iris is appropriately named, for the narrow, 16-inch leaves are indeed quite strong. The Indians used fibers from the edges of the leaves to make cord and rope. The species name is from the Latin word for tenacious. This is a Western species, growing from southwest Washington to northwest California, west of the Cascade Mountains. It blooms from April to June and the blossoms are large, delicate and a deep lavender color. This adaptable species needs moisture in the spring while in bloom but is able to withstand drier summer conditions.

I. missouriensis. Found from California, east to Colorado, this species blooms from May through July and grows to a height of 20 inches. The blossoms are large and pale blue or blue violet.

Iris douglasiana. The flowers of this species are 3 to 4 inches long and are reddish purple, pink, cream, or white. It is native from southern California to Oregon and blooms from March to May.

Dwarf crested iris

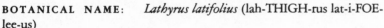

BOTANICAL NAME: *Lathyrus latifolius* (lah-THIGH-rus lat-i-FOE-lee-us)

COMMON NAME: sweet pea

FAMILY: Leguminosae

GROWING RANGE: all regions of the United States (may be difficult to control in the Midwest and some areas of the West)

NATURAL RANGE: Europe

BLOOMS: June — September

HEIGHT: trailing vine

COLOR: purplish pink

TYPE: perennial

DESCRIPTION: This trailing vine sometimes grows as long as 9 feet. The foliage is blue green and the blossoms an attractive pink or lavender. Under ideal conditions, sweet pea will cover the ground with more blossoms than leaves.

ENVIRONMENTAL PREFERENCE: This plant needs full sun or partial shade. It can take dry or moist conditions and seems to do quite well in heavy soils.

Sweet pea

PROPAGATION: This plant establishes colonies by putting out rhizome-bearing roots. It germinates readily from seeds sown in late winter or early spring. If the seeds are soaked in warm water for twenty-four hours before planting, they will sprout in fifteen days. The first blossoms will appear in two to three months.

Lathyrus latifolius is an escape plant from Europe. It is considered invasive or difficult to control in some parts of the country and should be used with care wherever it is planted. In a garden, it often crowds out its neighbors.

Other names for this species are sand pea and everlasting pea. The generic name is from the Greek word *lathyros,* which means "pea."

OTHER SPECIES: *L. venosus.* This native species is found from New Brunswick, south to Georgia and Texas. It blooms during late summer and needs good moisture, but it is an attractive meadow plant. Some of the species native to the western part of the country include *L. rigidus* and *L. polyphyllus.*

BOTANICAL NAME: *Lavatera trimestris* (lav-ah-TAIR-ah tri-MESS-tris)
COMMON NAME: tree mallow
FAMILY: Malvaceae
GROWING RANGE: Northeast, Pacific Northwest, Southeast, Southwest, West
NATURAL RANGE: Mediterranean
BLOOMS: July — September
HEIGHT: 36 — 72 inches
COLOR: white, rose, pink, red
TYPE: annual
DESCRIPTION: The leaves are roundish and toothed and resemble those of a maple tree. The large satiny flowers are single, measuring up to 4 inches across. They are similar to hollyhock blossoms.
ENVIRONMENTAL PREFERENCE: Best conditions include full sun and average to rich soil, with moderate amounts of moisture. This plant can take partial shade and seems tolerant of soil with a low pH.
PROPAGATION: Sow the seeds in spring as soon as the soil can be worked. They should germinate in two to three weeks. Sow the seeds where you want them, for they don't like to be moved. Thin the young plants to give each one room to spread. Tree mallow is easy to cultivate. Suggested planting rate is thirty pounds per acre.

Despite its common name, this is not a tree but a fast-growing, colorful, tall annual that is great to use in the back of the meadow. Its blossoms are large and showy and they add wonderful texture to the summer meadow.

Tree mallow

BOTANICAL NAME: *Layia platyglossa* (LAY-ee-ah plat-ee-GLOSS-ah)
COMMON NAME: tidy tips
FAMILY: Compositae
GROWING RANGE: Pacific Northwest, Southwest, Texas-Oklahoma, West
NATURAL RANGE: California
BLOOMS: March — May
HEIGHT: 12 inches
COLOR: yellow and white
TYPE: annual
DESCRIPTION: The flowers are large (1 to 1½ inches wide), showy, and daisylike: yellow ray flowers are tipped with white.
ENVIRONMENTAL PREFERENCE: Tidy tips will grow best in well-drained soil and full sun or partial shade. It is considered drought tolerant. Under ideal conditions it will compete well with grasses. It can take heavy soil but will not tolerate continually wet conditions.
PROPAGATION: This plant is easy to grow from seed. Sow it in early spring, outdoors, as soon as the soil is warm and the danger of frost is past. The seeds should sprout in eight days and the first blooms will appear in three months. Recommended planting rate for a pure stand is six pounds per acre.

Tidy tips

Since they bring good color to the meadow in spring and early summer, tidy tips should be planted in an area where they will be seen to greatest advantage. They are low growing, reaching a height of only 1 foot, so place them toward the front of the meadow. *Platyglossa* means "flat tongued" and refers to the shape of the ray flowers. The genus was named for George Tradescant Lay, a botanist who participated in plant explorations to California in the early 1800s.

BOTANICAL NAME: *Liatris pycnostachya* (lie-AT-riss pic-no-STAK-yah)
COMMON NAME: prairie blazing star
FAMILY: Compositae
GROWING RANGE: all regions of the United States
NATURAL RANGE: Indiana to South Dakota; south to Florida, Louisiana, and Texas
BLOOMS: August — September
HEIGHT: 24 — 48 inches
COLOR: violet, lavender
TYPE: perennial
DESCRIPTION: Growing from a woody corm or rootstock, this plant produces many grasslike, usually hairy leaves. The flower heads are rose or lilac colored and occur densely along a wandlike flowering stem.

Blazing star

ENVIRONMENTAL PREFERENCE: A basic requirement for the best results for this plant is full sun. If it is grown in the shade, it has a tendency to become rampant and unruly, producing only a few inferior flowers. If you don't have a sunny spot for this, don't plant it. In addition, it prefers moderately rich soils but cannot tolerate soggy winter soils. It is considered easy to grow.

PROPAGATION: Growing this genus from seed is a long process. Germination from fresh seed often takes up to six months, though cold stratification of the seeds might quicken the process. Suggested planting rate for most species is twelve pounds. Division of mature plants is the quickest means of propagation. Cut the corms as you would potatoes, leaving one or two eyes with each section. Plant these corms approximately 1 inch deep. The first year the flower spikes will probably not be well formed, but by the second year, flowering should be good.

Liatris is unusual for a member of the Compositae family in that the flowers are clustered on a dense spike. The flowers begin to open at the top of the spike and work their way downward. The flower heads are composed entirely of disk flowers and have no ray flowers. They make wonderful cut flowers. Best planted as individual specimens rather than in large groups, blazing stars add rich color to the autumn meadow.

OTHER SPECIES: *L. aspera.* The rough blazing star has long narrow, rough leaves and numerous purple heads. It blooms from mid August through September and is native from southern Ontario and Ohio to South Dakota, south to Texas and South Carolina.

L. scariosa. This blazing star has violet to lavender flowers. It is not as tall as other species, but the individual blossoms are larger. It can not tolerate too rich a soil; rich soil produces limp, ragged plants. It is native to the mountains from southern Pennsylvania to South Carolina and north Georgia.

L. spicata. The dense blazing star, or spiked gayfeather, likes a little extra moisture and well-drained, fairly rich soil. The seeds of this species also need cold stratification and should be placed in the refrigerator or planted outdoors in the fall. It grows to a height of 2 to 3 feet and blooms from July to September. It is hardy to -35° F. and is native to moist areas from Long Island to Michigan, south to Florida and Louisiana.

L. punctata. Dotted gayfeather is native from Michigan to Manitoba to Mexico. It is a perennial that blooms in September or October. It grows to a height of 2 feet, is drought tolerant, and is not particular about its soil. It needs full sun or partial shade. It has many common names including blazing star, gayfeather, and button snakeroot.

BOTANICAL NAME: *Lilium canadense* (LIL-ee-um CAN-ah-dense)

COMMON NAME: Turk's cap lily

FAMILY: Liliaceae

GROWING RANGE: Midwest, Northeast, Southeast

NATURAL RANGE: southern New Hampshire and Massachusetts; New York, south to Georgia and Alabama

BLOOMS: July

HEIGHT: to 108 inches

COLOR: orange

TYPE: perennial

DESCRIPTION: Tall arching stems bear many large, drooping orange flowers spotted with reddish brown. The petals and sepals are curved backwards, exposing the anthers and large brown anthers.

ENVIRONMENTAL PREFERENCE: Deep, moist rich soil and several hours of direct sunlight are basic requirements for this plant. It is quite a tall plant and should be planted in a protected spot, sheltered from high winds. An ideal site would be an open woodland area at the border of the meadow, protected by small trees or shrubs.

PROPAGATION: The native lilies are infamous for being difficult to propagate. They will certainly teach one patience! The seeds must go through both a cold stratification and two moist warm periods. To speed the germination period, the following procedure is suggested in Harry Phillips' book *Growing and Propagating Wildflowers:* prepare a jar or freezer container with damp sphagnum moss, place the seeds in this, seal and store at room temperature for six weeks, and then put the jar in the refrigerator for an additional six weeks. At the end of this period, plant the bulbs in a well-prepared site. The entire procedure should take approximately fourteen weeks, so begin in January or early February in order to be able to plant after the danger of frost has passed. These seedlings will be quite sensitive to any change in their environment so disturb them as little as possible. They will generally reach flowering size in five or six years. Another means of propagation is by using the small offshoots from the bulbs. Remove these and replant in the fall. Planting scales from large bulbs will produce new bulbs in one year. When purchasing plants from a nursery, be aware that these are difficult to propagate and will not be inexpensive. Check your source and make sure that the plants were not dug from the wild.

Turk's cap lily

The lily has always been an important symbol of the Christian faith. A legend says that the lilies came from Mary's tears when she found that she was to be a mother. Another legend says that the Easter lily was not white until picked by the Virgin Mary. The lily is the Christian symbol of purity, chastity, innocence, the resurrection and Easter. In more puritan times members of the church would remove the pistils and stamen from the blossoms before bringing lilies into the church so as not to offend anyone.

OTHER SPECIES: Our native lilies represent some of the most beautiful wildflowers found in the United States. They deserve our patience, time and attention. As with so many other types of our native plants, each region of the country will have different species that are indigenous. Call a local botanical garden or native plant society to find out which ones grow in your region and the best means of obtaining these plants.

Mountain phlox

BOTANICAL NAME: *Linanthus grandiflorus* (lin-AN-thus grand-i-FLOOR-us)
COMMON NAME: mountain phlox
FAMILY: Polemoniaceae
GROWING RANGE: Pacific Northwest, Southwest
NATURAL RANGE: California
BLOOMS: April — August
HEIGHT: 14 inches
COLOR: white, lavender, pink
TYPE: annual
DESCRIPTION: The flowers are a broad funnel shape and are delicate shades of pink and purple. They occur in open clusters along the flowering stem. The leaves are long and narrow.
ENVIRONMENTAL PREFERENCE: Since it needs light soil and full sun to partial shade, mountain phlox does better in the Western states than it does in the East. Although the plant will survive drought conditions, it will bloom longer and more fully if given moderate amounts of water.
PROPAGATION: Grown easily from seed sown in spring, this plant also reseeds itself readily.

Mountain phlox is also sometimes called California phlox because of its native range. It will bloom for two to three months or even longer with sufficient moisture. The genus name comes from two Greek words — *linon*, meaning "flax," and *anthos*, meaning "a flower," because the blossom resembles that of the flax.

BOTANICAL NAME: *Linaria maroccana* (lin-AIR-ee-ah mar-oh-CAN-ah)
COMMON NAME: spurred snapdragon
FAMILY: Scrophulariaceae
GROWING RANGE: Pacific Northwest, Southeast, Southwest, Texas-Oklahoma, West (some species may become serious pests)
NATURAL RANGE: Morocco

BLOOMS: April — July
HEIGHT: 30 inches
TYPE: annual
DESCRIPTION: The tiny delicate flowers of this species are less than an inch long with a very long spur. They are brightly colored and blotched with different colors on the lip.
ENVIRONMENTAL PREFERENCE: Plant snapdragon in light soil in full sun and supply it with moderate amounts of water.
PROPAGATION: This plant will grow quite well from seed, but for it to create a nice splash of color it should be sown in quantities. For a pure stand the planting rate is one half pound per acre.

Snapdragon

The best *Linaria* to grow within a meadow is *L. maroccana,* and what a little jewel it is! Although under ideal conditions it can grow to a height of 30 inches, in my own meadow it rarely reaches that height, which means that it is often overshadowed by larger plants. When you are walking through the meadow, however, it is quite a treat to find this delicate little flower. It competes well with grasses and is easy to grow. For the greatest show from this species, sow large amounts of the seeds in an area all to themselves.

The genus name is Latin and means "like flax." It refers to the leaves which are similar to those of flax. The species name, *maroccana,* was chosen because of the place of origin for the plant, Morocco.

OTHER SPECIES: Many species of *Linaria* have naturalized throughout the United States, and several of these have become serious pests.

L. genistifolia dalmatica. This plant is often incorrectly called *Linaria dalmatica.* It was introduced from Europe after World War II as an ornamental and adapted itself with such speed and ease to its new home that it now is considered a serious pest in Eastern Washington. It is especially troublesome in wheat fields and is difficult to get rid of for its waxy leaves are impervious to most general herbicides. This is a classic example of the introduction of non-native plant into an area with good intentions but disastrous results.

L. vulgaris. Butter and eggs is another European native that can become a pest in some areas. Although it does not seem to pose as serious a problem as *L. genistifolia,* it should be carefully controlled so it won't get out of hand. It is included within some mixtures, so watch out for it.

BOTANICAL NAME: *Linum grandiflorum rubrum* (LY-num grand-i-FLOOR-um)
COMMON NAME: red flax
FAMILY: Linaceae
GROWING RANGE: all regions except the Northeast
NATURAL RANGE: north Africa, southern Europe

BLOOMS: April — August
HEIGHT: 14 inches
COLOR: red
TYPE: annual
DESCRIPTION: The large, bright red flowers are borne on stems 1 to 2 feet tall. The blossoms last only a single day but occur in such profusion that this does not seem to matter. The leaves are long and narrow and needlelike.
ENVIRONMENTAL PREFERENCE: This plant is quite heat and drought tolerant. It needs well-drained soil and will not tolerate soggy winter soils. It prefers light soil and can be grown in full sun or light shade.
PROPAGATION: Scarlet flax grows well from seed and should be sown in quantity in the fall or early spring where you want it to grow. It reseeds readily. The seeds germinate in one to fifteen days at temperatures of 65° to 75° F. First blooms should appear in three months. It is difficult to divide, but stem cuttings can be taken in mid summer. The suggested planting rate is fifteen pounds per acre.

Red flax

Both the annual red flax and the perennial blue flax are nice additions to the meadow. The red flowers last only a single day and are not suitable for cut flowers, but they will bloom for long periods of time. The blue flowers close up by noon but still add a nice bit of color for mornings in the meadow.

Flax has served man longer than any other non-food plant. Linen cloth is made from flax, and for centuries a measure of a man's wealth was the amount of linen he had. Fibers from the stems were extracted when the stems reached a height of about 3 feet and then were separated and spun into cloth. Flax was first introduced to the American colonies to make clothing, but it was not cultivated extensively because of the popularity of cotton. Seeds from the plant were used in medicine for liniments, cough syrups, and salves. The paint industry also uses the seed for linseed oil, which is a drying agent put into paints and varnishes. Based on its many uses, the language of flowers associates flax with industry.

OTHER SPECIES: *L. perenne lewisii.* The blue flax seems to do quite well in most regions of the country except for the area north of Boston, where it is not considered hardy. It is a perennial, growing to a height of 2 feet. It prefers light soil, full sun, and dry conditions. The suggested planting rate for a pure stand is eight pounds per acre. This species is a prairie flower native to the Midwest. Although it is difficult to transplant, it is otherwise adaptable and easy to grow. The flowers open in the morning and are gone by noon. The blossoms, when pressed, keep their deep blue color.

BOTANICAL NAME: *Lobularia maritima* (lob-yew-LAIR-ee-ah mah-RIT-i-mah)

COMMON NAME: sweet alyssum

FAMILY: Cruciferae

GROWING RANGE: all regions

NATIVE RANGE: southern Europe

BLOOMS: April — August

HEIGHT: 12 inches

COLOR: white to rose to violet

TYPE: annual or tender perennial

DESCRIPTION: The blossoms of this low-growing plant occur in small clusters. Each individual flower is tiny and has four petals. The leaves are long and narrow and are ½ to 2 inches long.

ENVIRONMENTAL PREFERENCE: This plant is drought tolerant but likes soil rich in lime and full sun or light shade. It cannot take a heavy frost.

PROPAGATION: Sweet alyssum grows easily from seeds sown in spring after danger of frost is past and when the soil is warm. The suggested planting rate is two pounds per acre. It will germinate in five or six days, begin to bloom in six to eight weeks, and continue to bloom until frost if the spent blossoms are kept sheared. In mild regions it will bloom all year long.

Sweet alyssum

This species was formerly known as *Alyssum maritimum* and was originally considered a seaside plant — thus the species name. It was commonly found along the Mediterranean shore. It has always been a favorite in the garden because of its honey sweet scent. This makes a great plant to use in the front of the meadow for early spring color and is nice for borders in a more formal setting.

The genus name is from the word *lobulus,* which means "small pod" and refers to the fruit.

There are several dwarf forms of *Lobularia* available. Most of these should be planted at a rate of two pounds per acre for a pure stand.

BOTANICAL NAME: *Lupinus perennis* (lew-PINE-us per-EN-iss)

COMMON NAME: perennial lupine

FAMILY: Leguminosae

GROWING RANGE: all regions of the United States

NATIVE RANGE: Maine to southern Ontario, south to Florida and Louisiana

BLOOMS: May — June

HEIGHT: 12 — 24 inches

COLOR: blue, purple

TYPE: perennial

Perennial lupine

DESCRIPTION: The blue pea-like blossoms occur densely on an upright stem. The leaves, which grow in clumps, are palmately divided into seven to nine leaflets.

ENVIRONMENTAL PREFERENCE: Although adaptable to varying types of soils, the lupines need full sun to bloom and require well-drained soil. This species is evergreen in milder climates but does best in areas where summers are cool.

PROPAGATION: Germination from seeds is sporadic, but this can be helped by soaking the seeds in warm water for twelve to twenty-four hours before planting them. The *Praire Propagation Handbook* suggests sowing fresh seeds immediately into a mixture of peat moss and sand and transplanting the seedlings. The lupines, like many members of the Leguminosae family, are capable of nitrogen fixation, or taking nitrogen from the air and changing it to a usable form in the soil. For nitrogen fixation to take place, the correct bacteria must be present on the roots of these plants. To assure that this will happen, seeds of the pea family are often inoculated. Where colonies of lupines have already grown, inoculation is not always necessary. Where you are trying to establish a new colony, inoculation will probably be helpful. If you pretreat the seeds by scarifying and/or inoculating them, make sure you water sufficiently to get them established, for by breaking their dormancy, you are also destroying the seed's defense against cold or dry conditions. Established plants greatly resent being transplanted and rarely live once they have been dug up. The plants are rather short-lived and should be replaced every few years. If lupines are included in a seed mixture that you have put out, be patient in waiting for the lupine seedlings to appear. It may be two years or even longer before successful germination takes place.

The genus name comes from the Latin word *lupus,* which means "wolf." Lupines are often found growing in very poor soil and it was believed that the plant stole nutrients from the soil, just as wolves have an unfortunate reputation for stealing. Actually, because lupines are members of the legume family, they give more to the soil than they take away, for they are able to take nitrogen from the air and, with the aid of bacteria living on their roots, change it into a useable form — making the soil richer than before.

Another common name is sundial plant because the leaves follow the sun's path all day long, finally closing at night. The leaves fold together at night to reduce the amount of surface area and prevent unnecessary chilling. This is especially beneficial in parts of the West where the day and night temperatures vary greatly.

In the language of flowers lupine is voraciousness and imagination.

OTHER SPECIES: *L. densiflorus.* The golden lupine is native to California but will grow in the Pacific Northwest and the Southwest.

Given full sun, this species will grace the summer meadow with its golden spikes.

L. succulentus. The arroyo lupine, or succulent lupine, is a purple annual that grows well in the western states and blooms during the spring and summer. It grows to a height of 2 to 4 feet and will thrive in either clay or sandy soils with moderate amounts of water.

L. subcarnosus. The Texas bluebonnet has a well-deserved place in the heart of nearly every Texan. The Texas Department of Transportation has planted over one million miles of roadsides in wildflowers, most of them the bluebonnet. Roadsides in Texas in the late spring are a sight worthy of a trip to Texas. This species is native to its namesake and will grow well in states west to California. Germination can be increased by pretreating the seeds by soaking them in tepid water for twelve to twenty-four hours. Seeds take approximately twenty days to sprout, and you should have blossoms within four months. This is an extremely drought-tolerant species.

BOTANICAL NAME: *Lychnis chalcedonica* (LICK-niss kal-see-DON-i-kah)
COMMON NAME: Maltese cross
FAMILY: Caryophyllaceae
GROWING RANGE: all regions of the United States
NATURAL RANGE: Asia
BLOOMS: June — August
HEIGHT: 1 — 2 feet
COLOR: red
TYPE: perennial
DESCRIPTION: The bright red flowers occur in dense terminal clusters. The four petals are deeply cut and are 1 inch across. Maltese cross has an open growing habit and hairy leaves and stems.
ENVIRONMENTAL PREFERENCE: Full sun and dry, very well drained soil are the best conditions for this plant. It tends to be short-lived unless the soil is quite well drained. It is hardy to -35° F.
PROPAGATION: This plant is easy to germinate from seed. Sprouting takes place in two to three weeks when temperatures range from 70° to 80° F. The seeds need light to germinate so sow them on the surface. It reseeds easily.

Maltese cross

Maltese cross is often short-lived and sometimes considered a biennial. Other common names include Jerusalem cross, because of the shape of the flower, and scarlet lightning, because of the color of the blossom. The genus name is also based on the brightly colored flowers: *lychnis* comes from the Greek word meaning "lamp."

Prairie aster

BOTANICAL NAME: *Machaeranthera tanacetifolia* (mack-ee-ran-THAIR-ah tan-ah-set-i-FOE-lee-ah)

COMMON NAME: prairie aster

FAMILY: Compositae

GROWING RANGE: Midwest, Southeast, Southwest, Texas-Oklahoma, West

NATURAL RANGE: Alberta to South Dakota, south to north central Mexico

BLOOMS: July — October

HEIGHT: 18 inches

COLOR: lavender with yellow centers

TYPE: annual or biennial

DESCRIPTION: The foliage is like that of tansy, and the blossoms are very much like those of the asters. It is a many-branched, bushy plant.

ENVIRONMENTAL PREFERENCE: This plant likes partial or full sun and dry, sandy soils.

PROPAGATION: Prairie aster grows easily from seed. Germination generally takes five to ten days with temperatures of 60° to 70° F. First blooms will appear in three months, and bloom will continue until frost.

The genus name comes from the Latin word *machaera,* meaning "dagger," and *anthera,* meaning "anther." It refers to the anthers, which are pointed. The species name was chosen for the similarity of the leaves to those of tansy. It is also known as the Tahoka daisy. This genus differs from the true asters in that *Machaeranthueras* have spine-tipped leaves.

OTHER SPECIES: *M. canescens.* This plains species is taller, growing to a height of 24 inches. It is covered with bluish purple flowers with gold centers from August to October.

BOTANICAL NAME: *Mentzelia lindleyi* (ment-ZEE-lee-ah lind-LAY-eye)

COMMON NAME: blazing star

FAMILY: Loasaceae

GROWING RANGE: Midwest, Pacific Northwest, Southwest, Texas-Oklahoma

NATURAL RANGE: desert areas and central California

BLOOMS: March — June

HEIGHT: 12 — 48 inches

COLOR: yellow

TYPE: annual

DESCRIPTION: The star-shaped yellow blossoms have petals that are each nearly oval meeting at an orange reddish center. The leaves —

light green and rough with short hairs — look very much like dandelion leaves.

ENVIRONMENTAL PREFERENCE: Although it needs good drainage, this species will withstand heat, wind, and poor soil. It can take heavy or light, rich or sterile soil but needs full sun. It can survive drought conditions, but will perform better with moderate amounts of water.

PROPAGATION: Sow the seeds in prepared beds in late fall or early spring. Rake the soil lightly, tamp it, and keep it evenly moist until germination takes place, in about ten days. The sowing rate for a pure stand is four pounds per acre. This plant puts down such a deep taproot that it does not transplant well.

Another common name for this plant is stickleaf, because of the many tiny barbs found on the leaves. The Indians often roasted the seeds of this plant and ground them for meal. Most members of the Loasaceae family are native to the southwestern United States, Mexico, and the West Indies. The family was named for Christian Mentzel, a German botanist who died in 1701.

OTHER SPECIES: *M. decapetala.* Native from southern Canada to Texas, this large showy species opens late in the afternoon and then stays open during the morning. It has creamy petals with golden stamen.

Blazing star

BOTANICAL NAME: *Mirabilis jalapa* (meer-RAB-i-liss jal-AH-pah)
COMMON NAME: four o'clock
FAMILY: Nyctaginaceae
GROWING REGION: all regions of the United States (may become invasive and difficult to control in some areas)
NATURAL RANGE: tropical America
BLOOMS: July — September
HEIGHT: 36 inches
COLOR: red, pink, yellow, white
TYPE: perennial
DESCRIPTION: There is a profusion of dark green leaves and large, attractive, trumpet-shaped flowers. The flowers, measuring 1½ to 2 inches across, do not open until late in the afternoon, unless the day is cloudy.
ENVIRONMENTAL PREFERENCE: This is a very adaptable plant and a good one to use in the meadow because it can take full sun or partial shade and does not seem to mind growing under other plants, as often happens in a meadow situation. It can take dry or moist conditions, rich or poor soil, but it does prefer well-aerated soil. It seems to do particularly well in coastal areas.

PROPAGATION: This plant grows easily from seed, germinating in twelve to fourteen days with temperatures at 70° to 85° F. Sow the seeds directly into the meadow after the danger of frost is past in spring. Another method of propagation is from tubers which have been dug in fall and stored in a frost-free place. In cold climates this plant should be treated as an annual and planted each year.

Usually considered a garden flower, four o'clocks make good plants to use in urban areas for they seem impervious to dust and soot and fumes. When this plant is grown in its natural range as a perennial, the roots may weigh as much as forty pounds. This plant sometimes grows so prolifically that it might be difficult to control, particularly in the Midwest, Southwest, and Southeast.

The unusual blooming pattern has given rise to many different names. This pattern, of course, accounts for the name four o'clock. In France it is called *belle de nuit* and in Italy *bella di notte*. The genus was at one time called *Admirablilis*, but this was changed by Linnaeus to *Mirabilis*, from the Latin word meaning "wonderful." The family name comes from the Greek word *nyktos*, meaning "night" and based on the blooming habit of many plants in this family.

The plant has had many different uses. The powdered seeds were used by the Japanese in cosmetics. In China the flowers were soaked to extract their color and then used as a dye to color gelatin made from seaweed. The Hopi Indians used the root as a stomach soother and also to induce visions. Scientists have found that the plant is quite useful in the study of genetics and heredity.

OTHER SPECIES: *M. multiflora*. Native to southern Utah and Colorado, south to Texas and northern Arizona, this Western species looks much like *M. jalapa* but has brighter colored blossoms. It can become a very dense mound, up to 4 feet wide and 20 inches high, and it will bloom from July until frost.

Four o'clock

BOTANICAL NAME: *Monarda didyma* (moh-NARD-ah DID-i-mah)
COMMON NAME: bee balm
FAMILY: Labiatae
GROWING RANGE: all regions of the United States
NATURAL RANGE: New England, south to Georgia and Tennessee
BLOOMS: June — August
HEIGHT: 48 inches
COLOR: red
TYPE: perennial
DESCRIPTION: The heads of tubular scarlet flowers are found on top of sturdy, four-sided stems which sometimes reach as high as 6

feet. There are reddish or purplish bracts under each flower cluster. The leaves are large and opposite and give off a mint odor when crushed.

ENVIRONMENTAL PREFERENCE: Found naturally along stream banks or in wet meadows, this plant requires moist conditions and full sun to partial shade. It makes a good plant to use at the edge of a woodland area or stream bank bordering a meadow.

PROPAGATION: Seeds are best sown as soon as they ripen, but the seedlings grow very slowly so watch out for them. To encourage bushier plants, pinch out the tops several times during the growing stage. Plants grown from seed should bloom during the second year. Cuttings can be taken from mature plants any time during the summer and should be placed in a growing medium and kept evenly moist. The easiest method of propagation is by dividing the plants. They spread quickly and should be divided every two to three years to retain their vigor. Spring division is preferable, as plants divided in the fall often do not survive the winter.

Wild bergamot

Another common name for *Monarda didyma* is Oswego tea. The American explorer John Bartram found the Oswego Indians drinking mint tea made from the leaves. The tea can be made by using three to four dried leaves in a cup of boiling water and is best flavored with a little honey. The tea was found to be useful for soothing upset stomachs or cooling a fever. It was also used to soothe bee or insect stings, hence the common name.

The red and pink *Monardas* are wonderful plants for attracting hummingbirds. Not only do they like the color, but the long tubular configuration of the blossoms makes it difficult for anything but hummingbirds to pollinate it.

OTHER SPECIES: *M. fistulosa.* Wild bergamot has lavender or pink flowers and will bloom from late July until September. It grows to a height of 24 to 36 inches and is easily grown from seed, though germination seems to be helped by moist stratification. It will withstand drier conditions than *M. didyma*. It is native to North America east of the Rocky Mountains.

M. citriodora. This plant is native from Missouri to Nebraska, Utah, Texas, and Arizona. It is commonly called lemon mint for its scent. This species has pink or white flowers with purple spots. The seeds for this annual should be sown in late fall or early spring. It does best in soils rich in limestone and needs full sun or partial shade. It can tolerate drier conditions than many of the other species in this genus and can grow to a height of 24 inches.

BOTANICAL NAME: *Myosotis sylvatica* (my-oh-SO-tiss sil-VAT-i-kah)

COMMON NAME: forget me not

FAMILY: Boraginaceae

GROWING RANGE: all regions of the United States

NATURAL RANGE: Europe and Asia

BLOOMS: May — August

HEIGHT: 6 — 15 inches

COLOR: blue

TYPE: annual

DESCRIPTION: This is a well-branched, erect little plant with many small flowers, usually blue but sometimes pink or rarely white.

ENVIRONMENTAL PREFERENCE: Constant moisture is a must for this plant. If it dries out it will not last long. It prefers slightly acid to neutral soil with full sun or light shade.

PROPAGATION: This plant grows easily from seed and will germinate in ten to fifteen days. Sow it in late summer or early spring. It self-sows freely. Cuttings taken in summer root quickly.

There are several fairy tales and folk legends about how the plant got its common name. One of these tells how, when God was naming all the plants and animals, this little species could not remember its name. Finally, God leaned down and whispered, "Forget me not, that is your name." According to another story, two lovers were walking down a steep path in the mountains when the young girl saw this lovely little blue flower and asked her lover to get it for her. In doing so, the unfortunate man slipped and fell. As he threw her the blossom, he cried out "forget me not," and the plant has been called this since. Still another explanation is that the leaves of the plant are so bitter that once you taste them you will forget them not.

OTHER SPECIES: *M. laxa.* This smaller forget me not has much smaller blossoms but is native to North America and should be considered as an alternative species.

M. scorpiodes. A native of Europe and Asia, this plant is very much like *M. sylvatica* but the flowers are larger, measuring ¼ inch across. It needs very moist conditions and is a good plant to use as a ground cover for wet areas. The species name comes from the fact that when it is in bud it is coiled tightly, resembling a scorpion.

Forget me not

BOTANICAL NAME: *Nemophila menziesii* (nee-moe-FILL-ah men-ZEE-see-eye)

COMMON NAME: baby blue eyes

FAMILY: Hydrophyllaceae

GROWING RANGE: all regions of the United States

NATURAL RANGE: California

BLOOMS: March — May
HEIGHT: 10 inches
COLOR: blue
TYPE: annual
DESCRIPTION: The cup-shaped flowers are white toward the center and are found on top of stems branching from the base. Baby blue eyes blooms freely. The leaves are pinnately lobed.
ENVIRONMENTAL PREFERENCE: This species likes shade or partial shade, though it can tolerate full sun. It needs light soil and low to moderate watering. This species can not take hot and humid summer conditions.
PROPAGATION: Baby blue eyes grows from seed easily, taking about ten days to sprout and two to three months for the first blooms. Sow it either in spring or fall. In frost-free areas, it is good for winter or spring color. It will not transplant and will do best in an area with cool weather and moist soil. Under ideal conditions it will reseed itself. The recommended planting rate for a pure stand is eight pounds per acre.

Five spot

This delicate little plant is a prolific bloomer and is good for a border area or a part of the meadow that receives afternoon shade. They should provide good color in a shady spot throughout the summer. This species has been used in European gardens for over a century. The species was named for Archibald Menzies, a botanist who explored the Pacific coast in the 1700s. The genus name is from two Greek words — *nemos,* which means "a grove," and *phileo,* which means "to love" — and refers to the preferred habitat of some species.
OTHER SPECIES: *N. maculata.* Five spot, or buffalo eyes, has the same type of flower as *N. menzeisii* but is white with startling purple spots at the tips of the petals. It will grow in a variety of conditions including heavy clay or sand. This makes a nice bulb cover or is attractive planted in drifts in the meadow or in hanging baskets. Seeds should be sown thickly at a rate of twenty pounds per acre. If you set out plants, place them closely enough so that the leaves will shade the soil.

BOTANICAL NAME: *Oenothera biennis* (ee-no-THAIR-ah by-EN-iss)
COMMON NAME: evening primrose
FAMILY: Onagraceae
GROWING RANGE: all regions of the United States (some species may be difficult to control and become serious pests)
NATURAL RANGE: eastern North America
BLOOMS: July — frost
HEIGHT: 24 — 48 inches
COLOR: yellow

TYPE: biennial

DESCRIPTION: The yellow, lemon-scented flowers occur on long terminal spikes. The leaves are hairy and alternate with wavy margins often tinged with red. The blossoms open in late afternoon and close when the sun is up in the morning.

ENVIRONMENTAL PREFERENCE: This plant will grow in nearly any dry, sunny location. It is somewhat allelopathic and might inhibit the growth of plants growing close by.

PROPAGATION: Best propagation method is to sow seeds in the spring or fall. Germination takes place within five or six days. It transplants easily.

Evening primrose was taken from the New World to European gardens at a very early stage. It was described by European garden writers as early as 1600. The genus name is from the Greek word meaning 'wine imbibing'' and was given to this plant for its supposed power to increase one's desire for wine. Other common names include king's cure all, sand lily, and German rampion.

The young *Oenothera* plants make an excellent vegetable. Although they contain no opium as the Oriental poppies do, they were used medicinally as a sedative and sleep inducer. Pigment extracted from the blossoms was used to color medicines and wines. During the Middle Ages poppy juice was often given to infants to help them sleep, and the dried petals were used to calm children who had colic or whooping cough.

OTHER SPECIES: There are many, many species of this genus which can be grown in a meadow or garden situation. Some of these are quite difficult to control and will soon outgrow their welcome. One of the worst offenders in this category is *O. biennis,* which has the tendency to become invasive in the Midwest, Southeast, Northeast, and parts of the West. Members of the genus can be annuals, biennials, or perennials, depending on the environmental conditions as well as the genetic make-up of the plant. Members of the genus that open at night are called evening primroses. Those species that open during the day are called sundrops. Other species to be considered are:

O. caespitosa. The gumbo lily has wide, heart-shaped petals and a flower that measures up to 4 inches across. It opens so rapidly in the late afternoon that you can sit and watch it go from bud to full bloom.

O. lamarckiana. This annual grows to a height of 3 to 3 ½ feet. It needs little water and can take partial shade and soil with a high pH level. It has the added advantage of being less aggressive than many of the other species. Planting rate is two pounds per acre.

O. missouriensis. Native from Texas to Missouri and Nebraska, sundrops grow from 16 to 20 inches high. They prefer well-drained soil in full sun and will tolerate varying amounts of soil acidity. This plant can be very easily transplanted. Its growing habit makes it good

Evening primrose

to use for erosion control, and it is an attractive ground cover. Sowing rate is five pounds per acre. It blooms from May to August.

O. pallida. White evening primrose is a white species sometimes tinged with lavender. The blossoms are large and fragrant. It grows to a height of 14 inches and is excellent to use in sandy, coastal areas because it can form large clumps, binds the soil quite well, and is tolerant of salt spray. The recommended planting rate is five pounds per acre. It is native from California to the Rocky Mountains. It has a tendency to become invasive so use it sparingly.

O. speciosa. This plant is native to a large area stretching from Missouri to Mexico. It is low growing, has pink flowers, and blooms during the day.

O. hookeri. This evening primrose grows to a height of 24 to 36 inches and blooms from June to September. It is native from Washington to California and east to Texas and Colorado.

BOTANICAL NAME: *Papaver rhoeas* (PAH-pav-er RO-ee-us)
COMMON NAME: corn poppy
FAMILY: Papaveraceae
GROWING REGION: all regions of the United States
NATURAL RANGE: Eurasia and north Africa
BLOOMS: April — August
HEIGHT: 24 — 60 inches
COLOR: red
TYPE: annual
DESCRIPTION: The slender, hairy, branching stem bears large flowers 2 or more inches across. The foliage is finely dissected.
ENVIRONMENTAL PREFERENCE: This plant needs light soil, moderate watering, and full sun to partial shade. It likes open areas and cool soil, competes well with grasses, and prefers temperate climates.
PROPAGATION: Sow the seeds where you want them to grow for this plant transplants poorly. The seeds are very tiny — mix them with sand for more even sowing. Recommended planting rate is one pound per acre. For more continuous bloom, make several successive sowings. In mild regions the seeds will germinate in winter to give color in later winter and early spring. Elsewhere, sow in early spring.

Corn poppy

The corn poppy is often called Flanders poppy because after World War I great numbers of these plants began to bloom in Flander's field. Poppies had grown in this area for centuries but had been trampled underfoot during the four years of war and were able to bloom again only after the war was over. Actual soil counts were done and more than 2,500 poppy seeds per square foot were found.

OTHER SPECIES: *P. nudicaule.* The Iceland poppy is a perennial that is often grown as a biennial or annual. It will bloom the first year from seeds planted in the spring. It grows to a height of 12 to 24 inches and has yellow, cream, and orange blossoms. It is native to arctic regions in North America and Eurasia.

Beard tongue

BOTANICAL NAME: *Penstemon digitalis* (PEN-ste-mon di-ji-TAU-liss)

COMMON NAME: beard tongue

FAMILY: Scrophulariaceae

GROWING REGION: Midwest, Northeast, Southeast, Southwest, Texas-Oklahoma, West

NATURAL RANGE: Nova Scotia and Maine, to Minnesota and South Dakota, south to Alabama and Texas

BLOOMS: May — June

HEIGHT: 48 inches

COLOR: white

TYPE: perennial

DESCRIPTION: This species has a shiny stem with paired leaves and a terminal cluster of showy white tubular flowers.

ENVIRONMENTAL PREFERENCE: Beard tongue needs full to partial sun. It does not need excessive moisture but will tolerate wet soil.

PROPAGATION: Easily grown from seed or from cuttings taken in mid summer or from dividing mature plants, this penstemon will also readily self-sow.

Of the 250 known species of penstemons, only 2 are not native to North America. One is native to Central America and the other to northeastern Asia. The genus name is based on the Greek words *pente,* meaning five, and *stemen,* meaning stemen and refers to the four stamen and one staminode (non-functional stamen) found on the plants.

OTHER SPECIES: Climate is the determining factor for distribution of the different *Penstemon* species. For example, the Eastern and Southern species have upright herbaceous stems and are accustomed to great amounts of rainfall. The species that grow in the Southwest are very flat and creeping due to the lack of moisture. The rainy Pacific Northwest has shrubby species. Choose penstemons suited to your own climate, and you should have great success.

P. grandiflorus. This Western species is native from Illinois to North Dakota and Wyoming, south to Texas, and is considered an excellent garden plant. Its natural habitat is dry prairies and barrens, and it is best grown as a biennial. It grows to a height of 48 inches and blooms from July to August.

P. smallii. This species will grow in the Southeast, the Southwest, Texas and Oklahoma, and the West. It will not tolerate poorly drained soils as well as many of the other species, but it is a wonderfully showy and hardy plant to include in the meadow. There are sometimes as many as fifty flowers per plant, and a plant may bloom again if the flowering stem is cut back. The flowers are purple with white throats. The plant will grow to a height of 36 inches. The seeds can be collected in July and August (approximately six weeks after blooming) and should be sown immediately or stored in the refrigerator until spring. The plant is easily divided in the fall or early spring.

P. strictus. The Rocky Mountain penstemon needs good drainage and full sun. It has blue, snapdragonlike blossoms and grows on a stem 1 to 3 feet high. It is drought resistant and good for erosion control.

P. barbatus. The scarlet bugler is native from Utah to Mexico and is quite drought tolerant. It blooms in early summer on 2- to 4-foot stalks. Too much water results in tall, lank growth. Sow the seeds in the fall in an area that receives full sun or partial shade. To sow seeds in the spring, use cold stratification first.

P. eatonii. This native of southern California, Arizona, Nevada, and Utah grows to a height of 1 to 3 feet. It has scarlet but rather inconspicuous flowers.

BOTANICAL NAME: *Petalostemon purpureum* (pet-ah-low-STEM-on pur-pur-EE-um)
COMMON NAME: purple prairie clover
FAMILY: Leguminosae
GROWING RANGE: Midwest, Southeast, Southwest, Texas-Oklahoma, West
NATURAL RANGE: Indiana to southern Canada, south to Kentucky, Arkansas, and New Mexico
BLOOMS: June — August
HEIGHT: 12 — 36 inches
COLOR: purple red
TYPE: perennial
DESCRIPTION: The purplish flowers are found crowded along elongated cones. The individual flowers open from the base of the stem upward and have lovely orange gold anthers.
ENVIRONMENTAL PREFERENCE: Good drainage is a necessity, but prairie clover can grow in sandy or heavy soils. Full sun is needed for flowering.
PROPAGATION: Best grown from seed, the plants will often bloom the first summer. Seeds need moist stratification for ten days, or they can be planted in the fall. The sowing rate is eight pounds per acre. Division and transplanting of established plants is difficult.

Purple prairie clover

Although this species looks somewhat like common white clover in the initial stages, the advantages of using this plant are many. It is not as spreading or aggressive as the white clover, and rabbits do not seem to like to munch on it. The taproot makes a wonderful tea which is said to help reduce fever — particularly for measles victims. Other common names are voilet prairie clover and red tassel flower.

Desert bell

BOTANICAL NAME: *Phacelia campanularia* (fah-SEE-lee-ah kam-PAN-yew-lair-ee-ah)

COMMON NAME: desert bell

FAMILY: Hydrophyllaceae

GROWING RANGE: Pacific Northwest, Southeast, Southwest, Texas-Oklahoma, West

NATURAL RANGE: Colorado and Mojave deserts of southern California

BLOOMS: February — May

HEIGHT: 8 — 30 inches

COLOR: blue

TYPE: annual

DESCRIPTION: The deep blue corollas have five lobes and long golden stamen. They are arranged loosely on an open raceme. The leaves are slightly hairy with irregular edges.

ENVIRONMENTAL PREFERENCE: Adaptable to many types of soils, this species needs full sun, is drought tolerant, and adapts well to arid climates. It will perform best in rocky soils with good drainage.

PROPAGATION: Desert bells are easily grown from seed and should be planted in spring after danger of frost is past. Under good conditions, the plants will reseed. For a pure stand, the recommended planting rate is three pounds per acre.

OTHER SPECIES: *P. sericea.* Silky phacelia is native from British Columbia, south to Washington, and east to Colorado. It has violet-colored florets with long-silk-like filaments and has been described as looking like gold dust on royal velvet.

P. tanacetifolia. This species is called tansy phacelia because of the finely dissected foliage. The flowering stalks are curled. It will grow to a height of 36 inches. It should be sown at a rate of three pounds per acre. It is native from central California to Arizona, south to Mexico.

BOTANICAL NAME: *Phlox drummondii* (FLOCKS drum-MON-dee-eye)

COMMON NAME: annual phlox

FAMILY: Polemoniaceae

GROWING RANGE: all regions of the United States
NATURAL RANGE: south central Texas
BLOOMS: June — September
HEIGHT: 10 — 20 inches
COLOR: red
TYPE: annual
DESCRIPTION: The showy red flowers are borne on top of short, sticky stems that are covered with hairs.
ENVIRONMENTAL PREFERENCE: Well-drained, light soil that is rich in organic matter and full sun give this species the best growing conditions. It is rather adaptable, however, and seems to do fine in less perfect circumstances. It can withstand dry periods, but moderate watering will prolong the blooming season. Under good conditions, it tends to become bushy.
PROPAGATION: The seeds do best kept in continual darkness until germination takes place — usually within about ten days. Sow them in fall or spring after danger of frost has passed and the soil has warmed. Seeds can be started indoors in late winter in order to have plants to set out for earlier bloom.

Annual phlox

This Texas native is a bright addition to any meadow. The red flowers bloom in profusion and add a nice contrasting color to many areas that seem predominantly yellow during the summer months.

The word *phlox* is from the Greek word meaning "flame" and is descriptive of the color of many species. Nearly all the phloxes have a very sweet scent. Phlox was one of the earliest New World plants taken back to Europe by plant explorers, and it was hybridized and greatly valued in European gardens. It was reintroduced to America as a garden plant by European horticulturists.

Phlox leaves were made into a tea that supposedly was useful in curing an upset stomach. In the language of flowers phlox is a proposal of love and the hope for sweet dreams.

OTHER SPECIES: There are many native phlox species, most of which seem to like at least partial shade and woodsy conditions.

P. divaricata. The blue phlox is native from Quebec to Michigan south to Georgia and northern Alabama. While it is usually considered a woodland species, it will bloom in full sun if given sufficient moisture. It grows to a height of 8 to 12 inches and blooms in early spring. Cut the flowering stem back after the blooms fade and new green growth will appear and stay until frost. Although the seeds are difficult to collect, the plant is easily propagated by dividing clumps in spring or early fall.

P. pilosa. The prairie phlox is native to the area from southeastern Connecticut to southern Florida, west to Wisconsin and Texas. The blossoms are reddish purple, and it blooms from mid-May to early July. It grows 12 to 24 inches tall. The seeds have an unpredictable ger-

Coneflower

mination rate, but stem cuttings can be taken or the clumps can be divided.

BOTANICAL NAME: *Ratibida columnaris* (rah-TIB-id-ah kol-lum-NIF-er-ah) (same as *Ratibida columnifera*)

COMMON NAME: prairie coneflower

FAMILY: Compositae

GROWING RANGE: all regions of the United States

NATURAL RANGE: southwestern Canada to northern Mexico, east to Minnesota and Texas

BLOOMS: June — August

HEIGHT: 36 inches

COLOR: yellow, or yellow and red

TYPE: perennial

DESCRIPTION: There are two varieties of this species, one all yellow and one with red ray flowers touched with yellow. Both have ray flowers that droop at the base of an upright 1- to 2-inch-tall brownish cone. They have an airy, open growth pattern and branches often above the base.

ENVIRONMENTAL PREFERENCE: This plant needs full sun and dry, well-drained soil. Although it prefers soil rich in limestone, it is adaptable to many different types of soil and is quite drought tolerant.

PROPAGATION: The seeds may be sown in fall or spring and should germinate within five to ten days, blooming the second growing season. Prairie coneflower is considered hardy and easy to grow.

The *Ratibida* genus was once placed in the same genus as *Rudbeckia,* but morphological differences were great enough to warrant separate genera. Both the common and the species names refer to the elongated center cone that is so conspicuous in this plant. The Indians extracted a dye from the blossoms and made tea from the leaves and flower heads.

BOTANICAL NAME: *Rudbeckia hirta* (rood-BECK-ee-ah HER-tah)

COMMON NAME: black-eyed Susan

FAMILY: Compositae

GROWING RANGE: all regions of the United States (may be difficult to control in some areas)

NATURAL RANGE: Appalachian highlands, Pennsylvania to Georgia and north to Maine, west to Illinois

BLOOMS: June — August

HEIGHT: 24 — 36 inches

COLOR: yellow

TYPE: short-lived perennial

DESCRIPTION: Stout stems covered with rough barbs bear terminal blossoms composed of bright yellow orange ray flowers and dark brown disk flowers. The leaves are thick and covered with hairs.

ENVIRONMENTAL PREFERENCE: This is a versatile plant with the ability to grow in heavy or light, rich or sterile soils. It will perform best with regular watering but is also able to withstand periods of drought.

PROPAGATION: The seeds need no period of stratification; they do best when planted as soon as they are ripe. If seeds are held until spring, sow them when danger of frost is past and the soil is warm. Seeds should germinate in ten to fifteen days. The tiny seedlings look like miniature cacti with their round leaves and dark hairs. This is a short-lived perennial, so plan to reseed each year and replant the largest seeds. For a pure stand, the planting rate is suggested at two pounds per acre.

Rudbeckia hirta is often considered a weed and may be somewhat difficult to control. In Hawaii it is considered a real pest, and its potential for becoming a problem should be taken into consideration when you include it within a meadow or garden area.

The *Rudbeckia* genus was named for a Swedish botanist who is considered the "father of modern botany" — Olaf Rudbeck. It is the state flower of Maryland and has been the subject of many hybridizations resulting in some lovely garden varieties. A solution made from the plant was used to treat skin disorders, and modern testing has found that the plant does indeed contain antibodies that are effective in combating certain types of infections.

Many cultivars have been developed from *Rudbeckia hirta*, including the Gloriosa daisy.

Black-eyed Susan

OTHER SPECIES: *R. fulgida.* This coneflower is a perennial that grows to a height of 16 to 22 inches, blooming during the summer and fall. It needs rich soil with plenty of humus and regular watering during the summer. It is native from New Jersey to Illinois, south to Alabama.

R. laciniata. Blooming in midsummer, this coneflower grows to a height of 3 to 8 feet. The individual flowers are small, measuring only 1½ to 2 inches long, but they are borne in profusion. It has the advantage of blooming as well in the shade or woodland border as in full sun if given sufficient moisture. This plant is native to a broad area ranging from Quebec to northern Florida, west to the Rocky Mountains, and beyond.

R. amplexicaulis. This is actually an old name for *Dracopis amplexicaulis* (drah-KOE-pis am-plecks-i-CALL-iss), the clasping coneflower. It is an annual native to Georgia, west to Texas, and north to Kansas. It blooms from midsummer to fall at a height of 2 feet. It needs full sun but requires little water. The suggested planting rate is three pounds per acre.

Sage

Catchfly

BOTANICAL NAME: *Salvia coccinea* (SAL-vee-ah cock-SIN-ee-ah)
COMMON NAME: scarlet sage
FAMILY: Labiatae
GROWING RANGE: all regions of the United States
NATURAL RANGE: South Carolina to Florida, west to Texas and Mexico
BLOOMS: June — July
HEIGHT: 24 inches
COLOR: red
TYPE: perennial
DESCRIPTION: Bright red tubular flowers are widely spaced on an upright square stem. The leaves are triangularly shaped and grow opposite one another below the flowers.
ENVIRONMENTAL PREFERENCE: This plant needs full sun and somewhat sandy soil, and it needs low to moderate amounts of water.
PROPAGATION: Scarlet sage is best planted indoors in late winter and then transplanted to the meadow in the spring. The seeds can be sown outdoors when all danger of frost has passed and the soil has warmed. The seeds should be covered with the growing medium when planted, because the germination will be lowered if they are exposed to light. Suggested planting rate is eight pounds per acre.

The genus name is from the Latin word meaning "safe" or "healthy" and refers to an ancient belief in the medicinal value of the sages. Scarlet sage is an excellent species to use to attract hummingbirds.
OTHER SPECIES: *S. lyrata.* This plant is sometimes included within a wildflower seed mixture for meadows, but it is generally considered too weedy and insignificant to make any kind of show. The flowers are light lavender and occur in whorls around the square stem. It blooms in April and May.

BOTANICAL NAME: *Silene armeria* (sigh-LEE-nee ar-MARE-ee-ah)
COMMON NAME: catchfly
FAMILY: Caryophyllaceae
GROWING RANGE: all regions of the United States
NATURAL RANGE: Europe
BLOOMS: June — August
HEIGHT: 24 inches
COLOR: pink, lavender
TYPE: annual or biennial
DESCRIPTION: Bright lavender-pink flowers are borne in tight clusters on small bushy plants. the individual petals are deeply notched.

ENVIRONMENTAL PREFERENCE: Grown in full sun or partial shade, this plant will adapt to heavy or light soils and needs low to moderate watering.

PROPAGATION: Catchfly is easily grown from seeds planted either in the spring or fall. Germination should take place in ten to fifteen days. The suggested planting rate is one pound per acre.

The genus name is from the Greek word *sialon,* which means "saliva" and refers to the sticky sap present in members of this genus. The sap catches small flying insects — thus the common name. Other common names are garden catchfly and none-so-pretty.

Blue-eyed grass

BOTANICAL NAME: *Sisyrinchium angustifolium* (sis-i-RIN-kee-um AN-guss-ti-FOE-lee-um)
COMMON NAME: blue-eyed grass
FAMILY: Iridaceae
GROWING REGION: all regions of the United States
NATURAL RANGE: eastern North America
BLOOMS: May — June
HEIGHT: 6 — 10 inches
COLOR: blue
TYPE: perennial
DESCRIPTION: The leaves are grasslike, and the sky blue flowers have three petals and three similar sepals, each with a pointed tip. The centers are yellow, providing nice color contrast.
ENVIRONMENTAL PREFERENCE: Blue-eyed grass can form large clumps if supplied with well-drained, slightly acid, sandy soil.
PROPAGATION: Blue-eyed grass is easily propagated by dividing and replanting the clumps nearly anytime, even when in full bloom. It reseeds easily, but the seeds that set soon after blooming is finished will not germinate until the following spring. Though the flowers are tiny, they produce rather large seeds.

Blue-eyed grass flowers last only a single day, but the blooming season is relatively long, resulting in a nice show. The name *Sisyrinchium* is from the Greek word meaning "pig grubbing," for wild pigs loved to grub for the roots.
OTHER SPECIES: *S. bellum.* The Western blue-eyed grass is very similar to *S. angustifolium* in appearance and growing requirements. The blossoms of this species are slightly larger than those of *S. angustifolium.* The planting rate is eight pounds per acre.

BOTANICAL NAME: *Solidago* (sol-i-DAY-go)
COMMON NAME: goldenrod
FAMILY: Compositae

GROWING RANGE: all regions of the United States (some species may become difficult to control)

NATURAL RANGE: throughout the United States

BLOOMS: late summer to fall

HEIGHT: varies from 24 to 72 inches

COLOR: yellow

TYPE: perennials

DESCRIPTION: Most goldenrods are yellow, have graceful arching plumes of flowers, and have stout sturdy stems.

ENVIRONMENTAL PREFERENCE: Most species will tolerate poor soil that is neither extremely dry or soggy. Most need full sun.

PROPAGATION: The germination rate from *Solidago* species is generally poor, so sow the seeds thickly either in the fall or spring. When gathering seeds, wait until they are an off-white or gray color. White seeds are not yet mature. When transplanting young plants, do not allow the lower leaves to come into contact with the soil or the plant will rot. The easiest means of getting new plants is dividing clumps in late winter. Lift the entire clump, divide it, and replant immediately.

European gardeners have long used goldenrods to add bright color to the late summer garden. We would do well to do the same.

Tea was often made from the leaves of the goldenrods, especially during the Revolutionary War when imported tea was so difficult to get. If you try goldenrod tea yourself, be careful: a fungus often grows on these plants, which will make you sick if taken internally. The name *Solidago* is from the Latin, meaning ''to heal'' or ''to make whole,'' and refers to the supposed healing power of the plants. The American Indians put goldenrod in an herbal bath used to steam pain out of a sick person. However, little medicinal value is attributed to the plant today.

Goldenrod has long been a symbol for treasure and good fortune. For instance, one old superstition says that he who carries a piece of the goldenrod will soon find treasure.

OTHER SPECIES: There are more than eighty-five species of goldenrods native to the United States, and many of these interbreed frequently, making identification of many species difficult. There is a goldenrod native to every region. The best way to choose a species for your garden is to look along the roadsides and in fields and see which species grow naturally in your area. Not all of the goldenrods are suitable for cultivation. Many of them like to ''stretch their roots'' when they get in a garden or meadow situation and give you more goldenrod than you had bargained for. However, many are excellent flowers to include within your area and, along with the asters, should be the backbone of the meadow in late summer and fall. Most goldenrods are hardy and easy to grow and are rarely bothered by pests

Goldenrod

or disease. They are rarely included within seed mixtures because of the unreliability of germination and because the seeds are difficult to harvest. This should not deter you from including them within your meadow. Contrary to popular belief, goldenrods do not cause hay fever. Either collect the seeds yourself and sow heavily or buy nursery plants to set out. Some of the best goldenrods for cultivation are the following.

S. altissima. Tall goldenrod is native from Quebec to Florida, west to North Dakota, Kansas, and Arizona.

S. californica. This plant is native from southwest Oregon to Baja California.

S. canadensis. Meadow goldenrod is native from British Columbia to central California, east to the Rocky Mountains.

S. erecta. This is a very showy species, blooming in late summer through fall and needing full sun to partial shade and well-drained soil.

S. juncea. The early goldenrod blooms from July — September, grows to a height of two to four feet and has smooth, stalkless leaves. It is easily transplanted in fall or spring.

S. nemoralis. The gray goldenrod has leaves that have a grayish cast. The blooms are one sided, the stalks only grow to 2 feet, and it will tolerate very poor soil. Native from Ontario to Alberta, south to Kentucky, Arkansas, Texas, and Arizona, it is one of the best species to use in a garden.

S. odora. When the leaves of scented goldenrod are crushed, they give off an anise-like scent. It blooms from July to frost and grows to a height of 3 feet.

S. pallida. From the great Plains, this species is not particular about soils and is drought resistant and non-spreading.

S. rugosa. Rough-leaved goldenrod has crinkled bronze leaves, similar to the foliage of ajuga, that are attractive even when the plant is not in bloom. Delicate sprays of yellow blossoms appear in September and October and make this one of the most beautiful of all goldenrods and one especially well suited to the meadow environment. The clumps spread readily, so they should be placed at least 3 feet from their neighbors. Divide the clumps every other year to keep them from outgrowing their allotted space. It is native from Newfoundland to Ontario, south to West Virginia and Kentucky.

S. sempervirens. The seaside goldenrod does not require wet conditions but it will tolerate soggy soils, brackish conditions, and salt spray. It needs full sun, blooms in September and October, and reaches a height of 6 feet. It is native to coastal areas from Newfoundland to New Jersey and locally in Virginia, but it will grow in almost every region of the United States.

S. spathulata. This plant is native to Washington and northern Oregon and to the Rocky Mountains.

S. speciosa. Showy goldenrod is one of the prettiest and best species to use in the garden or meadow. It grows to a height of 6 feet and blooms from August to October.

Stoke's aster

BOTANICAL NAME: *Stokesia laevis* (STOKES-ee-ah LEE-viss)
COMMON NAME: Stoke's aster
FAMILY: Compositae
GROWING RANGE: Northeast, Pacific Northwest, Southeast, Southwest, Texas-Oklahoma, West
NATURAL RANGE: South Carolina, to Louisiana and Florida
BLOOMS: May — June
HEIGHT: 24 inches
COLOR: purple to blue
TYPE: perennial
DESCRIPTION: A small "button" of center flowers is surrounded by a ring of larger ray flowers. The unopened flower buds are conspicuous due to long, finely toothed bracts that surround the bud. The blossoms are 3 to 4 inches wide, and the leaves are long, narrow, and smooth.
ENVIRONMENTAL PREFERENCE: Stoke's aster requires regular watering. It will grow best in well-drained, average soil in full sun or partial shade. This plant does not always overwinter in cold climates.
PROPAGATION: This plant is easily grown from seed, particularly if the seeds are planted in a cold frame or prepared seeding bed and the young plants are moved to the meadow. Seeds should germinate in two to three weeks. Established plants can be divided in fall or spring. The clumps will need dividing every four years to retain shape and vigor.

A lovely but often overlooked species, Stoke's aster is not a true aster, though it is in the same family. The genus was named for Dr. Jonathan Stokes, an English physician and botanist who wrote extensively about plants and their medicinal uses. The species name means "smooth" and refers to the leaves of this plant.

Wind poppy

BOTANICAL NAME: *Stylomecon heterophylla* (sty-low-ME-con het-er-oh-FILL-ah)
COMMON NAME: wind poppy
FAMILY: Papaveraceae
GROWING RANGE: Pacific Northwest, Southwest
NATURAL RANGE: California
BLOOMS: May — June
HEIGHT: 24 inches
COLOR: reddish orange
TYPE: annual

DESCRIPTION: The four tangerine-colored petals have a purple spot underneath at the base of the flower. The stems are slender and graceful, the buds nodding.

ENVIRONMENTAL PREFERENCE: This species needs at least partial shade and moderate amounts of water. It requires good drainage but will grow in light or heavy soils. It is a good plant to use in a woodland border.

PROPAGATION: Wind poppy is easily grown from seed. The recommended planting rate for a pure stand is twelve pounds per acre.

Although this makes a poor cut flower, the brightly colored blossoms create quite a display. It is particularly useful for a border area or a part of the meadow that might receive afternoon shade.

Creeping thyme

BOTANICAL NAME: *Thymus serpyllum* (TY-mus sir-PY-lum)
COMMON NAME: creeping thyme
FAMILY: Labiatae
GROWING RANGE: all regions of the United States
NATURAL RANGE: northwestern Europe
BLOOMS: June — August
HEIGHT: 3 inches
COLOR: reddish purple
TYPE: perennial
DESCRIPTION: The individual flowers are tiny — only 1/8 inch wide — but they are grouped on dense racemes above a mat of creeping stems.
ENVIRONMENTAL PREFERENCE: This species prefers a temperate climate, well-drained soil, and full sun to partial shade.
PROPAGATION: The fastest ways to increase the number of plants are dividing the clumps in early spring or rooting the runners. It self-sows readily.

Other common names for this species are wild thyme or mother of thyme. It is a very low growing plant that is well suited to rock gardens or borders. A place in the meadow should be chosen with care so the plant can be seen among the taller species. Many plants that are offered for sale with this name are actually different species.

Cutting off the flowering stem after the blossoms fade will help the plant retain its shape and vigor. The leaves have quite a nice scent and are sometimes used in making aromatic essences or in cooking.

BOTANICAL NAME: *Tradescantia virginiana* (tray-des-CAN-tee-ah ver-jin-ee-AY-nah)
COMMON NAME: spiderwort
FAMILY: Commelinaceae
GROWING RANGE: all regions of the United States (may be difficult to control in some areas)
NATURAL RANGE: Connecticut to Georgia, west to Missouri

BLOOMS: June — August
HEIGHT: 12 — 24 inches
COLOR: purple or white
TYPE: perennial
DESCRIPTION: The three roundish petals of purple or white are all the same size. There are six rather conspicuous stamens and a hairy stem. Spiderwort grows in clumps and the summer foliage may get rather ungainly, detracting from the appearance of the plant.
ENVIRONMENTAL PREFERENCE: This plant will put up with many adverse conditions including poor light, poor soil, and poor drainage. Ideal conditions for it include moist, well-drained soil rich in humus and full sun.
PROPAGATION: Although it can be easily grown from seed sown in spring (taking approximately ten days to sprout), the fastest means of propagation is by dividing the clumps in early spring.

Although spiderwort is generally an attractive plant, if given very good conditions, it will soon outgrow its allotted space in the meadow or garden. In poor conditions, its growth is less rank, but it is also less attactive and does not bloom as profusely. It has the tendency to become invasive, particularly in the Northeast.

The common name spiderwort has several possible origins. The most widely accepted one is from the fact that the leaves are twisted at the stems and could resemble the legs on a spider. Another explanation is that the plant was once used to cure the bite of a spider.

When the blossoms fade they do not shrivel up and fall off like most other spent blooms. An enzymatic reaction within the plant causes the blossoms to turn to a runny blob instead. This has given rise to other common names including Moses in the bulrushes and widow's tears.

Researchers have found that spiderwort is particularly sensitive to varying levels of pollution and will undergo a mutation that causes the blossoms to change color when exposed to great amounts of certain chemicals.

OTHER SPECIES: *T. ohiensis.* The Ohio spiderwort is native from southern New England to Florida and west to Minnesota and Texas. It blooms in June and July, producing clusters of blue to rose-colored flowers. It grows 2 to 3 feet tall and should be divided in spring or fall.

Spiderwort

BOTANICAL NAME: *Trifolium incarnatum* (try-FOE-lee-um in-car-NAY-tum)
COMMON NAME: crimson clover
FAMILY: Leguminosae
GROWING RANGE: all regions of the United States
NATURAL RANGE: Europe
BLOOMS: May — August
HEIGHT: 8 — 14 inches

COLOR: deep red

TYPE: annual

DESCRIPTION: The small, deep red to purplish flowers appear on 1-inch-long cones above hairy stems. The leaves are also slightly hairy.

ENVIRONMENTAL PREFERENCE: An adaptable plant, this species will tolerate a wide range in soil fertility and moisture.

PROPAGATION: Crimson clover grows easily from seed sown in spring or fall.

This is a favorite plant to use along the highways in the southeastern United States. Like all members of the legume family, it adds nitrogen to the soil and is therefore a good plant to have in the meadow to improve the quality of the soil. When a meadow is planted from a seed mixture only, this clover is often used as a nurse grass to establish the area before some of the slower growing species have a chance to germinate. Do not use it too heavily — it can crowd more desirable seedlings. The planting rate for a pure stand is sixteen pounds per acre. Do not confuse it with some other species of clovers that could become established and then be nearly impossible to eradicate.

Crimson clover

BOTANICAL NAME: *Venidium fastuosum* (ven-ID-ee-um fas-too-OH-sum)

COMMON NAME: cape daisy

FAMILY: Compositae

GROWING RANGE: Southeast, Southwest, Texas-Oklahoma, West

NATURAL RANGE: South Africa

BLOOMS: June — August

HEIGHT: 24 inches

COLOR: orange

TYPE: annual

DESCRIPTION: The bright orange, daisylike flowers measure nearly 5 inches across and have a purplish brown base. Cape daisy has a bushy growing habit, and the young flower heads look like cobwebs when they first form.

ENVIRONMENTAL PREFERENCE: This plant needs a moderate amount of water and full sun, but can grow in heavy or light soils.

PROPAGATION: Cape daisy grows easily from seed sown outside in the spring after the last frost, and when the soil has warmed, it will germinate in approximately eight days when temperatures are around 70° F. The seeds need light to germinate, so seeds should be sown on the surface of the growing medium. The first blooms should appear in about four months. The planting rate is five pounds per acre.

The blossoms of this bright, cheerful little plant not only add beauty to the meadow and garden but also make wonderful cut flowers. The genus name is said to be based on the Latin word *vena,* meaning "a vein", for the fruits of some species are ribbed or have prominent veins.

Cape daisy

Hoary vervain

BOTANICAL NAME: *Verbena stricta* (ver-BEE-na STICK-tah)
COMMON NAME: hoary vervain
FAMILY: Verbenaceae
GROWING RANGE: all regions of the United States (it may become difficult to control in some areas)
NATURAL RANGE: Massachusetts to Montana, south to New Mexico
BLOOMS: June — August
HEIGHT: 24 — 36 inches
COLOR: purple
TYPE: perennial
DESCRIPTION: One to several erect spikes bear small (½ inch wide), deep purple flowers. The foliage is downy, and there are many paired toothed leaves.
ENVIRONMENTAL PREFERENCE: The hoary vervain needs moderate amounts of water, lean to rich soils, and full sun.
PROPAGATION: This plant reseeds quite easily, but the seeds need continual darkness until germination takes place. Sow seeds in the spring when the soil has warmed. It will take about twenty days for the seeds to sprout and three months until the first bloom. Germination may be helped by a period of cold stratification.

Many species of vervains, including *V. stricta,* are considered invasive and aggressive. They seem to be particularly troublesome in the Midwest.

The vervains have been used in medicines since the time of the Druids in ancient England. The plant was held in such esteem that the genus was named from the Latin words for "sacred plant." Some species were later used to scent soaps and perfumes.

Verbena has been thought to hold wonderfully magical powers for centuries. Water scented with verbena and sprinkled in the dining room was thought to make the guests merry. It was thought to ward off witchcraft, prevent poisoning, and cure the bite of rabid animals.

OTHER SPECIES: *V. goodingii.* The southwestern verbena is native from California to Utah, south to Arizona. In mild climates, it will bloom throughout most of the year. In colder regions, blooms will last until frost. It grows to a height of only 6 inches. The recommended planting rate is six pounds per acre.

V. bipinnatifida. This is a very drought-tolerant, low-growing plant that is good to use as a ground cover in an area that gets full sun but has poor soils. It is easily grown from seed. It is native from South Dakota to Alabama and west to Arizona.

BOTANICAL NAME: *Vernonia altissima* (ver-NON-ee-ah al-TISS-i-mah)
COMMON NAME: ironweed
FAMILY: Compositae
GROWING RANGE: Midwest, Northeast, Southeast, Texas-Oklahoma, West

NATURAL RANGE: New York to Missouri, south to Georgia and Louisiana

BLOOMS: late July — August

HEIGHT: 60 inches

COLOR: vivid purple

TYPE: perennial

DESCRIPTION: The leaves are long, narrow, and downy underneath. The flowers are borne on tall, erect stems and are in loose clusters with many disk flowers and no ray flowers. The blossoms are an extremely brilliant and vivid purple.

ENVIRONMENTAL PREFERENCE: This plant needs moist soil and full sun to partial shade, but it is quite adaptable to many different types of soil. It will perform best if given ample moisture and seems to like constantly moist conditions.

PROPAGATION: Ironweed is easily grown from divisions made in the spring or late fall. The seeds need a period of cold stratification and should be sown in the fall or stored in the refrigerator. Seeds are generally ready to be collected one month after blooming. The percentage of seeds that will germinate is predictably low, so be sure to sow plenty of seeds. The plants can also be grown from stem cuttings taken in June or July.

OTHER SPECIES: *V. noveboracensis.* The New York ironweed is similar in appearance and cultural requirements, but grows taller (3 to 6 feet) and blooms sooner than *V. altissima.* It is native to Massachusetts to Mississippi.

    V. fasciculata. This prairie species grows from 2 to 5 feet tall and blooms in July and August. The seeds can be collected in October and should be sown immediately. This species does well in a meadow or prairie because it needs competition from other plants to keep it in check.

Ironweed

Johnny-jump-up

BOTANICAL NAME: *Viola cornuta* (vee-OH-lah kor-NEW-tah)

COMMON NAME: Johnny-jump-up

FAMILY: Violaceae

GROWING RANGE: all regions of the United States

NATURAL RANGE: Spain and Pyrenees

BLOOMS: April — August

HEIGHT: 5 — 8 inches

COLOR: yellow and purple

TYPE: tender perennial

DESCRIPTION: The cheery little faces of the Johnny-jump-ups are colored in yellow, orange, red, blue, purple, and white or combinations. They are small, tufted plants with leaves that are smooth and wavy on the edges.

ENVIRONMENTAL PREFERENCE: With ample shade and moisture, these plants will bloom continuously through the summer. They prefer rich, well-drained soil and full sun to partial shade. They are good to set out under deciduous trees that allow full sun during the cool spring but will offer light shade during the hottest part of the summer.

PROPAGATION: Where winters are mild, seeds can be sown in late summer, providing late winter and early spring color. In colder regions, the seeds can be sown in September to provide blossoms for late spring and early summer. The seeds need continual darkness to germinate so keep them covered with the growing medium until they sprout — in about ten days.

As with most flowers, keeping the faded blossoms picked will prolong the blooming period. This member of the *Viola* family is named Johnny-jump-up because of its bright and cheery little face, which looks like a miniature pansy. A Greek legend said that this flower was all white until it was wounded by one of Cupid's arrows. Shakespeare referred to this in his *A Midsummer Night's Dream* when he wrote of the flower "once white and now purple with love's wound." There is much magic attributed to the small violas and pansies, much of it to do with love and matchmaking.

BIBLIOGRAPHY

Brown, Lauren. *The Audubon Society Nature Guide's Grasslands.* Alfred A. Knopf, New York; 1985.

Browse, Philip McMillan. *Simon and Schuster Plant Propagation Step by Step Encyclopedia.* Mitchell Beazley Publishers Limited, New York; 1979.

Bruce, Hal. *How to Grow Wildflowers and Wild Shrubs in Your Garden.* Alfred A. Knopf, New York; 1976.

Bush-Brown, James and Louise. *America's Garden Book.* Charles Scribner's Sons, New York; 1980.

Donaldson, Anthony and Rene. "Prairie, A Landscape Alternative." *Garden Magazine,* May-June; 1981.

Drew, John K. *Pictorial Guide to Hardy Perennials.* Merchants Publishing Company, Kalamazoo, Michigan; 1984.

Frese, Paul F. "The Return of the Wildflowers." *Flower and Garden Magazine,* April-May; 1984.

Haughton, Claire Shaver. *Green Immigrants: The Plants That Transformed America.* A Harvest/HBJ Book, Harcourt Brace Jovanovich, New York; 1978.

Hebb, Robert S. *Low Maintenance Perennials.* Demeter Press Book, The New York Times Book Co.; 1975.

Horticultural Data Processors. "The Flowering Meadow." 1977 Avant Gardener 10 (10); October 15, 1977.

Johnson, Charles C., and Robert S. Lemmon. *Wildflowers of North America in Full Color.* Hanover House, Garden City, New York; 1961.

Kenfield, Warren G. *The Wild Gardener in the Wild Landscape: The Art of Naturalistic Landscaping.* Hafner Publishing Co., Connecticut; 1966.

Martin, Laura C. *Wildflower Folklore.* The East Woods Press, Charlotte, North Carolina; 1984.

McDonald, Elvin. *How to Grow Flowers from Seed.* Van Nostrand Reinhold Co., New York; 1979.

McHarg, Ian L. *Design With Nature.* Natural History Press, New York; 1969.

Miles, Bebe. *Wildflower Perennials for Your Garden.* Hawthorne Books, New York; 1976.

Missouri Botanical Garden. *Directory to Resources on Wildflower Propagation.* National Council of State Garden Clubs; 1981.

Morrison, Darrel G. "The 'Wild' Moves in on the Backyard." *Landscape Architecture Magazine;* March, 1979.

Morrison, Darrel G. "Restoring the Midwestern Landscape." *Landscape Architecture Magazine;* October, 1975.

National Wildlife Federation. *Gardening With Wildlife,* Washington; 1974.

New England Wild Flower Society. *Nursery Sources, Native Plants, and Wild Flowers,* Framingham, Massachusetts; 1984.

Penn, Cordelia. *Landscaping with Native Plants.* John F. Blair, Winston-Salem, North Carolina; 1982.

Phillips, Harry R. *Growing and Propagating Wild Flowers.* University of North Carolina Press, Chapel Hill, North Carolina; 1985.

Phillips, Harry R. "Spreading the Native-Plant Idea." Garden Magazine; May-June, 1984.

Proulx, E.A. "Return of the Natives." *Horticulture Magazine;* October, 1984.

Raymond, Dick. *Garden Way's Joy of Gardening.* Garden Way Publishing Co. Pownal, Vermont; 1982.

Rock, Harold W. *Prairie Propagation Handbook.* Alfred L. Boener Botanical Gardens, Whitnall Park, Hales Corners, Wisconsin; 1981.

Schuler, Stanley. *Simon and Schuster's Guide to Garden Flowers.* Simon & Schuster, New York; 1983.

Scott, Jane Harrington. "Natives from Nurseries: A Cautionary Tale." Garden Club of America Bulletin; 1985.

Smyser, Carol. "A Meadow of Your Own." *House and Gardens;* August, 1980.

Soil Conservation Society of America. *Sources of Native Seeds and Plants;* 1982.

Sperka, Marie. *Growing Wildflowers: A Gardener's Guide.* Harper & Row, Publishers, New York; 1973.

Steffeck, Edwin F. *The New Wild Flowers and How to Grow Them.* Timber Press, Portland, Oregon; 1983.

Sunset Magazine. "What About A Wild Border." *Sunset Magazine;* September, 1985.

Taylor, Kathryn S., and Stephen F. Hamblin. *Handbook of Wildflower Cultivation.* Macmillan Publishing Company, New York; 1963.

Time-Life Books. *Time-Life Gardening Yearbook.* Time-Life Books, Alexandria, Virginia; 1978.

Watts, May T. *Reading the Landscape of America.* Collier Books, New York; 1975.

Wilson, William H. *Landscaping with Wildflowers and Native Plants.* Ortho Books, Chevron Chemical Co., San Francisco; 1984.

Check the end of each regional chapter for lists of books with information pertinent to each region.

INDEX

Numbers in bold indicate the principal description and illustration.